DEATH AND SERVICE

The Commonwealth War Graves of Somerset

First Published in Great Britain 2021 by Mirador Publishing

First edition: 2021

References to places and people are made with due respect. Any offence caused by references in the narrative is completely unintentional.

A copy of this work is available through the British Library.

ISBN: 978-1-914965-23-4

Mirador Publishing
10 Greenbrook Terrace
Taunton
Somerset
UK
TA1 1UT

DEATH AND SERVICE

The Commonwealth War Graves of Somerset

By

Richard Cooper-Knight

FOREWORD

I moved to Somerset a matter of weeks before the coronavirus pandemic changed our lives irrevocably. I knew Glastonbury like the back of my hand but didn't really have an idea of the other towns and villages the county had to offer.

So, as the initial lockdown began to lift, I set out to discover the places I hadn't been able to explore. I've been a keen photographer all of my life, so set myself a project of taking my camera on an alphabetical journey of the villages of Somerset, ready to post my findings online.

As I took shots of the churches in these out of the way places, the bright marble war graves caught my eye. An eager amateur genealogist, I wondered if it would be possible to research the lives of the people behind the names on the headstones, and so a new addiction was born.

Over the last year, and using a variety of online tools, I have pieced together stories of joy and tragedy, love and family from across Somerset. These are stories of youth and experience, stories of hope and drive, stories of doing one's duty for King and Country. These are stories not solely of the heroics of the trenches of the Western Front; these are the stories of the men and women who served on the Home Front, who died on home soil and were therefore buried here.

The lives uncovered in this book feature the souls who fell during the First World War; that conflict holds more of a direct interest to me, and documentation on those who died as a result of that war is more readily – and publicly – available than any later conflict.

There are more than 840 First World War graves in the county; the pages of this book feature less than a third of those. Where possible, I have aimed to record details of *all* Great War gravestones in a churchyard or cemetery. There are those whose graves no longer exist, or cannot be pinpointed, however, and, in some of the larger cemeteries, there is no guarantee that I have been able to record the details of every Commonwealth War Grave. My aim has always been, however, to be as comprehensive as possible.

Similarly, the information in this book is based on the research available at the time. I have retained spellings consistent with contemporary records – Serjeant as well as Sergeant, for example – and any newspaper quotes are verbatim, and so errors in those reports have not been corrected.

For me, this is only the beginning. I still have nearly 600 Somerset graves to photograph. There are lives still to be uncovered.

Richard Cooper-Knight

October 2021

Name: Adams, Albert

Rank: Lance Corporal

Regiment: Devonshire Regiment

Date of death: 9th February 1919

Age at time of death: 40

Cause of death: Malaria and pneumonia

Grave location: St John's Cemetery, Bridgwater

Albert James Adams was born in Somerset in September 1878, the fifth of ten children to Robert and Mary. Robert was a mason, who sadly passed away when Albert was only 11 years old. Mary lived on as the head of the household, and by the 1901 census, she had four of her five sons living with her, three of them also stonemasons.

Albert had taken a different route in life and found work as a postman. He married Annie King, a young woman from Taunton, in 1910, and they set up home in the village of Selworthy near Minehead. Albert was the village postman, and the young couple lived there with their sons – Albert and Robert – and Mary.

When war came, Albert enlisted, joining the 6th Battalion of the Devonshire Regiment. While his military records are scattered, his battalion served in India and Mesopotamia; during their three years in the Middle East, the 6th Battalion lost twice as many men to illness – influenza, pneumonia, malaria – as to enemy action.

Lance Corporal Adams was not immune to sickness; while I have been unable to unearth exact dates for his military service, his cause of death is recorded as malaria and pneumonia. He passed away on 9th February 1919, at the age of 40 years old.

Albert James Adams lies at rest in St John's Cemetery in Bridgwater, Somerset.

Name: Adams, James

Rank: Stoker Petty Officer

Regiment: Royal Navy

Date of death: 22nd December 1917

Age at time of death: 34

Cause of death: Killed in action

Grave location: Wembdon Road Cemetery, Bridgwater

James Adams was born in June 1883, son of Robert and Eliza Adams from Bridgwater in Somerset. Robert was an agricultural labourer; James was one of seven children.

James was keen to get out and see the world. In November 1905 – aged just 12 years old – he enlisted in the Royal Navy as a stoker. After training in Devonport, Plymouth, Stoker Adams served on a number of different vessels, including HMS Victorious, Ramillies, Amphitrite, Monmouth, Andromeda and Halcyon.

By the time war broke out, James had been promoted to Leading Stoker and was assigned to HMS Cornwall. This was an armoured cruiser that was involved in the Battle of the Falklands in December 1914.

Promoted to Stoker Petty Officer in October 1915, James continued to serve on HMS Cornwall until he was transferred to the brand-new ship, HMS Valkyrie. The vessel was involved in offensive sweeps and convoy escorts based out of Harwich.

On 22nd December 1917, the Valkyrie was part of the escort for a convoy travelling to the Netherlands, when she struck a mine. In total, nineteen men were killed, twelve instantly; this included Stoker Petty Officer Adams. He was 34 years old.

James Adams lies at rest in the Wembdon Road Cemetery in his home town or Bridgwater.

Name: Alston, Jack

Rank: Private

Regiment: Somerset Light Infantry

Date of death: 7th April 1916

Age at time of death: 51

Cause of death: Unknown

Grave location: St Mary's Cemetery, Taunton

John Thomas Alston, also known as Jack, was born in Chorley, Lancashire, in 1865 and was one of thirteen children to Richard and Elizabeth Alston. Before he died in 1878, Richard was a stripper and a grinder in a cotton mill, and it was millwork that the majority of his and Elizabeth's children went into.

When he left school, Jack and his siblings worked as cotton piecers in the mills, tying together any threads that broke on the machines. This was a job aimed at children, whose hands were often the only ones small enough to reach into the equipment.

By 1895, Elizabeth too had passed away. Jack, who was 30 by this point, had moved from Chorley to nearby Oswaldtwistle, and met Mary Ellen Wilcock. She was a widow with two children, and the couple married on 14th February 1897. Their marriage certificate shows that she was the daughter of a weaver, while Jack was working as a furnace man in the mill. The couple went on to have a child together, Amy, who was born in 1900.

The couple settled into if not a comfortable life, then a continued existence. While Mary and her two older children were working in the cotton mill, Jack began labouring at the local chemical works. The family lived in a small, two-up, two-down cottage right next to Mary and the children's place of work, and life continued apace.

War was coming however, and Jack volunteered to do his bit. His service records no longer exist, but it can only be assumed that he joined of his own accord; he would have been 50 when hostilities commenced, and so exempt from the initial call-up.

Private Alston was assigned to the Somerset Light Infantry and was based at their depot in Taunton. Little information about his time there is available, and sadly, the next accessible document is his pension record. This confirms that he died on 7th April 1916, from "*shock caused by a fall while on duty*". There is no other reference to what or how this happened, so the circumstances will remain a mystery. He was 51 years old when he passed away.

It seems that his widow may not have had the funds to bring Jack back home; instead, he lies at rest in St Mary's Cemetery in Taunton, Somerset, close to the depot where he was based.

Name: Andrews, Herbert

Rank: Private

Regiment: Gloucestershire Regiment

Date of death: 10th September 1918

Age at time of death: 22

Cause of death: Bright's disease and haemoptysis

Grave location: St Peter's Churchyard, Evercreech

Herbert Arthur John Andrews was born in July 1896, the eldest of seven children of Hugh (known as Henry) and Jane Andrews from Evercreech, Somerset.

By the time war broke out, Herbert was helping out on his grandfather's farm in nearby Thornford. He enlisted into the army on 15th November 1915, joining the Gloucestershire Regiment.

Private Andrews served in France from March 1916, eventually spending eighteen months on the front line (not counting leave), and received a gunshot wound to the face on 27th August 1917. (He was treated in France and remained there for a further five months.)

Herbert seems to be the only member of his family to have seen active service. His brother Norman was the only one of his siblings to have been old enough to enlist and, while he did so in 1917, he was assigned to the Experimental Company of the Royal Engineers, testing munitions and gases in Porton.

It appears that while Herbert was on leave in February 1918 he fell ill. Ultimately, he was discharged as medically unfit for service on 7th September. Just three days later, he passed away three days later, succumbing to a combination of chronic Bright's disease (a kidney complaint) and haemoptysis. He was just 22 years old.

Private Herbert Andrews lies at rest in the graveyard of St Peter's Church in his home village of Evercreech.

Name: Antell, Frank

Rank: Private

Regiment: Devonshire Regiment

Date of death: 27th December 1916

Age at time of death: 37

Cause of death: Suicide

Grave location: All Saints' Churchyard, Martock

Frank Antell was born in 1880, one of seven children — six sons — to Thomas and Harriett Antell. Thomas was a groom, and Harriett a dressmaker and the family lived in the village of Martock in Somerset.

After Thomas died in 1893, Frank left school and became a carpenter. By the time of the 1901 census, he was living with his mother and youngest brother. Income seems to have been short — there were three other people boarding and lodging with the family.

In August 1904, Frank married Augusta Ring, and together they had five children — Lily, Ada, Leslie, Ronald and Freda.

Frank enlisted in the 13th (Works) Battalion of the Devonshire Regiment; this had been formed in the summer of 1916, so it can only be assumed that he was called up at the start. The battalion was based in Plymouth, so it is likely that Private Antell did not see fighting on the Western Front.

Private Frank Antell's death is also a bit of a mystery. All that there is to confirm what happened is one stark sentence on his pension ledger: *Wounds self-inflicted during temporary insanity whilst on active service.*

This one statement covers a multitude of sins but does nothing to explain the mystery of what happened. There is no coverage of the incident or funeral in contemporary newspapers, so I have been unable to find any further explanation.

Frank Antell was a man with a young family. His regiment was based in England and was to be so for the duration of the war. One cannot imagine what thoughts were going through his head at the time he took his own life. That the 37-year-old felt this was his only option is tragic. He died on 27th December 1916.

Frank Antell lies at rest in the graveyard of All Saints' Church in his home village of Martock in Somerset.

Frank's widow Augusta went on to marry again in 1919, to a Joseph Maunder. She died in 1951 at the age of 73 years old.

Name: Ashford, Arthur

Rank: Private

Regiment: Dorsetshire Regiment

Date of death: 22nd December 1916

Age at time of death: 42

Cause of death: Accidental injury

Grave location: St Peter's Churchyard, Evercreech

Arthur James Ashford was born in the Dorset village of Okeford Fitzpaine, to John and Tryphina Ashford. His father died when Arthur was only seven years old, leaving Tryphina to raise him and his three siblings.

Arthur had had a military career before the start of the Great War. He had enlisted into the Dorsetshire Regiment in 1891 and, while I have not been able to locate his records from that time, the regiment had been stationed in Ireland in the 1890s.

In 1899 he married Amy Upshall, at which point he was employed as a labourer. The couple had six children, though sadly, two of them – Arthur George and Elsie May – died in childhood.

He enlisted within months of the First World War beginning, returning to the Dorsetshire Regiment he had previously served on 30th September 1914. (It is interesting that on his enlistment papers he said that he had previously served for 12 years, although the dates don't fully tally up.) This time, however, Private Ashford served on the Home Front, in Dorchester and Portland.

On the evening of 22nd December 1916, Arthur fell down a gulley in Portland. He was taken to the Verne Military Hospital in the town but died of his injuries – a fractured skull – in the early hours of the following day.

Private Arthur Ashford was buried in his home village of Evercreech on Thursday 28th December 1916.

Name: Ashton, Frederick

Rank: Private

Regiment: Royal Berkshire Regiment

Date of death: 27th August 1918

Age at time of death: 26

Cause of death: Died of wounds

Grave location: St Mary's Cemetery, Taunton

Frederick John Ashton was born in Taunton, Somerset, in 1892. He was one of eight children to scavenger and labourer Thomas Ashton and his wife Susanna.

When he left school, Frederick found work as a carter, and this is the job he was doing in 1913, when he married local woman Ethel May Lock. The young couple went on to have two children, Olive and Phyllis.

War was on the horizon, and Frederick enlisted in June 1916. Initially assigned to the Royal Berkshire Regiment, Private Ashton was shipped off to France within a couple of months.

During his time there, he was promoted to Lance Corporal, but requested being reverted back to his previous rank a few months later. By this point, he had been transferred to the Labour Corps, the regiment in which he served for the rest of his time.

In March 1918, Frederick was badly wounded, and found himself invalided back to England. He was admitted to the Northumberland War Hospital in Newcastle-upon-Tyne, where his right leg was amputated. Sadly, it appears that the treatment came too late, and Private Ashton passed away on 27th August 1918. He was just 26 years old.

Frederick John Ashton lies at rest in St Mary's Cemetery in his home town of Taunton.

Name: Athay, Albert

Rank: Private

Regiment: Labour Corps

Date of death: 22nd June 1918

Age at time of death: 31

Cause of death: Pneumonia

Grave location: Milton Cemetery, Weston-super-Mare

Albert Athay was born in 1887, one of eight children to Thomas and Emily. Thomas was a labourer for the local council in Weston-super-Mare, and the family lived in a small house on a road leading inland from the seafront.

Thomas died when Albert was only 14 years old, and, having left school, he found labouring work to help support his now widowed mother and younger siblings.

In August 1910, Albert married Mable Dunstone, a cowherd's daughter from Somerset. The couple continued to live with Albert's mother and brother right up until the outbreak of war. They went on to have three children, Millicent, Freda and Charles.

Albert, by this time, had been volunteering with the local Labour Battalion; he formalised his military service in June 1917, officially enlisting in the Labour Corps. He served as part of the territorial force, in and around Salisbury Plain.

Private Athay fell ill in the summer of 1918 and was admitted to hospital on 11th June with pneumonia. Sadly, as the days progressed, so did the condition, and he passed away from it just eleven days later. He was just 31 years old.

Brought back to Weston-super-Mare, Albert Athay was laid to rest in the Milton Cemetery in his home town.

Name: Baber, Henry

Rank: Colour Sergeant

Regiment: Somerset Light Infantry

Date of death: 12th April 1915

Age at time of death: 56

Cause of death: Unknown

Grave location: St Mary's Churchyard, Yatton

Henry Matthew Baber was born in the spring of 1859, the second of six children to Henry and Jane Baber. Henry Sr was a cordwainer – or shoemaker – and the family lived in Bristol. Or, at least, most of them did. The 1871 and 1881 censuses show Henry Sr and Jane happily living with their children, but Henry Jr is noticeable in his absence.

In August 1887, Henry married Sarah Jane Hardwidge in the village of Paulton, bear Bath. His younger brother Alfred and two of his sisters, Annie and Ellen, all bear witness to the wedding, at which Henry gives his profession as coachman.

The newlyweds settled down in Weston-super-Mare, and went on to have two children, Henry and Kathleen. Sadly, the couple's happiness was to be cut short, when, in 1891, Kathleen passed away, followed just two years later by Sarah, at the age of just 32 years old.

With a young boy to bring up, Henry sought a new companion and, just over a year after Sarah's death, he married Alma Quantick, who was fourteen years Henry's junior. Together, they went on to have six children and, by the time of the 1901 census, the family were living in the Somerset village of Yatton. Henry, by this time, was working as an insurance agent for Prudential, a profession that was to last him through to the start of the First World War.

From the early 1890s, Henry had enlisted in the local Yeomanry. While only a reserve force, he had a short spell in Egypt, fighting at Tel-el-Kibir in 1882. Harry worked his way up through the ranks, eventually attaining the role of Colour Sergeant. He was brought out of reserve status on 4th

August 1914, at the age of 55, and was assigned to the 4th Battalion of the Somerset Light Infantry.

There is little else to confirm his military career during the Great War; he was discharged in November 1914, but there is nothing to confirm whether he had seen active service during those four months or not.

Colour Sergeant Baber's passing is also shrouded in mystery. He died on 12th April 1915, but the cause of his death is lost to time. He was 56 years old when he died.

Henry Matthew Baber lies at rest in the graveyard of St Mary's Church in Yatton, Somerset.

Henry and Alma's eldest son William Albert Baber is also interred in the family grave and within eighteen months, Alma had lost both her husband and her eldest son.

Name: Baber, William

Rank: Private

Regiment: London Regiment

Date of death: 16th October 1916

Age at time of death: 21

Cause of death: Died of wounds

Grave location: St Mary's Churchyard, Yatton

William Herbert Baber was born in May 1895, the oldest of six children to Henry and Alma Baber. By the time of William's birth, Henry was an insurance agent for the Prudential insurance company and brought his family up in the Somerset village of Yatton. William's father had been widowed early on, and so, in addition to his five younger siblings, he also had an older half-brother, also called Henry.

By the time of the 1911 census, William was working as a clerk in a coal office, and the family were living in a five-room house not far from the village centre.

Little remains documented about William's military service. He enlisted in the Somerset Light Infantry but transferred to the 24th Battalion of the London Regiment. He was involved in the Battle of High Wood – part of the Somme offensive – and was wounded during the skirmish.

Evacuated back to home soil, Private Baber was treated in one of the Military Hospitals in Cardiff. Sadly, he was to succumb to his wounds, and passed away on 16th October 1916. He was just 21 years old.

William Herbert Baber lies at rest in the family grave in the churchyard of St Mary's in Yatton.

William's father Henry Matthew Baber is also interred in the family grave; within eighteen months, his mother Alma had lost both her husband and her eldest son.

Name: Bailey, Newman

Rank: Engine Room Artificer

Regiment: Royal Navy

Date of death: 23rd November 1918

Age at time of death: 32

Cause of death: Influenza

Grave location: St James' Cemetery, Taunton

Newman Joynt Bailey was born on 1st August 1887, the eldest of five children to Newman Bailey and his wife Anna (née Joynt). Newman Sr worked as a switchman and signalman for Great Western Railway and had been born in Bath. He married Anna (whose maiden name was Joynt, and who had been born in Ireland) in 1885 and, after a short stint living across the county border in Devon – where Newman Jr was born – he settled his young family in Taunton.

When Newman Jr left school, he became an office boy, but he soon found himself following in his father's footsteps. He became a fitter for the railways and, by 1910, was living within spitting distance of the GWR depot in the town.

It was here, in William Street, that he set up home with his new wife, Lily Gill, who he had married on 31st July 1910. Lily was the daughter of a Taunton lamplighter, and, to help make ends meet, worked as an ironer at the town's collar factory.

War was on the way, and in July 1915, Newman enlisted in the Royal Navy. After initial training aboard Vivid II, the shore establishment in Devonport, he was deployed on HMS Blake as an Engine Room Artificer.

HMS Blake was an auxiliary ship designed to provide maintenance support to a flotilla of destroyers or other small warships. With his experience with steam engines at GWR, his knowledge of mechanics would have made him ideally suited to this type of role.

While he survived the war, Artificer Bailey was to be struck down with something much closer to home. In the immediate post-war period, the Spanish Flu pandemic swept the globe, and Newman was to fall victim to it. Admitted to the Royal Naval Hospital in South Queensferry, near Edinburgh, he passed away from the lung condition on 23rd November 1918. He was just 32 years old.

Brought back home, Newman Joynt Bailey was laid to rest in St James' Cemetery in his home town of Taunton.

Name: Baker, Ernest

Rank: Private

Regiment: Somerset Light Infantry

Date of death: 16th April 1915

Age at time of death: 36

Cause of death: Bronchitis and pneumonia

Grave location: St Mary's Cemetery, Taunton

Ernest Baker's early life is a bit of a muddle; born in 1878 in Somerset, it's a challenge to unpick specific details, as there are two Ernest Bakers, both of whom have parents of the same name – Henry and Sarah – and have siblings with similar names too. Was Ernest's father, therefore, a thatcher from Meare near Glastonbury or a travelling draper from Taunton?

In fact, it was a newspaper article from April 1915 that helped unlock the confusion.

The Taunton Courier and Western Advertiser confirmed that Ernest's full name was Ernest Bond Baker, and that his father – who had passed away by the time of Ernest's death – was from Bishop's Hull, a village near Taunton.

This would seem to confirm, therefore, that his father was a travelling draper.

Ernest was one of ten children. His father died when he was only fifteen years old, by which time Ernest had left school and found employment as a basket weaver, a trade which was prevalent on the Somerset Moors.

Sarah, a widow at only forty, took in laundry to make ends meet. Of Ernest's two older brothers, one had passed away as a teenager, while the other had gone on to have a wife and family of his own. It was left to Ernest, therefore, to remain at home and support his mother and younger siblings.

Ernest met and married local butcher's daughter Bessie Glover in 1900, and the couple went on to have seven children. After a spell living in Wiltshire, the young family moved back to Somerset, settling in Bridgwater, where Ernest continued to ply his trade.

Ernest's military service records are lost to time; he enlisted in the Somerset Light Infantry, joining the 5th Battalion at some point early in the war (certainly before October 1914). Private Baker's battalion seems to have been part of a territorial/reserve force, and he was based in his home town of Taunton.

In early April 1915, Ernest fell ill, and was admitted to the Voluntary Aid Detachment Red Cross Hospital in Yeovil, suffering from bronchitis and pneumonia. Sadly, the lung conditions were such that he was to succumb to them, and he passed away on 16th April 1915. He was just 36 years old.

Ernest Bond Baker lies at rest in St Mary's Cemetery in his home town of Taunton, Somerset, the same cemetery where his father and brother were buried.

Name: Baker, Thomas

Rank: Private

Regiment: Devonshire Regiment

Date of death: 22nd February 1917

Age at time of death: 40

Cause of death: Pneumonia

Grave location: Churchyard of Blessed Virgin Mary & All Saints, Meare

Thomas Baker was born in 1877, the youngest of four children – all boys – to John and Anna Baker from Meare in Somerset. John was a farm labourer, and it was rural trades that his four sons followed, Thomas himself also becoming a farm worker.

Thomas married in August 1896; Phoebe Ann Willis was also from Meare and was just seventeen when the couple married. While I am sure there was love involved, something more practical might have prompted such a young marriage as, six months later, the couple had their first child, Henry.

Thomas and Phoebe went on to have four children, three of whom – Henry, Florence and Amy – survived. By the time of the 1911 census, the family were living in their home village of Meare, with Henry following in his father's – and grandfather's – line of work.

Full details of Thomas' military service are not available. He enlisted in the Devonshire Regiment as part of the 13th Works Battalion and, while there is no documentation to confirm when he joined up, it was probably early in 1917.

Thomas and Phoebe's son Henry had enlisted in 1915, joining the Gloucestershire Regiment. It seems likely he fought on the Somme, and he was killed in action in November 1916, aged just 20 years old. It may have been this loss that prompted Thomas to do his duty, albeit on the Home Front.

Whenever it was that Private Thomas Baker had enlisted, it was Phoebe that was to suffer the ultimate price. Having already lost a child young, her boy had died in the fields of France, and her husband was also about to add to that loss.

Thomas contracted pneumonia in the winter of 1916-17 and passed away in a Military Hospital on 22nd February 1917. He was 40 years old.

Thomas lies at rest in the graveyard of the Church of the Blessed Virgin Mary & All Saints in his home village of Meare in Somerset.

Name: Batten, Arthur

Rank: Private

Regiment: Devonshire Regiment

Date of death: 12th March 1919

Age at time of death: 19

Cause of death: Died of wounds

Grave location: St James' Cemetery, Taunton

Arthur Henry Reed Batten was born in the spring of 1900, the only child to Henry and Alice. Henry was a gardener, and the young family lived in the Somerset town of Taunton.

There is little documentation about Arthur's short life. When war broke out, he enlisted in the 1st Battalion of the Devonshire Regiment. While there is nothing to confirm the date he joined up, it may well have been a reaction to the passing of his mother, who died on 1st September 1914, at the age of 47 years old.

Private Batten's battalion initially fought on the Western Front during the war, before moving to Italy in November 1917, then back to France the following April. It seems likely that it was during this second stint in France at some point late in 1918 that Arthur was caught up in the fighting.

He received a gunshot wound and was shipped back to England for treatment. Admitted to the Military Hospital in Stockport, Greater Manchester, he seems to have suffered for a long time, passing away from his injuries on 12th March 1919, three months after the Armistice was signed. He was just 19 years of age.

Arthur Henry Reed Batten was brought back to Taunton for burial, and lies in the family grave in St James' Cemetery, alongside his mother.

Name: Bellham, William

Rank: Private

Regiment: Coldstream Guards

Date of death: 10th December 1917

Age at time of death: 29

Cause of death: Pneumonia

Grave location: St Mary's Cemetery, Taunton

William Harry David Bellham was born in September 1888, the only child to William and Rosina Bellham. William Sr was a foreman for a collar manufacturer, and the young family lived in Taunton, Somerset, in a house they shared with Rosina's mother, Mary Hale.

Life continued pretty much unchanged. When William Jr left school, he became a stenographer for a coal merchant, and when war erupted in 1914, he didn't sign up as soon as you would expect for someone of his age.

William enlisted in February 1916 and was assigned to the Coldstream Guards – given he stood 5ft 11ins (1.8m) tall, this probably went in his favour. Initially placed on reserve duty, Private Bellham was eventually mobilised in January 1917, and sent to Caterham for training.

Within a matter of weeks, William had an accident. Slipping on some ice, he suffered an inguinal hernia, which subsequently became strangulated, causing him severe pain. After initial treatment in hospital, he was discharged, but was then admitted again five months later when the hernia returned. A further operation was ruled out by the medical examiner, and he was discharged from the army on medical grounds at the end of June 1917.

Once back in Taunton, it *did* become necessary for William to undergo an additional operation. This was carried out in the local hospital and, according to the records, was a success. Sadly, however, William subsequently contracted pneumonia, and he died on 10th December 1917. He was just 29 years old.

William Harry David Bellham was buried in St Mary's Cemetery in his home town of Taunton.

Cruelly, the contemporary local media had a less sympathetic take on the incident that caused William's troubles. The Taunton Courier and Western Advertiser [on Wednesday 26th December 1917] suggested that he "*was not really strong enough to stand the strain and hardships of military training and was invalided out after some months' service.*" Not exactly the picture that his medical records had outlined.

Name: Bellringer, Albert

Rank: Private

Regiment: Somerset Light Infantry

Date of death: 5th December 1918

Age at time of death: 30

Cause of death: Syphilis?

Grave location: Wembdon Road Cemetery, Bridgwater

Albert George Bellringer was born in April 1889, the youngest of three children to Charles and Sarah. Charles was a sawyer in a timber yard, and his son followed suit.

Little detail of Albert's early life remains, but he married Elizabeth Burge in December 1909, and the couple went on to have three children – Albert Jr, Cecil and Charles.

Albert enlisted when war appeared inevitable, joining the Somerset Light Infantry in June 1914. When his training was complete, his troop – the 2nd Battalion – were shipped off to India, and this is where Private Bellringer spent the majority of the war.

Distance from home and family made some soldiers act in ways they otherwise wouldn't. On 15th August 1917, Albert was admitted to hospital with a venereal sore. He was then admitted to the Dinapore (now Danapur) Station Hospital on 2nd December 1917, "*in a very excited condition. He was childish, silly and had grandiose delusions.*"

Things were not going well for Private Bellringer's health. He was transferred back to England for treatment on the Hospital Ship Wandilla – this was torpedoed on the journey home, although the device failed to explode. While on board, he was seen to be "*exalted in his ideas, and to have physical signs of GPI [General Paresis (or Paralysis) of the Insane].*"

The ship arrived back in England on 25th April, and Albert was admitted to the Royal Victoria Hospital in Netley, Hampshire. The medical report again showed that "*he was foolish, demented and [that] the physical signs of GPI were marked.*"

Moved to Dykebar Hospital in Paisley – a mental health institution – for specialist attention, Private Bellringer was eventually discharged from the army. Medical grounds were the reason for his dismissal, and his last day of service was 5th July 1918.

Sadly, however, Albert's health faltered; he was transferred again, this time to the Somerset and Bath Asylum in Somerset, and it was there that he passed away. Albert George Bellringer died on 5th December 1918; he was 30 years old.

Albert lies at rest in the Wembdon Road Cemetery in his home town of Bridgwater.

So, what was the cause of Albert's illness and death? His initial hospital admission identified a venereal sore, and, based on his subsequent decline, it is likely that this was syphilis. One of the last symptoms of the disease is mental illness – insanity – and so this underlines the probable diagnosis.

However, mental illness only usually appears on average 10 to 30 years after the STI is first contracted, and then only if it is not treated (which, given that this would have been Victorian England, it is likely not to have been).

What this suggests, therefore, is that Albert contracted syphilis before the war, probably before his marriage to Elizabeth, and he may not have been unfaithful while serving in India.

Name: Bentley, Arthur

Rank: Second Lieutenant

Regiment: Yorkshire Regiment

Date of death: 2nd December 1918

Age at time of death: 35

Cause of death: Unknown

Grave location: St Mary's Cemetery, Taunton

Arthur Webb Butler Bentley was born on 1st January 1884 to Dr Arthur Bentley and his wife Letitia. The oldest of five children, they were a well-travelled family. Dr Bentley had been born in Devon, but his and Letitia's first two children were born in Singapore, while their second two were born in Ireland, where Letitia herself had been born.

By the time of the 1891 census, the family were living in Paddington, London, where Arthur's father was a medical practitioner.

Arthur Jr looked set to follow in his father's footsteps, becoming a student of medicine in Edinburgh, although it seems his life was destined to take a different route.

By 1905, his father was working at a practice in Egypt. It was around this time that his mother made the newspaper headlines:

VICTIM OF CHLORODYNE

A painful story was told at the Clerkenwell Sessions when Letitia Bentley, the wife of a doctor holding an official position in Cairo, pleaded guilty to the theft of a diamond and ruby ring from the shop of Messrs. Attenborough, Oxford Street [London]. It was stated that Mrs Bentley was addicted to the drinking of spirits and chlorodyne, and that 240 empty bottles which had contained the latter drug had been found in her rooms in Bloomsbury.

Dr Bentley said he would keep his wife under strict supervision in the future, and she was bound over.

Shetland Times: Saturday 3rd June 1905.

The ring concerned was valued at five guineas (around £700 in today's money), and another report confirmed that her husband "*supplied her with ample means*" [financially].

In the 19th century, chlorodyne was readily used as a treatment for a number of medical conditions. Its principal ingredients were a mixture of laudanum (an alcoholic solution of opium), tincture of cannabis, and chloroform, and it readily lived up to its claims of relieving pain and as a sedative.

Letitia does not appear in any other contemporary media; sadly, however, she passed away "*at sea*" in June 1907, presumably on the way to or from Cairo, where Arthur Sr was still working. She was just 47 years old.

Arthur seems to have taken the decision to move away, and he emigrated to Canada, settling in Winnipeg. Leaving England behind, he left the idea of medicine with it, finding work as a lineman instead, constructing and maintaining telegraph and power lines.

Arthur's father is the next member of the family to appear in the local newspapers. Working in Cairo during the winter and Llandrindod Wells in the summer, he travelled to Wales in April 1911. One evening he collapsed and died while in the smoking room of his hotel. The media reported that he was "*formerly Colonial Surgeon to the Straits Civil Service, Singapore*" and that "*he was going to deliver a lecture at Owen's College [now the Victoria College of Manchester] on tropical diseases, upon which he was an expert.*"

Arthur Jr was now 27 and had lost both of his parents. War was on the horizon, though, and he seemed keen to become involved. He enlisted in December 1915, joining the Canadian Expeditionary Force. His sign-up papers gave him as just short of 32 years old, standing at 5ft 8ins (1.72m) tall, with a fair complexion, blue eyes and brown hair. The document also recorded his next of kin as his brother, William, who was living near Cairo.

Arthur arrived in England on 25th September 1916; during his time in the army, he remained on English soil, primarily at a signal base in Seaford. Transferred to a reserve battalion in January 1917, he was eventually discharged seven months later, although there is no record as to why that happened.

It may well be that the reason for Arthur's discharge was his transfer from the Canadian Expeditionary Force to the Yorkshire Regiment. He is recorded as enlisting in the latter with a commission, although there is no confirmation of when this happened.

Second Lieutenant Bentley was assigned to the 3rd Special Reserve Battalion but never saw action in Europe. The troop's main duties were to train men for service overseas and to provide coastal defences. While there is no confirmation of exactly where Arthur was based, there were units in and around Hartlepool, County Durham.

Sadly, there is little further information about Arthur. By the end of the war, he was living in Taunton, Somerset, where his younger sister Eileen had settled. Second Lieutenant Bentley survived the war, but passed away not long afterwards, on 2nd December 1918. There is no cause given for his death. He was just 35 years old.

Arthur Webb Butler Bentley lies at rest in St Mary's Cemetery in Taunton, Somerset.

Name: Beresford, Cecil

Rank: Major

Regiment: Royal Defence Corps

Date of death: 9th October 1917

Age at time of death: 42

Cause of death: Unknown

Grave location: Milton Cemetery, Weston-super-Mare

Cecil William Beresford was born in June 1875, the oldest of five children. He shared the same first name as his father, so became known as William. Cecil Sr was a barrister in London and he and his wife, Caroline, brought the family up in Kingsbury, London.

Things certainly went well for the Beresford family. By 1901, Cecil was a county judge, and had relocated the family to Devon. William, by this time, was training to be a barrister, and lived with his parents, siblings and four servants in Weare Hall, overlooking the village of Weare Giffard, near Bideford.

From this point on, information about William is a bit sketchy. He does not appear on the 1911 census – by this time Cecil and Caroline had moved to Weston-super-Mare, where Cecil died a year later. It is likely that William had enlisted in the army by this point and was posted overseas.

William's military records are not available, but when war broke out in 1914, he joined the Royal Defence Corps and, through his service, had attained the rank of Major.

In October 1917, a number of the local newspapers ran this brief report:

> *The death has occurred in a military hospital at Weymouth of Major Cecil William Beresford (RDC), eldest son of his Honour, the late Judge Beresford and Mrs Beresford, late of Wear Gifford Hall, and subsequently of Penquarry, Weston-super-Mare. He was 42 years old.*
>
> *Western Times: 17th October 1917*

Sadly, this is all that remains to document Major Beresford's passing. There is nothing to confirm whether he had been wounded or had fallen ill, and there are no newspaper reports around his funeral.

Cecil William Beresford was laid to rest in the Milton Cemetery in his mother's adopted home town of Weston-super-Mare.

Name: Betty, Alfred

Rank: Lieutenant

Regiment: Rifle Brigade

Date of death: 23rd March 1917

Age at time of death: 48

Cause of death: Illness

Grave location: St Mary's Cemetery, Taunton

Alfred William Betty was born early in 1869, one of ten children to John Betty and his wife Hannah. John was a blacksmith, and the family lived in Taunton.

After leaving school, Alfred found work as a *silk throwster*, twisting silk into thread or yarn. This was not the long-term career that he sought, however, and in 1887 he enlisted in the Rifle Brigade. During a period of service that lasted 21 years, he fought in India and South Africa, rising to the rank of Quartermaster-Sergeant by the end of his tenure in 1908.

In 1896, Alfred had married Elizabeth Johnson, also from Taunton, who was herself the daughter of a soldier. The couple went on to have three children, two of whom survived – daughters Ella and Hazel.

By the time of the 1911 census, the family had set up home in Taunton. Alfred, now back on civvy street, was working as a clerk and had become involved in the town's Holy Trinity Men's Club.

War was on the horizon, however, and when hostilities broke out, Alfred quickly re-enlisted. Within a month of re-joining the Rifle Brigade, he was given a commission in the 13th Battalion. After initially being based in Winchester, by the summer of 1915 Lieutenant Betty found himself on the front line. He was involved in some of the fiercest fighting and was caught up in the Battle of the Somme.

It was here that Alfred fell ill. While full details of his condition are not readily available, he contracted a prolonged illness, as a result of "*hardship and exposure*" *[Western Daily Press, Saturday 24th March 1917]*.

Whatever the condition, it was serious enough for Lieutenant Betty to be invalided back to England and out of the army, and he returned to his family home in Taunton.

Sadly, Alfred's condition was to take its toll on him, and he finally succumbed to it on 23rd March 1917. He was 48 years old.

Alfred William Betty lies at peace in St Mary's Cemetery in his home town of Taunton in Somerset.

Name: Blackmore, Alfred

Rank: Private

Regiment: Somerset Light Infantry

Date of death: 6th July 1918

Age at time of death: 49

Cause of death: Suicide by drowning

Grave location: St Mary's Cemetery, Taunton

Alfred Blackmore was born on 25th October 1868 in the village of Thurlbear, near Taunton. Documentation varies and names cross over, but it appears that he was one of numerous children to farm labourer William Blackmore and his wife, Mary Ann.

Details of Alfred's early life are a bit hazy – again, in a rural location, names often cross over, so it is a challenge to totally confirm that they relate to the right person. His mother appears to have passed away by the time of the 1881 census, and Alfred was living with his father and three of his siblings and working as a farm hand.

Alfred again disappears off the radar for a while; in July 1894, he married Lucy Charlotte Yard, and the couple went on to have two daughters, Lucy and Beatrice. By 1901, the young family were living in the village of Frampton Cotterell, just to the north of Bristol, and Alfred had found employment as a marine fireman.

Ten years later, Lucy and the girls were still living in Frampton Cotterell, but Alfred was back in Taunton, lodging with a 75-year-old widow called Mary Croker and working as a labourer. This separation may have signalled the beginning of the end for the couple's marriage.

War broke out, and it is evident that Alfred enlisted as a Private in the Somerset Light Infantry. Sadly, his service records are lost to time, but it appears that he served for at least three years.

The next time Alfred appears in documentation, it is a newspaper report on his passing, under the heading *"Taunton Soldier's Death"*.

FOUND DROWNED AT BLACKBROOK

Mr F Foster Barham, coroner for West Somerset, held an inquest at the Blackbrook Inn, Ruishton, on Monday, relative to the death of Alfred Blackmore, aged 49, a private in the Labour Company at Taunton Barracks, whose body was found in the stream at Blackbrook on Saturday morning.

William Cozens, farmer... gave evidence of identification, and stated that on Friday he saw the deceased sitting by the hedge... about 400 yards from where the body was found.

William Richard Radnidge, butcher... stated that on Saturday morning he found the body in the stream dividing Ruishton from Taunton St Mary's... His cap, belt and cape were on the bank. The deceased was lying face downward, his face and arms being in the mud below the surface.

PC Jenkins stated that at 10:45am on Saturday he received a communication from PC Wathen, in consequence of which he proceeded to Blackbrook, where he found the body lying under a hedge. He searched the body, and on it found a summons, returnable at Taunton on 29th June, for having failed to comply with a maintenance order obtained by his wife, Lucy Blackmore, on 25th September 1915, the sum of £2 13s [approx. £300 today] being due. On the back of the summons was written: "This is what my old cow has done for me."

There was also the following letter: "When my body is found, don't you give a farthing to my old cow. What I have got to come give to my brother, Edward Blackmore... Signed A Blackmore." At the back of the letter was written: "Goodbye to all that I love."

The deceased had left his lodging at nine a.m. on June 29th to attend the Taunton Police Court, but did not do so.

An officer stated that the deceased's conduct during the three years he had been in the army had been satisfactory.

The Foreman of the jury said that according to the evidence they found that the deceased met with his death by drowning whilst temporarily insane.

Taunton Courier and Western Advertiser: Wednesday 10th July 1918

Alfred Blackmore took his own life on 6th July 1918. He was 49 years old [the war grave gives a different age].

Alfred lies at peace in St Mary's Cemetery in Taunton, Somerset.

Name: Bond, Alert

Rank: Private

Regiment: Royal Army Service Corps

Date of death: 4th November 1918

Age at time of death: 30

Cause of death: Pneumonia

Grave location: St Leonard's Churchyard, Butleigh

Albert Victor Bond was born in 1887, the only child of John and Sarah Bond. John was an engine driver, with a steam roller, and the family lived in the Somerset village of Butleigh.

Albert started working for the local baker and, by the time of the 1911 census, when his parents were celebrating their 25th wedding anniversary, this is the job he was doing.

He enlisted in March 1915, joining the Royal Army Service Corps. While his complete service record is not available, Private Bond's service was relatively short-lived. He was discharged as medically unfit in February 1916, having served for just 332 days.

He was discharged with pneumonia, and this seems not to have cleared up and he was eventually admitted to the Military Hospital in Wool, Dorset. Albert passed away from the disease on 4th November 1918, just a week before the Armistice. He was 30 years old.

Albert Bond lies at rest in the graveyard of St Leonard's Church in his home village of Butleigh.

Name: Boon, Henry

Rank: Private

Regiment: Devonshire Regiment

Date of death: 23rd December 1916

Age at time of death: 36

Cause of death: Apoplexy

Grave location: St Mary's Cemetery, Taunton

Henry Boon was born in May 1880, the youngest of ten children to Edwin and Fanny Boon. Edwin worked in service – consecutive census records list him as a manservant, coachman and gardener – and the family lived in the Somerset town of Taunton.

Henry was working as a packer in a factory when he met Alice Mockridge. The couple married in June 1902, and went on to have three children – Henry, Dorothy and Vera.

By the time of the 1911 census, Henry had put the factory behind him and was working as a labourer in the local sewage works. Employed by the town council, it is likely that the job paid more, particularly with a young family to support. Alice was also working, doing ironing and sewing to help them make ends meet.

Storm clouds were gathering over Europe, however, and soon Henry was needed to do his duty. Full details of his military service are not readily available, but he joined the Devonshire Regiment early on in the conflict and was assigned as a Private to the 13th (Works) Battalion.

Private Boon seems to have been based in England for the duration, although full details of his movements are not clear. He was certainly living in Taunton by December 1916, and it was here that he fell ill.

Admitted to hospital with apoplexy, it seems that it was this haemorrhage or stroke that killed him. Private Boon passed away on 23rd December 1916. He was just 36 years of age.

Henry Boon lies at rest in St Mary's Cemetery in Taunton, Somerset.

Name: Bourne, Eustace

Rank: Air Mechanic 2nd Class

Regiment: Royal Flying Corps

Date of death: 2nd May 1917

Age at time of death: 20

Cause of death: Accidental drowning

Grave location: Westonzoyland Cemetery

Eustace Lionel Bourne was born in 1897, one of six children to Robert and Eve, from Westonzoyland, Somerset. Robert was a wheelwright and carpenter and, after leaving school, Eustace followed in a similar vein, becoming an apprentice to an ironmonger.

When war broke out, Eustace's interest in engineering led him to join the Royal Flying Corps, where he was appointed as an Air Mechanic. His enlistment papers – dated November 1915 – give his trade or calling as "motor cyclist", so it is obviously a passion that he had.

Air Mechanic Bourne was assigned to Milton Airfield near Abingdon, Oxfordshire and it was there that he served for nearly eighteen months. He seems to have enjoyed his time off as much as his time working and boating on the Thames nearby was a hobby. Sadly, it was also to be his undoing.

On 2nd May 1917, he was out on the river at Culham Reach; the local newspaper account picked up the story:

> *Accidentally drowned was the verdict returned at the inquest last Saturday on Eustace Lionel Bourne, 21 [sic], attached to the mechanical department of the RFC, stationed at Milton.*
>
> *It appeared that while sculling with a colleague in Culham Reach on May 2nd, he lost a scull. His companion, who had dropped a rudder-line, was turning round at the time. Deceased, in leaning over to pick up the scull, fell into the river and disappeared. It was twilight at the time, and a search was unavailing.*

The other man, who could neither swim nor scull, was left in the boat, which was half filled with water.

The body was discovered on Friday morning near Sutton Weirs.

Reading Mercury: Saturday 19th May 1917

Eustace Lionel Bourne was just 20 years old when he drowned. He lies at rest in the cemetery of Westonzoyland, his home village.

Name: Bowyer, Cecil

Rank: Ordinary Seaman

Regiment: Royal Navy

Date of death: 11th October 1918

Age at time of death: 18

Cause of death: Illness

Grave location: Wembdon Road Cemetery, Bridgwater

Cecil Henry Bowyer was born in October 1900, the oldest of four children to Harry and Bessie Bowyer. Harry was a carter and, at the time of the 1901 census, the family lived in a small house in the middle of Bridgwater, with Harry's sister, Bessie's mother and an additional boarder.

Bessie was keen to earn her way, becoming a musical instrument dealer, while her husband moved on to work as a foreman for a coal merchant. By this time, the family had moved round the corner from their former home, and Harry and Bessie lived there with Cecil, his younger siblings Leslie, Henry and Doris, and another boarder.

Harry found himself before the Bankruptcy Court in 1913. By this time, he was carrying on business as a gramophone and cycle agent, as well as his carter business. Bad debts and living expenses were his downfall, however, and he found himself with a deficiency of £83 15s 5d. The examination was declared closed, according to the Wells Journal, but no outcome was reported.

War was looming, and the family did their bit. Harry joined up, enlisting in the Royal Engineers as a sapper. He was shipped to Salonica, Greece, where he served for much of the war.

Cecil, however, chose the seafaring route. He had to wait until he came of age before enlisting, however, and so it was late September 1918 before he joined the Royal Naval Voluntary Reserve. He started his training at the training base in Crystal Palace but was only there for a couple of weeks before he fell ill.

Contracting pneumonia, Ordinary Seaman Bowyer was admitted to hospital, but sadly this took him quickly, and he passed away on 11th October 1918. He had just turned 18 years old.

Cecil Henry Bowyer was brought back to Bridgwater to be buried; he lies at rest in the Wembdon Road Cemetery there.

Name: Boyce, Henry

Rank: Private

Regiment: British West Indies Regiment

Date of death: 24th October 1918

Age at time of death: 46

Cause of death: Pneumonia

Grave location: St Leonard's Churchyard, Butleigh

Henry Leslie Boyce was born on 14th June 1872 in the parish of St Michael, Barbados, then the British West Indies. His parents were Samuel and Mary Boyce.

Further details of his early life are scant, but Henry appears to have moved to England at some point in the early 1890s. The 1911 census shows him living in Ilford, Essex, and working as an iron and metal merchant. His wife Rosanna, a dressmaker, was born in Wincanton, Somerset, and they married in 1896. The young couple had two children; sadly, they both died young.

Henry was quick to do his duty when war broke out, joining up in September 1914. He enlisted in the British West Indies Regiment, and after training on the Home Front, served in France from April 1917. While there, he was promoted to Acting Corporal, but contracted bronchial pneumonia and was sent back to England to recuperate after only five months.

A medical report from November 1917 states that Acting Corporal Boyce remained unfit for military service, and he was discharged from the army at the end of that year. The same report showed him as a former commercial traveller, living in Forest Gate. It marks him as having a very good military character: "*Judging from his records, he is a steady, sober, well-conducted man*".

While no information after that point is available for him, it seems that he succumbed to the disease less than a year later.

Henry Leslie Boyce died on 24th October 1918. He was 46 years old.

He lies at rest in the graveyard of St Leonard's Church in Butleigh, Somerset, presumably close to his widow's family.

Name: Bracey, Victor

Rank: Second Lieutenant

Regiment: Royal Flying Corps

Date of death: 22nd September 1917

Age at time of death: 19

Cause of death: Flying accident

Grave location: St Mary's Churchyard, Wedmore

Victor Charles Edelsten Bracey was born in October 1897, the only child of William and Florence Bracey. William was a physician and surgeon, practicing in Lancashire when Victor was born. The young family soon moved south, however, and by the time of the 1901 census, they were living in Wedmore, Somerset, where William had taken up as the village's general practitioner.

Military records for Victor are not available, but his life can readily be pieced together from newspaper reports of his death and the *de Ruvigny's Roll of Honour*, published after the war.

TWO PILOTS KILLED IN THE NEW FOREST

Two air fatalities have occurred within twenty-four hours of each other in the New Forest. On Saturday [22nd September 1917] Second Lieutenant Ernest Hargrave's machine nose-dived from the height of 200ft and crashed to earth.

Second Lieutenant Victor Bracey was flying on Sunday morning at a height of 300ft, when his machine turned and came down in a spinning nose-dive.

At the inquests verdicts of "Death by misadventure" were returned.

Western Gazette: Friday 28th September 1917

BRACEY, VICTOR CHARLES EDELSTEN, 2nd Lieut., RFC, only child of William Edelsten Bracey, LRCP [Licentiate of the Royal College of Physicians], Lieut. (Hon.) RAMC (retired), by his wife, Florence Marion, dau. of the late James Canning Gould.

[Victor was] educated St Peter's School, Weston-super-Mare, and Blundell's School, Tiverton, where he was a member of the OTC [Officers' Training Corps]; passed into the Royal Military Academy in April 1915; joined the Inns of Court OTC in December 1916; was gazetted 2nd Lieut. RFC [Royal Flying Corps] 27 April 1917, obtaining his wings in July, and was killed in an aerial accident at the Beaulieu Aerodrome, Hampshire, 23 September, while testing a new machine.

A brother officer wrote that he was "a gallant gentleman and a most skilful pilot." He was a keen cricketer and footballer, and while at Blundell's played in the First Cricket XI and the Second Football XV, and was also captain of the First Hockey XI; later played for the Royal Military Academy, Woolwich, and the RFC Rugby Football XV at Oxford.

de Ruvigny's Roll of Honour, 1914-1919

A note on Second Lieutenant Bracey's Roll of Honour states that he was ineligible for medals as he saw no overseas service; this seems to have been challenged by Victor's father in 1921, but nothing confirms whether anything was subsequently awarded.

Victor Charles Edelsten Bracey lies at rest in the churchyard of St Mary's in Wedmore, where his father continued to practice. He died, aged just 19 years of age.

William's prominence in the village played a big part in Victor's legacy. A Memorial Fund was set up; this helped fund "*necessitous cases for medical requirements and for conveying patients to hospitals*". The Victor Bracey Cup was also awarded into the 1940s for sporting achievement in the schools he had attended.

Name: Bradbeer, William

Rank: Second Lieutenant

Regiment: Royal Garrison Artillery

Date of death: 8th August 1920

Age at time of death: 32

Cause of death: Unknown

Grave location: Wembdon Road Cemetery, Bridgwater

William James Bradbeer was born in the spring of 1888, the youngest of eight children to Alfred and Jane Bradbeer from Bridgwater in Somerset. Alfred was a carriage trimmer, fitting out the train coaches for the local railways.

Sadly, William lost both of his parents in 1910; by this point he was 22 and was working as a schoolmaster along with his older brother Alfred. Five of the Bradbeer siblings were living together by this point, along with Sidney Palfrey, a photographer, who was boarding with them.

On 27th December 1911, William married Selina Nurse, who was also from Bridgwater, and whose father was a master mariner. The couple did not have any children together.

There is little evidence of William's life after his marriage. He was enlisted in the Royal Garrison Artillery during the war, although no details of his military service are available. The battalions provided support in key forts primarily along the south coast of England, but also in places like the Channel Isles, Malta and Sierra Leone. Without Second Lieutenant Bradbeer's records, it is impossible to know specifically where he served, but it would seem likely that he remained in England during the war.

The last years of William's life are also shrouded in mystery; he passed away on 8th August 1920, at the age of 32. I have been unable to uncover a cause of death, but it seems likely to have been an illness, as there is nothing in the contemporary media to suggest anything unusual or untoward.

William James Bradbeer lies at rest in the Wembdon Road Cemetery in his home town of Bridgwater. Sadly, though, his grave is also lost to time, and I was unable to pinpoint its location. In death, as in his later years, William remains a mystery.

Note: The photo shows a Bradbeer family grave, situated in the same cemetery.

Name: Brandao, Joaquim

Rank: Trabalhador

Regiment: Corpo de Lenhadores Portugueses

Date of death: 3rd October 1918

Age at time of death: Unknown

Cause of death: Unknown

Grave location: St Mary's Cemetery, Taunton

In a quiet corner of the St Mary's Cemetery in Taunton, Somerset, sit a pair of headstones.

Both are adorned with the word Portugal and have the word *Trabalhador* (translated as *Worker*) and the phrase *Corpo de Lenhadores Portugueses* (or *Portuguese Forestry Corps*) inscribed on them.

During the Great War, vast quantities of timber were required by the army in France. Initially imports from Canada provided most of what was needed but, as the war progressed, ships were required for other essential supplies, so imports of timber fell dramatically.

In 1916, the British Government asked the country's oldest ally, Portugal, to send workers to assist with the war effort. Soon both the Portuguese Forestry Corps and Canadian Forestry Corps had teams working all across the United Kingdom, totalling many thousands of men.

This side of the war effort was not without its casualties, and those serving were accorded Commonwealth War Graves.

There is no information readily available for Joaquim Maria Brandao. He would have come to England from Portugal at some point in 1916, but the only record of him is that of his passing.

He died on 3rd October 1918, although the cause of his death and the age at which he passed are lost to time.

Joaquim Maria Brandao lies at rest in St Mary's Cemetery in Taunton, Somerset.

Name: Brine, Gerald

Rank: Able Seaman

Regiment: Royal Navy

Date of death: 1st July 1918

Age at time of death: 20

Cause of death: Accidental shooting

Grave location: Holy Trinity Churchyard, Binegar

Gerald Montague Brine was born in October 1897, the youngest of seven children to John and Annie Brine. John was a potter, and, while the children were born in Dorset, the family soon moved to the Somerset village of Binegar.

Gerald's three older brothers all went to work in a local stone quarry, as an engineer, breaker and foreman respectively. When Gerald left school, he found work with the local blacksmith as a striker. It was while employed there, in 1912, that his mother Annie passed away, aged just 50 years old.

War was on its way, however, and where his brothers enlisted in the army, Gerald was bound for the sea. He enlisted in the Royal Navy on 3rd November 1915 and, as an Ordinary Seaman, was assigned to HMS Iron Duke. He was aboard the vessel when it became embroiled in the Battle of Jutland in May 1916 and was subsequently transferred to HMS Discoverer.

Promoted to Able Seaman in April 1918, the Discoverer headed back to Chatham a couple of months later. A Somerset newspaper picks up on Gerald's sad tale from there:

> *When one of His Majesty's ships was returning to port, and her crew were looking forward to "leave", an unfortunate tragedy occurred by which Gerald Montague Brine, a young Able Seaman [and] a native of Binegar, lost his life. It appears that in the course of storing gear, a loaded revolver was removed by mistake to the armourer's room, instead of to the officer's cabin, and was placed on a table.*

*Curiosity led Peter Macfarlane, another able seaman, to handle
it, and as he was bringing it to his side from an upward position,
he, to use his own words, unconsciously pulled the trigger. It
fired, and the bullet entered Brine's body just under his left
shoulder, fracturing his spine and producing paralysis of his
lower limbs.*

Wells Journal: Friday 12th July 1918

Gerald's parents had a telegram to say that he was seriously wounded and in the Royal Naval Hospital, Chatham. They travelled at once to Chatham and found him very ill, but conscious. They remained with him until he died a week later, on 1st July 1918. He was just 20 years of age.

At the inquest, Macfarlane described Brine as his best chum, and all witnesses agreed that "*the best possible relations existed between the members of the crew.*" According to the doctor's evidence at the inquest, Gerald was unable to be saved. The jury reached a verdict of Accidental Death.

Able Seaman Gerald Montague Brine was brought home to Binegar and lies at rest in the graveyard of Holy Trinity Church.

Gerald's grave also acts as a memorial to two of his older brothers.

Arthur Brine, who had been the stone breaker in the quarry, emigrated to Canada after his mother had died, finding work there as a fireman. The Great War brought him back to European shores, however, and he enlisted in the Canadian Expeditionary Force, joining the 188th Battalion.

Private Brine arrived in England in October 1916; he transferred to the 28th Canadians and set off for France the following January. He was caught up in the Battle of Arras and was hit and killed by a piece of shrapnel on 15th April 1917. He was just 29 years old.

Arthur Brine lies at peace in the Ecoivres Cemetery to the north-west of Arras in Northern France.

Herbert Brine had been the foreman at the stone quarry. He married Sarah Lucy James shortly before his mother's death in 1912; the couple went on to have two children, Arthur and Kenneth.

Herbert was mobilised in July 1917, initially joining the 3rd Reserve

Battalion. He was drafted, as an Able Seaman, to the Hood Battalion, Royal Naval Division (RND) in November 1917, before re-joining his RND Battalion at Flesquières, near Cambrai, two months later.

In early March 1918, the Germans started bombardments in preparation for a major offensive. For ten days from 12th March, the Flesquières salient was drenched with nearly a quarter of a million (mostly mustard) gas shells, and there were over 2,000 resultant casualties in the RND. After this preparatory shelling, the Germans attacked in enormous numbers.

By the end of the day, the situation was precarious, and the Division was forced to retreat in steps, through Bertincourt, Ypres and the Metz lines, through the old Somme battlefields.

Able Seaman Brine was first reported missing on 24th March but was only accepted as having been killed in action on that date nine months later. As such, Herbert is commemorated by name on the Arras Memorial; his name also resides on Gerald's gravestone back home in Binegar.

The Great War took its toll on the Brine family. Three of the four brothers died during those tumultuous years, leaving only John's oldest son, Wallace, to carry on the family name. John himself died in 1942, aged 84, and lies with his wife and youngest boy in the small Binegar churchyard.

Name: Britton, Edward

Rank: Sapper

Regiment: Royal Engineers

Date of death: 26th August 1918

Age at time of death: 48

Cause of death: Drowned

Grave location: St John's Cemetery, Bridgwater

Edward Britton was born in Bridgwater in 1870, one of nine children to Edward and Eliza Britton. Edward Sr was a mariner, and the family lived on the main road from the town to Bath.

There is a gap in the documentation for Edward Jr; when we next meet him on the 1911 census he is married with children of his own. His wife is Ada Olive Martin, the daughter of a bricklayer from Topsham in Devon. They had eight children, six of them girls, and, according to the document, Edward was working as a 'deal carrier', moving wood from the ships arriving in Bridgwater to the timber yard.

Sadly, Edward's service records are also sparse. He enlisted in the Royal Engineers as a Sapper and, given his age, it is likely that this was not early in the conflict. He was involved in the Inland Water Transport Division – given his father's work as a mariner, this doesn't come as a surprise.

The Army Register of Soldiers' Effects provides a surprising insight into Sapper Britton. It gives the date of his death, but notes the cause as *"Drowned, River Stour, Kent."* I have not been able to find out anything further – surprisingly, none of the contemporary newspapers report on the incident.

Sapper Britton's death remains something of a mystery, as did his early life. He passed away on 26th August 1918, at the age of 48.

Edward Britton lies at rest in St John's Cemetery in his home town of Bridgwater, Somerset.

Name: Budgett, James

Rank: Guardsman

Regiment: Coldstream Guards

Date of death: 4th May 1917

Age at time of death: 36

Cause of death: Aneurysm

Grave location: St Michael's Churchyard, Stoke St Michael

James Budgett was born in October 1880 and was one of nine children to Henry and Eliza Budgett. Henry was a labourer, and the family lived in the small village of Stoke St Michael, near Shepton Mallett in Somerset.

While initially following his father in to labouring, James was drawn to the military as a career. He enlisted in the army in August 1899 and was assigned to the Coldstream Guards. James' bearing would certainly have stood him in good stead for this wing of the army; his medical examination shows he was 6ft 1in (1.85m) tall.

Guardsman Budgett's initial service was for twelve years; during this time, he spent six months in Australia, but his records show that most of his time was spent on home soil.

When his term ended in August 1911, he enrolled for a further four years. Initially assigned to the Reserve Battalion, he was formally mobilised when war broke out. Sent to France as part of the British Expeditionary Force in August 1914, he was wounded in the foot two months later, and was sent home for treatment.

According to Guardsman Budgett's medical records, the treatment unearthed two other issues. One was that he was suffering from syphilis, which was treated. The other was that an x-ray identified an aneurysm in his aortic arch. This was considered harmful enough for him to be medically dismissed from the army, and he left active service on 25th March 1915.

After this, details of James' life get a bit hazy. His pension records show that he married a woman called Bessie, but there is nothing to confirm when the marriage took place.

The next record for James Budgett is confirmation of his passing. He died from an aneurysm on 4th May 1917, at the age of 36. He lies at rest in the graveyard of St Michael's Church in his home village of Stoke St Michael, Somerset.

Name: Burgess, Donald

Rank: Ordinary Seaman

Regiment: Royal Navy

Date of death: 8th October 1918

Age at time of death: 17

Cause of death: Pneumonia

Grave location: St Barnabas' Churchyard, Queen Camel

Donald Burgess was born in 1901 in the village of Queen Camel in Somerset. His father, Frank Luther Burgess was the local schoolmaster, and he and his wife Frances had four children, all sons.

By the time of the 1911 census, Donald and his three brothers – Claud, Wilfred and William – were all at school, and Frank was, by now, the village headmaster.

Donald seems to have volunteered as soon as his age allowed. He joined the Royal Naval Voluntary Reserve in September 1918 and was stationed at HMS Victory in Crystal Palace. He was training to become a wireless operator, but his time there seems to have been cut cruelly short.

Able Seaman Burgess contracted pneumonia and was admitted to the 4th London General Hospital in nearby Camberwell. Sadly, he succumbed to the condition and passed away on 8th October 1918, after just a few weeks' service. He was just 17 years of age.

Donald Burgess lies at rest in sight of his father's school, in the graveyard of St Barnabas' Church.

Name: Burke, Albert

Rank: Lance Corporal

Regiment: Somerset Light Infantry

Date of death: 13th March 1921

Age at time of death: 23

Cause of death: Suicide by poison

Grave location: St Mary's Cemetery, Taunton

Sometimes, researching war graves can throw a bit of a curve ball, and the things you uncover can make you stop in your tracks. Such is the story surrounding Lance Corporal Albert Burke, and a media report surrounding his death in March 1921.

SCHEME OF VENGEANCE

Taunton Suicide's Amazing Last Letter

Toll On Young Women

A sensational affair has occurred at Taunton Barracks. On Sunday morning, Albert (or Alfred James) Burke, aged 23, a Lance Corporal in the Somerset Light Infantry, was found to have taken his life by inhaling chloroform, his dead body being found on a bed at the military hospital, where he was employed as an orderly.

On Saturday night, according to the evidence, the deceased appeared to be in his usual health and spirits. The next morning, a comrade found his dead body with a chloroform bottle by its side and near his face a large piece of cotton wool which he had evidently used for the purpose of inhaling the poison.

Some light was thrown on the tragedy by a letter addressed to a Taunton young woman, found on his clothing, and which was read at the inquest yesterday.

It was of an extraordinary character, and began "You wish to know what my intentions are in regard to you. Well, in the first place let me tell you I am not, as the coroner who holds the inquest will adjudge me, insane. In fact, I don't think I was ever so rational or level-minded as at the present moment, although I have had a glass or two.

"Well, Beatrice, mine is a rather long and interesting story. I married Louisa Wills some time in 1917, and I think the least said about her the better, but I wish to say this, that I have never knocked across a beast to equal her for violence. I am afraid the people around Brentford, Middlesex, could give you a far better account of her than I can."

The writer went on to make certain allegations against the woman, and then referred to other towns where, he said, he had ruined girls before coming to Taunton and joining the Somerset Light Infantry. He added that he spent Friday night, when he was supposed to go out with Beatrice, with another girl in the barracks.

He said his father committed suicide owing to a "thing" who called herself a woman, and he (deceased) got a feeling with him that he would like to pay it back on a few girls. In conclusion, Burke expressed his satisfaction at knowing the condition Beatrice was in, and that he had been able to add another to the list of those on whom he wished to have his revenge.

Evidence was given by Alec Treeby, civilian orderly at the Barracks, who found deceased. In reply to the coroner, witness said that he knew the man was keeping company with a girl, but was not aware that there was any trouble about her.

PC Carter stated that the police had made enquiries, and a telephone message had been received that nothing was known of the man or of a wife and family of the name at Brentford...

[The] medical officer at Taunton Barracks said deceased was a steady, hard-working man, and, so far as he knew, perfectly sane.

The jury returned a verdict of "suicide while of unsound mind".

Western Times: Wednesday 16th March 1921

The newspaper report confirms the Lance Corporal's name as either Albert or Alfred James Burke; the coroner also went on to say that he had also used the aliases of Povery and Pavey. Sadly, research around these names – and that of Louisa Wills – have either led to frustrating dead ends, or to results too vague to concretely connect them to Lance Corporal Burke.

The life and loves of Lance Corporal Burke are destined to remain a mystery. All that can be confirmed is that he took his own life on 13th March 1921; he was 23 years old.

Albert Burke lies at peace in St Mary's Cemetery in Taunton, Somerset. He was accepted for commemoration as war dead on 27th May 2016 and was afforded a gravestone by the Commonwealth War Graves Commission.

Name: Burleton, Percy

Rank: Sapper

Regiment: Royal Engineers

Date of death: 17th September 1918

Age at time of death: 32

Cause of death: Illness

Grave location: St Peter's Churchyard, Draycott

Percy Edward Burleton was born on 24th July 1885, the youngest of seven children to George and Lucy Burleton. George was a quarryman, and the family lived in the village of Draycott, near Wells in Somerset.

Percy's older brother Lewis worked for the railways, and this is a trade that his younger sibling followed. By the time of the 1911 census he was living with his brother in Glastonbury and worked as a carman, delivering goods to and from the local station.

In February 1914, Percy appeared as a witness in an inquest about the death of a colleague, George Gillett. George had gone missing one night after the two had met for a drink in a local pub. The alert was raised when George's coat was found hanging on a branch on the banks of the River Brue, to the south of the town; the waters were dredged, and George's body found.

At the inquest, Percy confirmed that the two men had had a drink in a local pub, and that George had seemed a little strange, but not the worse for drink. He reported that the deceased man had been quieter than usual at the railway stables for a week or so. George had left the pub at 10:55 that evening, and that was the last time that Percy had seen him.

Part of a carman's duty was to collect money for the goods they had delivered; this was then paid to the station clerk on a daily basis. In the week leading up to his death, the stationmaster had been advised of some financial discrepancies, and on the day that he drowned, Percy had been spoken to and advised the matter would be reported to the police if the missing amount was not paid back.

The place where George's coat was found was not on his way home from the pub, and he would have had to have gone out of his way to get there. When considering their findings, the jury returned a verdict of suicide during temporary insanity, citing that the financial situation George had apparently gotten himself into.

When war broke out, Percy seemed to have been keen to get involved. Initially joining the Devonshire Regiment in September 1914, his experience with his job saw him transferred to the Railway Operating Division of the Royal Engineers.

Shipped to France on 22nd September 1915, his service saw him awarded the Victory and British Medals and the 1915 Star. Sapper Burleton was moved to the Eastern Front and served in the Balkans for three years. According to the Central Somerset Gazette, which reported his passing, he contracted 'a chill' on the boat back to England and was admitted to Frensham Hill Hospital in Surrey.

Sadly, the chill seems to have been more severe than the report suggested, and Sapper Burleton passed away on 17th September 1918. He was 32 years old.

Percy Edward Burleton lies at rest in the graveyard of St Peter's Church in his home village of Draycott, Somerset.

Name: Burnett, James

Rank: Private

Regiment: Devonshire Regiment

Date of death: 29th February 1920

Age at time of death: 32

Cause of death: Unknown

Grave location: St Lawrence's Churchyard, Lydeard St Lawrence

James Burnett was born in 1888, the second son of James and Sarah Ann Burnett. James Sr was a farm labourer, and his son quickly followed his line of work.

James enlisted in the Devonshire Regiment in February 1916. He was noted as being 5ft 2ins (1.58m) tall and weighed in at 7.5st (47.6kg).

Private Burnett's medical record notes that his sight was such that he should wear glasses constantly, and, in fact, he was signed off medically as Category B1 ("*Free from serious organic diseases, able to stand service on Lines of Communication in France, or in garrisons in the tropics. Able to march 5 miles, see to shoot with glasses, and hear well.*")

After training, Private Burnett was mobilised in September 1916, but transferred to the Agricultural Company (of the Labour Corps) in the summer of 1917.

Sadly, however, I have been unable to locate any details of James' passing. He died on 29th February 1920 and lies at rest in the local churchyard of his home village, Lydeard St Lawrence, Somerset.

Name: Burroughs, George

Rank: Pioneer

Regiment: Royal Engineers

Date of death: 8th April 1917

Age at time of death: 18

Cause of death: Meningitis

Grave location: Somerton Cemetery

George William Burroughs was born in 1899, the eldest of two sons to harness maker Stratton Burroughs and his wife Alexandra. George was born in Warminster, Wiltshire, but the family soon moved closer to Alexandra's family in Somerton, Somerset.

The 1911 census found the young family living in Market Place in the centre of Somerton, with a visitor, fancy goods seller Joseph Cazes from Constantinople.

George seems to have enlisted almost as soon as he was old enough to do so, giving up his job as a school teacher (surprising given he was only 17 at the time). He signed up for the Royal Engineers in January 1917, gaining the role of Pioneer.

Sadly, his time in the services was very short. Within weeks of being posted, Pioneer Burroughs was admitted to hospital with meningitis, an illness that was becoming more widespread within the armed forces.

Tragically, after a month in the Norton Barracks Military Hospital in Worcestershire, George passed away from the disease. He was just 18 years old.

George William Burroughs lies at rest in the cemetery of his home town of Somerton.

Name: Cassidy, Charles

Rank: Company Serjeant Major

Regiment: Somerset Light Infantry

Date of death: 13th February 1916

Age at time of death: 60

Cause of death: Heart failure

Grave location: St Mary's Cemetery, Taunton

Charles Cassidy's early life is a bit of a challenge to uncover. He was born in County Antrim, Ireland in around 1856, but there is little concrete information to identify his parentage or his movements before the late 1870s.

A newspaper report of his passing confirms that his military career began early. He joined the Somerset Light Infantry, and *"saw active service in the Zulu campaign in 1879, and in Burmah 1885-1887."* [Western Times: Tuesday 15th February 1916]

In around 1890, he married a woman called Annie; she came from Wareham in Dorset, and the couple went on to have three children – Daisy, Charles and Margaret.

After completing his military service, Charles continued to work as a messenger for the regiment. However, when war came, he was called up again, acting as Company Serjeant Major in the Taunton Barracks.

Charles' military service was not to be prolonged, however. On 13th February 1916, he was in the Sergeants' Mess in the barracks, when he suddenly collapsed with heart failure, dying almost instantaneously. He was 60 years old.

Charles Cassidy lies at rest in St Mary's Cemetery in Taunton, next to the barracks where he so readily did his duty.

Name: Cawley, Henry

Rank: Private

Regiment: Somerset Light Infantry

Date of death: 21st February 1916

Age at time of death: 45

Cause of death: Illness

Grave location: St James' Cemetery, Taunton

Henry Cawley was born in September 1871, one of eight children to John and Ann Cawley. John worked as a blacksmith in the village of Corfe, near Taunton, Somerset, but when Henry left school, he found work as a butcher's assistant in Bristol.

Henry disappears from the radar for a while. John died in 1884, but the next information available for his son comes in the form of his war medals. This confirms that he enlisted in the Somerset Light Infantry in the summer of 1915, and that he was assigned to the depots as a Private. He was awarded the Victory and British Medals, as well as the 1915 Star, but then fell ill early in 1916.

Private Cawley was medically evacuated back to England and was admitted to a sanatorium in Taunton. Sadly, whatever illness he contracted, he succumbed to, and he passed away on 21st February 1916, at the age of 45 years old.

Henry Cawley was laid to rest in St James' Cemetery in Taunton.

Henry's war pension was given to his mother, Ann. After her husband's death, she continued to live in Corfe and, based on the available information, lived into her 80s.

Name: Chapman, John

Rank: Sapper

Regiment: Royal Engineers

Date of death: 2nd June 1916

Age at time of death: 23

Cause of death: Pneumonia

Grave Location: Churchyard of St Mary the Virgin, Croscombe

John Chapman was born in October 1892 in the small Somerset village of Ashwick, just to the north of Shepton Mallet. One of five children to Albert and Mary Ann, John followed his father into mining, and, by the time of the 1911 census, he was listed as a coal mining hewer.

In November 1914, he married Louisa Elizabeth Perkins from Shepton Mallet. The war had begun by this point, and before the couple had even been married a year, John had enlisted.

His background made him ideal for the Royal Engineers, and soon Sapper Chapman was bound for France with the British Expeditionary Force. He seems to have been abroad for around six months and was shipped back to England at the end of April 1916.

John was admitted to a Military Hospital in Brockenhurst, Hampshire, with bronchial pneumonia, and this is what he succumbed to a matter of weeks later. He died on 2nd June 1916, at the age of 23 years old.

John Chapman is buried in the village of Croscombe, Somerset, where his widow now lived.

An additional tragedy to the loss of this young life is that Louisa was pregnant at this point. The birth of their daughter, Selina, was registered between April and June 1916, and, while I have been unable to pinpoint an exact date of birth for her, it is likely that John never got to see his daughter.

Name: Chinn, Hedley

Rank: Air Mechanic 1st Class

Regiment: Royal Naval Air Service

Date of death: 2nd January 1921

Age at time of death: 29

Cause of death: Unknown

Grave location: Holy Cross Churchyard, Middlezoy

Hedley Walter Chinn was born in April 1900, one of six children to Walter and Kate Chinn. Walter was the butcher in the Somerset village of Middlezoy, and this is where the family had made their home.

There is little information on Hedley's pre-war life, beyond the two census records of 1901 and 1911. With war breaking out and his older sister Lilian dying while nursing the troops (see next entry), it seems that Hedley was eager to do his duty.

Within months of Lilian's death in 1917 – and basically as soon as his age allowed – Hedley enlisted in the Royal Naval Air Service as a mechanic. He carried out his initial training on the land-based ships President II, Impregnable and Cranwell, before officially joining the newly formed Royal Air Force in May 1918.

Air Mechanic Chinn continued his service at Calshott, where he worked as a wireless operator for the flying boats guarding the Solent around Southampton. He continued in the role for the remainder of the war and beyond.

Hedley was eventually transferred to the RAF Reserve in February 1920, when, presumably, he returned to the family home in Somerset.

Little further is evident of Hedley's life, but he passed away less than a year after being demobbed. There is nothing to confirm the cause of his death; given he died more than two years after the war, it is likely that it was as a result of an illness, although this is a presumption on my part. Either way, he died on 2nd January 1921, aged just 29 years old.

Hedley Walter Chinn lies at rest in the peaceful graveyard of Holy Cross Church in Middlezoy, Somerset.

When researching Hedley's life, I ran through the contemporary newspapers to trace his name. Nothing evident came up, although Hedley's father, Walter's name *did* appear.

In 1910, he declared himself bankrupt after being unable to pay for meat for his shop, that he had bought at auction. It appears that he had run up debts of over £300 (approximately £23,500 in today's money) over a number of years; he put these debts down to a number of factors – "*illness of my children, bad debts, having to maintain my mother for 14 years; and loss on sale of Middlezoy House, Middlezoy, three years ago, which realised £200 less than the amount I gave for it, and the amount expended on improvements*".

Walter's debts were finally cleared in 1928 and the bankruptcy annulled.

The gravestone in Holy Cross Churchyard is a haunting memorial to the tragic lives of the Chinn family.

Walter and Kate had six children and would outlive every one of them. The stone confirms that each of their children lies in the grave:

- Clarence Joseph (born 1891, died 1907)
- Myrtle Amy (born 1892, died 1893)
- Lilian Ella (born 1893, died 1917)
- Hilda Kate (born 1895, died 1896)
- Hedley Walter (born 1900, died 1921)
- Hilda Godfrey (born 1903, died 1904)

The grave's epitaph – *God moves in a mysterious way, his wonders to perform* – sounds cruelly hollow to 21st century ears. The only comfort to take, I guess, is that the whole family was destined to be together again: both Kate (who died in 1927) and Walter (who died in 1933) are also buried in the family grave.

Name: Chinn, Lilian

Rank: Nurse

Regiment: Voluntary Aid Detachment

Date of death: 24th June 1917

Age at time of death: 23

Cause of death: Meningitis and peritonitis

Grave location: Holy Cross Churchyard, Middlezoy

Lilian Ella Chinn was born in 1893, one of six children to Walter and Kate Chinn. Walter was the butcher in the Somerset village of Middlezoy, and this is where the family had made their home.

There is little recorded of Lilian, and the information is confusing – another Lilian Chinn was born around the same time a few miles away, so it's a challenge to identify the correct details.

What *is* known, is that, with the war raging, Lilian felt that she needed to do what she could – and enlisted in the Voluntary Aid Detachment in 1916. Serving as a nurse, she was based at the Military Hospital in Devonport, Plymouth.

Sadly, it is evident that nursing staff were not immune to the ailments and illnesses of the soldiers they were treating. Lilian contracted meningitis and peritonitis, passing away on 24th June 1917, aged just 23 years old.

Lilian Ella Chinn lies at rest in the peaceful graveyard of Holy Cross Church in Middlezoy, Somerset.

Lilian's brother Hedley also served – and perished – as a result of the Great War. Read the previous entry to learn more.

Name: Chubb, Oliver

Rank: Private

Regiment: Canadian Infantry

Date of death: 17th December 1918

Age at time of death: 33

Cause of death: Lymphatic leukaemia

Grave location: St John's Cemetery, Bridgwater

Oliver Job Chubb was born on 3rd December 1884 in the village of Smallbridge in Devon. He was one of six children to Job Chubb, who was an agricultural labourer, and his wife Louisa. Oliver did not seem to be one for settling down; after his parents had moved the family to Ilminster in Somerset when he was just a child, by 1901 he was living in Lyme Regis, working as a carter in a market garden.

In 1902, at the age of 17, Oliver enlisted in the Somerset Light Infantry. Eighteen months later he transferred to the Royal Navy, serving as a Stoker on a number of ships during what would become twelve years' service, including the Royal Oak, Skirmisher and Newcastle.

In 1906 he married Rosina Keirle, a brickmaker's daughter from Somerset. The wedding was in Bridgwater, and the couple went on to have three children, Olive, Albert and Cecil.

There is a sense that Oliver either had perpetually itchy feet, or that he was always running from something. The 1911 census found him aboard HMS Suffolk in the Mediterranean, where he listed himself as single. By the end of his naval service in November 1915, however, Stoker Chubb disembarked in the port of Victoria, British Colombia, and immediately signed up for military service with the Canadian Expeditionary Force.

Again, however, indecision seems to have set in. He listed his marital status as 'single' and confirmed his next of kin as his sister Elsie, but on his military will, he left everything to Rosina.

Private Chubb was assigned to the 29th Battalion of the Canadian Infantry;

they served on the Western Front from early in 1915 through to the end of the war. He was involved in the fighting at Ypres, and, in September 1916, was treated in England for an inguinal hernia. After three months' recovery, he returned to the front.

While Private Chubb seems to have had a good overall manner, there were blips in his character. In May 1917, he was sentenced to three days' field punishment for being absent without leave for 21hrs. In March 1918, he was sentenced to another five days' field punishment for going AWOL for 48 hours. On 11th April 1918, Private Chubb received 14 days' field punishment for drunkenness on duty.

In December of that year, Oliver was invalided back to England for medical treatment; he was admitted to the Fort Pitt Military Hospital in Chatham with lymphatic leukaemia. Sadly, Private Chubb passed away shortly after being admitted, dying on 17th December 1918. He was 34 years old.

Oliver Job Chubb lies at rest in St John's Cemetery in Bridgwater, where his family still lived.

Name: Clarke, Charles

Rank: Serjeant Major

Regiment: Royal Army Service Corps

Date of death: 8th August 1915

Age at time of death: 31

Cause of death: Suicide by shooting

Grave location: Milton Cemetery, Weston-super-Mare

Charles Edward Nesbit Clarke was born in December 1884, the son of Ralph Clarke. Sadly, there is little documentation to flesh out his early life. He had at least one sibling, a sister called Nellie, and was born in London, possibly in Hampstead.

Charles seemed to have been mechanically minded; when he left school, he found work with a motor vehicle fitter, before going on to get employment as an electrical engineer.

He met a woman called Elizabeth Bertha Gould, and the couple married in Islington in November 1908. Four years later, the couple had a child, Edward. The boy's baptism record shows that the family were living in the St John's Road Workhouse in Islington, so things seemed to have been really tough for them. (There are no other workhouse records available, so it may be that it was a temporary residence, while Edward was born, but this cannot be confirmed either way.)

The Great War broke out, and Charles enlisted straight away. He had found employment as a foreman fitter by this point, and joined the Army Service Corps, in the Motor Transport Division. A week later he went to France, as part of the British Expeditionary Force, and served there for seven months.

When he returned to England, having gained the 1914 Star and the British and Victory Medals for his service, he was assigned to the military camp at Burnham-on-Sea, Somerset.

Five months later, a local newspaper picked up the sorry story of what happened next:

At Weston-super-Mare Hospital... Dr S Craddock held an inquest on the body of Staff Sergeant Major Charles Clark [sic], Army Service Corps, who was admitted to that institution suffering from a mortal and self-inflicted wound received at the Burnham military camp on Sunday morning.

Captain Budibent deposed that at the time the deceased was detained in camp as the result of having been absent from duty for four days without leave. On hearing of his return, witness (who liked the man and recognised his great value, having served with him in France) went to the tent to see him. Deceased was very upset, and in reply to a question said "I can't account for staying away; I must have been mad." Witness tried to cheer him up, reminding him that it was not "a hanging matter", to which Clark replied "No, sir, I wish it was." When they were in France together Clark confided to witness that a girl who once lived with him desired him to marry her on his returning from the Front, but he stated that he could not do so, as he loved another girl. As he was depressed, witness advised him on returning home to see the girl who considered she had a claim upon him, and, if it were a matter of money, to settle it, and then marry the other girl. On later returning to the Front from England, deceased said his troubles were over, that he had married the other girl, and that he could now do his work with a good heart. Witness, however, believed other troubles had arisen.

Sergeant Belt, ASC, said he had slept in the same tent with the deceased. Clark had a good night, but next morning became very depressed over the fact that half the Company were leaving the camp for another destination, and would be losing close friends. He remarked "The last hour has been the worst in my life." Later, when outside the tent, witness heard a rifle shot and, rushing in, found Clark lying in bed with a rifle wound in his chest. Deceased admitted that he had fired the rifle himself. Death occurred in Weston Hospital, whither he was removed the same night. The medical evidence revealed terrible internal injuries, the bullet having practically severed deceased's liver.

The jury returned a verdict that Clark committed suicide while temporarily insane.

Taunton Courier & Western Advertiser: Wednesday 18th August 1915

The newspaper report spell's Sergeant Major Clarke's name without an 'e'; this is, however, an error on their part. In addition, it raises some further questions, particularly Captain Budibent's comments. By the time of the First World War, Charles was married to Bertha. There is no record of him having married anyone else, so where the girl he loved, and the other who loved him came into it, it is impossible to say.

Sergeant Major Clarke had taken his own life at the age of just 31 years old. Bertha and their son were living in Chatham, Kent, at the time, and it seems likely that the cost of moving him closer to home may have ruled that out.

Charles Edward Nesbit Clarke's body was buried instead in the Milton Cemetery in Weston-super-Mare.

Name: Coates, Bertram

Rank: Private

Regiment: London Regiment

Date of death: 31st March 1917

Age at time of death: 27

Cause of death: Measles

Grave location: St Mary's Churchyard, Walton Clevedon

Bertram Noel Coates was born in the sleepy Somerset village of Walton-in-Gordano in the spring of 1890. He was the middle of three children to Herbert and Florence Coates. Herbert was a solicitor, and clerical work seemed to have been in the Coates' blood.

While he did not follow in his father's exact footsteps, by the time of the 1911 census, Bertram had found work as a bank clerk, and was boarding with his employer, James Barry, in Chipping Sodbury, Gloucestershire.

Bertram was obviously made very welcome in Chipping Sodbury, as, on 27th May 1914, he married his employer's daughter, Mary Barry. The couple would go on to have a daughter – Eileen – who was born in February 1916.

By the time of his wedding, Bertram had moved to London, and was working as a bank clerk in South Woodford, so was obviously showing an ambitious streak.

War was beckoning, however, and in December 1915, Bertram enlisted. Placed in the Army Reserve, he was finally mobilised in January 1917, and assigned to the 28th Battalion of the London Regiment, which was also known as the Artists Rifles.

Tragically, Private Coates' military service was to be a short one. While training, he contracted measles, which turned septic with additional complications. He sadly passed away on 31st March 1917, less than three months after being mobilised. He was just 27 years old.

Bertram Noel Coates was returned to Somerset. He lies at peace in the churchyard of St Mary's in Walton Clevedon, near his parents' home.

Name: Coggan, William

Rank: Staff Serjeant

Regiment: Royal Army Service Corps

Date of death: 29th July 1920

Age at time of death: 38

Cause of death: Unknown

Grave location: St John's Cemetery, Bridgwater

William Reginald Coggan was born in Twerton, near Bath, at the end of 1882. His father, also called William, was a railway guard, and with his mother, Annie, he would go on to raise nine children, six of them girls.

William Jr became known as Reginald, presumably to avoid confusion with his father. He didn't follow his father onto the railways but found a way to serve his country. In the 1901 census, he was working as a baker for the Army Service Corps and was based at the Stanhope Lines Barracks in Aldershot (along with more than 1800 others).

Ten years later – by the time of the 1911 census – William had left the army but continued his trade. He was listed as a baker of confections in Glastonbury and was living above the bakery with his wife of four years. I have been able to find little information about his wife, Kate, other than that she came from Dublin.

William's life becomes a little vague after the census. A newspaper report confirms that he had served in the South Africa war (1899-1902), and that he had seen five years' service in France. The report – and William's pension records – confirm that he had continued in the Army Service Corps, gaining the rank of Staff Sergeant.

William had died in Ireland, and his death registered in Fermoy, thirty miles to the north of Cork. The report confirmed that:

> *Nothing is yet known of how he came by his death, although a request was made for a post-mortem examination.*
> *Taunton Courier and Western Advertiser: Wednesday 11th August 1920.*

I can find no further information about his death and, unusually, his Pension Record gives the date, but not the cause. Staff Sergeant Coggan died on 29th July 1920, aged 38 years old.

William Reginald Coggan's body was brought back to England for burial. He lies at rest in St John's Cemetery in Bridgwater, Somerset.

Name: Coleman, Walter

Rank: Driver

Regiment: Royal Field Artillery

Date of death: 10th April 1915

Age at time of death: 28

Cause of death: Fell from horse

Grave location: St James' Cemetery, Taunton

Walter Coleman was born in the spring of 1887, one of seven children to James and Emily Coleman. James was a hairdresser and the family lived in the Somerset town of Taunton.

Walter didn't follow his father's trade; instead, after a spell working at a collar factory when he left school, he was soon employed as a groom.

On Christmas Day 1910, he married Kate Norris, and the couple set up in a two-up, two-down in the middle of the town.

War was on the horizon, however, and when it broke out, Walter signed up straight away. He joined the 72nd Brigade of the Royal Field Artillery as a Driver and trained at the Bulford Camp on Salisbury Plain. It was while he was here on 10th April 1915 that he had an accident and fell off his horse. Sadly, Driver Coleman fractured his skull and died of his injuries that day. He was just 28 years old.

Walter Coleman lies at rest in the St James' Cemetery in his home town of Taunton.

Walter's older brother Henry James Coleman also served in the Great War. Posted to France as part of the Labour Corps, he died of wounds on 12th April 1918. He was 33 years old and left behind a widow and four children. He is buried at the Longuenesse Souvenir Cemetery in France.

Name: Collard, William

Rank: Lance Corporal

Regiment: Royal Army Medical Corps

Date of death: 18th April 1915

Age at time of death: 23

Cause of death: Unknown

Grave location: St Mary's Churchyard, Wedmore

William Collard was born in August 1891, the youngest of two children to William and Agnes Collard from Wedmore in Somerset. William Sr was a carter for a local miller and his son followed him into labouring when he left school.

William's life seems to have been a tragic one. His mother died in 1910, while his sister Mabel passed a year later.

William married Eva Heal, a woman from the same village, in April 1914. The couple didn't go on to have any children.

There is limited information relating to William's military service. What *is* apparent is that he enlisted in the Royal Army Medical Corps, presumably at some point after the start of the Great War.

Private Collard's battalion, the 3rd South Midlands, were based in Essex and were shipped to France in March 1915. There is, however, no evidence that William went with his troop. His training must have gone well, however, and he was promoted to Lance Corporal.

Details of his death are vague; William's gravestone confirms he passed on 18th April 1915; the cause was not reported. He was 23 years of age.

A brief notice in a local newspaper gives a little more information:

> *Mr W Collard [Senior], of Wedmore, one of the patients at the Country Sanatorium, received last week the news of the death of his soldier son. The funeral took place on Thursday at Wedmore in the same grave as the mother and only other member of the family, a sister of the deceased.*
> *Shepton Mallet Journal: Friday 30th April 1915*

William Collard lies at rest in the churchyard of St Mary's Church in his home village of Wedmore, Somerset.

William is remembered on a plaque in Bristol Cathedral; this commemorates the fourteen members of the 3rd South Midland Field Ambulance who fell during the war.

Comment should also be made of William's father. In the space of four and a half years, he had lost his wife and both his children. He was already in a sanatorium when his son died. He too passed away, in December 1924, at the age of 58.

William's widow, Eva, never remarried. She went on to live to the age of 96, and passed away in Poole, on the Dorset coast.

Name: Collins, William, aka Clark, Geoffrey

Rank: Private

Regiment: Army Veterinary Corps

Date of death: 25th October 1918

Age at time of death: 32

Cause of death: Unknown

Grave location: Christ Church Graveyard, Coxley

One of the things I have found during this research is that occasionally a mystery will come to light. In the case of the gravestone in the Somerset village of Coxley – nestled on the main road between Wells and Glastonbury – it was the very identity of a person buried there that threw me.

The headstone in question simply says "WG Collins served as Private G Clark in the Army Veterinary Corps", but the research tools I normally use drew blanks.

The Commonwealth War Graves Commission website confirmed that the second name is Geoffrey Clark, but does not give full names for WG Collins.

Unfortunately, the Find A Grave website does not have the burial listed under either name, so that too was a dead end.

The British Newspaper Archives site – a record of media across the UK covering 250 years – similarly has no entry for either name around the time of his death, which suggests it was either not 'out of the ordinary' (not headline-grabbing) or his death and funeral were just not submitted to the local paper.

Fold3 – which stores military records – *does* have a document for 9978 Private Geoffrey Clark. The Register of Soldiers' Effects confirms that a war gratuity was awarded to his sister, Ada Jane Waldron, after his death.

And, as it turns out, it was Ada who proved the key to the mystery of her brother. Working on the basis that Ada's maiden name was Collins, I used Ancestry.co.uk to try and track her down. The site presented a family tree featuring both an Ada Jane Collins and, more importantly, a William George Collins, and the game was afoot...

William George Collins was born in the Somerset village of Coxley in the summer of 1889. He was the youngest of seven children – Ada was his oldest sister – to James Collins, an agricultural labourer, and his wife Jane.

Following the death of his mother in 1901, and his father a decade later, it's evident that William wanted to make his way in the world. By the 1911 census, he had moved to Wales, working as an attendant at the Glamorgan County Lunatic Asylum. The asylum, which was in Bridgend, South Wales, was home to nearly 900 patients, and William acted as one of the 120 staff looking after them.

War was on the horizon, however, and the mystery surrounding William returned once more. Military records for William (or Geoffrey) are limited; he enlisted in the Royal Army Veterinary Corps in the summer of 1915 and was shipped to France in September of that year.

There is no record why he enlisted under the name Geoffrey Clark, nor does there seem to be any evidence of either names in his family. As to his passing, there is nothing to give a hint as to how he died. All that can be confirmed for certain is that he passed away at the University War Hospital in Southampton on 25th October 1918, at the age of 32.

William's probate records give his address as Railway Terrace in Blaengarw and show that his effects went to his sister, Ada.

William George Collins – also known as Geoffrey Clark – lies at peace in the graveyard of Christ Church, in his home village of Coxley.

Name: Comer, Frederick

Rank: Gunner

Regiment: Royal Field Artillery

Date of death: 5th December 1918

Age at time of death: 25

Cause of death: Died from wounds

Grave location: Milton Cemetery, Weston-super-Mare

Frederick George Comer was born on 8th July 1893, the older of two children to Fred Comer and his wife Fanny. Fred Sr was a decorator and raised his family in his town of his birth, Weston-super-Mare.

While his younger brother Clifford followed in his father's footsteps and became a decorator, Frederick Jr had set his sights elsewhere. The Western-super-Mare Gazette and General Advertiser reported on 31st December 1910, that he had gained a certificate by Pitman's Shorthand with a speed of 60 words per minute. Within a year, he was working as a news reporter in the local area.

War was on the horizon, but sadly this is where Frederick's trail goes a bit cold. He enlisted in the Royal Field Artillery, although existing documents do not confirm a date for this. Gunner Comer definitely served overseas, however, and was wounded in action.

Sadly, the other information available confirms that Gunner Comer died from his wounds on 5th December 1918. He was just 25 years old.

Frederick George Comer's body was brought back to Weston-super-Mare; he lies at rest in the Milton Cemetery in his home town.

Name: Cook, Harold

Rank: Private

Regiment: Suffolk Regiment

Date of death: 4th October 1917

Age at time of death: 18

Cause of death: Accidental shooting

Grave location: Street Cemetery

Harold Cook was born in February 1899, the youngest of nine children to George and Amelia Cook from Street. George worked as a bootmaker, presumably for the Clark's factory in the town.

Harold lost his mother at a young age; Amelia passed away in 1901, aged just 41 years old.

By the time of the 1911 census, George, his two older sons – Maurice and George Jr – and his four daughters – Beatrice, Florence, Alice and Gladys – were all employed by the factory. In fact, the only member of the family *not* employed by Clark's was Harold himself, who was still at school.

Harold's military records are not available, but from the information I have been able to gather, it appears that he enlisted as soon as his age allowed. He joined the Suffolk Regiment and was in training when an accident occurred.

The local newspaper – the Central Somerset Gazette – picks up his story:

> It appears that about 11pm on August 24th [Private Cook was] in bed and suddenly got up, saying he was lying on something. This proved to be the oil bottle of his rifle and he said he would put it away. He got hold of his rifle and turned it muzzle downwards in order to put the oil bottle in the butt. When he closed the butt-trap the rifle went off.
>
> He at once exclaimed "Who put the safety catch forward?". Corporal Butler and [Private Johnson] then bandaged Private Cook's foot (which was drilled clean through) and he was taken away at once.

From subsequent evidence by the Adjutant, it transpired than the rifle had been faultily loaded and that the safety catch had been broken.

Deceased had received every possible attention at the American Hospital in Cambridge, but his leg had to be amputated and subsequently septicaemia set in and to this he succumbed.

The jury, in accordance with the Coroner's summing up, returned a verdict of "Accidental Death."

Central Somerset Gazette: Friday 19th October 1917

Private Cook died on 4th October 1917, aged just 18 years old. His body was brought back to his home town of Street, and he lies at rest in the local cemetery.

Name: Cottrell, William

Rank: Private

Regiment: Canadian Infantry

Date of death: 9th January 1919

Age at time of death: 33

Cause of death: Died of wounds

Grave location: St Mary's Churchyard, Wedmore

William Cottrell was born in April 1885, the third of twelve children to Henry and Annie Cottrell from Bampton, Devon. When William left school, he became an assistant to the village baker, but new opportunities lay ahead.

In May 1907, William married Maria Wall, the daughter of a stonemason from Wedmore in Somerset. Within weeks, the young couple had embarked for a new life, boarding the Empress of Britain in Liverpool, setting sail for Canada. Settling in Manitoba, William became a labourer, and he and Maria had three children – Leslie, Ronald and Kathleen.

War came, and William enlisted in the Canadian Expeditionary Force in August 1915. Shipped to England in the spring of the following year, Annie followed suit, returning to Somerset with the three children.

Private Cottrell was assigned to the 44th Battalion Canadian Infantry, setting off for France in August 1916, just weeks before his fourth child – Ruby – was born.

The battalion was involved in some of the fiercest fighting of the war, and it was during the Somme Offensive that William was shot in the left arm. Initially treated in the field, he was soon shipped back to England to recover in a Military Hospital in Epsom. Discharged after three months, he was returned to his battalion in early 1917.

The fierce fighting continued, and Private Cottrell was wounded again in October 1918. Further treatment back in the UK was needed, and he was admitted to the 1st Eastern General Hospital in Cambridge.

Details of William's injuries at the Somme are readily available, but information on his second lot of injuries is scarcer. They must have been pretty severe, however, as he was not discharged. He lost his final battle after four months, succumbing to his wounds on 9th January 1919. He was 33 years old.

William Cottrell lies at rest in the graveyard of St Mary's Church in his widow's home village of Wedmore, Somerset.

William's gravestone is also a memorial to his eldest son, Leslie, who was killed during the Second World War.

Details of his military service are sketchy, but he enlisted in the Queen's Own Royal West Kent Regiment. His battalion – the 1st – was involved in the fighting in Italy, and it was here that he lost his life. He was killed on 8th February 1944 and is buried in the Sangro River War Cemetery, in Abruzzo.

Name: Counsell, Stanley

Rank: Private

Regiment: Worcestershire Regiment

Date of death: 2nd May 1919

Age at time of death: 23

Cause of death: Influenza

Grave location: Glastonbury Cemetery

Stanley John Counsell was born in September 1896 to George and Ellen, farmers in Glastonbury.

The youngest of five children, Stanley was an apprentice carpenter by the time he enlisted with his brothers Lawrence and Wilfred.

Private Counsell joined the Worcestershire Regiment in 1915 and was sent into action in France in September 1916.

He suffered medically during the war, succumbing to tonsillitis and diarrhoea during his time in France. A bout of tuberculosis in late 1918 saw Stanley shipped back to the UK and admitted to a hospital in Newcastle-upon-Tyne.

The end of the Great War came and went, and Stanley was finally discharged from the army in March 1919, as no longer medically fit for war service.

On 2nd May 1919, less than six weeks after being discharged, Private Stanley Counsell passed away. He was 23 years old and was a victim not of the war, but of the subsequent influenza pandemic, which killed 250,000 people in the UK alone.

Stanley John Counsell lies at peace in the cemetery of his home town, Glastonbury.

Name: Coward, Albert

Rank: Private

Regiment: Devonshire Regiment

Date of death: 29th September 1918

Age at time of death: 18

Cause of death: Unknown

Grave location: Shepton Mallet Burial Ground

Albert Reginald Robert Coward was born on 26th August 1900, the middle of three children – all boys – for James and Florence Coward. James was a labourer and drayman for the railways, and the family lived in Shepton Mallet, Somerset.

Little remains of Albert's military service records. His older brother Arthur was a Corporal in the Somerset Light Infantry. He died in France in April 1918, which may have been a contributing factor to his sibling's decision to do his duty.

Albert enlisted in the 53rd Battalion of the Devonshire Regiment and, given his age, I would presume that this was as soon as he was able to – sometime in 1918.

Whether Private Albert Coward saw any military action is not known. He is listed as having passed away at a Military Hospital on 29th September 1918, although, as I have been unable to find a cause of death, it is likely to have been an illness, rather than an injury. Albert was aged just 18 years old.

Albert Reginald Robert Coward lies at rest in the cemetery of his home town.

Albert's brother, Corporal Arthur William James Coward, is commemorated on the Arras memorial in France. He was 23 years old when he died.

Name: Cowles, Henry

Rank: Private

Regiment: Bedfordshire Regiment

Date of death: 26th April 1920

Age at time of death: Unknown

Cause of death: Unknown

Grave location: Milton Cemetery, Weston-super-Mare

In a quiet corner of a cemetery in Somerset stands a gravestone to Private HJ Cowles. It confirms that he passed away on 26th April 1920, and that he was in the Bedfordshire Regiment during the First World War.

Little additional information on HJ Cowles is available. One document, the Medal Roll Index Card, confirms his first name as Henry, and that he had initially joined the Somerset Light Infantry. He was awarded the British Medal for his war service.

Cowles is a fairly common name in the Somerset area, and, without any additional information – date of birth, familial connections – it is impossible to narrow down the name on the gravestone to a specific Henry Cowles from the area or beyond.

There is also nothing in any contemporary newspapers to suggest that Private Cowles' passing was anything out of the ordinary.

Sadly, therefore, he remains a name lost to history. Henry J Cowles, whoever he was, and however he died, lies at rest in the Milton Cemetery in Weston-super-Mare, Somerset.

Name: Criddle, Charles

Rank: Private

Regiment: Hampshire Regiment

Date of death: 7th November 1919

Age at time of death: 19

Cause of death: Illness

Grave location: St James' Cemetery, Taunton

Charles Pretoria Criddle was born on 18th June 1900, the second of five children to Charles and Mary Criddle. Charles Sr was an army reservist, who worked as a labourer for the local council, and the family lived in Taunton, Somerset.

Sadly, little detail of Charles Jr's life is documented. The Great War broke out when he was only 14, so was too young to enlist at the beginning of the conflict. However, he *did* volunteer, albeit later on, and joined the 15th Battalion of the Hampshire Regiment at some point in 1918.

Private Criddle's was one of those lives to be cut tragically short, not by conflict, but by illness. He survived the war but was subsequently admitted to a Military Hospital in Brighton, Sussex, where he passed away 'from disease' on 7th November 1919. He was just 19 years of age.

Charles Pretoria Criddle lies at rest in the St James' Cemetery in his home town of Taunton, Somerset.

Tragedy was to strike again for Charles Criddle Sr. Less than a week after his son had passed, he was called upon to identify the body of his sister, Emma Cable. She had taken her own life after suffering an increasing number of fits over the previous few years.

Emma was a widow, and, since the previous winter, had become increasingly depressed and less physically able, having suffered a debilitating bout of influenza. Early on the morning of Sunday 16th November 1919, she took herself out, dressed in only her nightgown and a pair of boots, and had drowned herself in the River Tone.

At the inquest into her passing, her doctor noted that he had seen her on the previous Thursday "*but her condition was not such that he could certify her as insane, but she had been violently hysterical.*" [*Taunton Courier and Western Advertiser: Wednesday 19th November 1919*]

The coroner recorded a verdict that the deceased drowned herself while of unsound mind.

Emma Cable was 52 years old.

Name: Crook, Gordon

Rank: Private

Regiment: Hampshire Regiment

Date of death: 31st March 1921

Age at time of death: 21

Cause of death: Unknown

Grave location: Shepton Mallet Burial Ground

Gordon Spencer Crook was born in 1900, one of thirteen children to William and Elizabeth Crook from Somerset. William, like his father, was a gardener, and the family lived in Lower Lane, a small lane sandwiched between the railway and a stream in the centre of Shepton Mallet.

The military records for Gordon, who seems also to have gone by the name of George, are a challenge to piece together. His older brothers Walter and Bertram both died as a result of the fighting, both in 1916, and it seems likely that Gordon was keen to do his bit as soon as he could, to honour their memories.

He enlisted in the Hampshire Regiment, whose battalions served both in France and on the Home Front. There is conflicting information about his service, but Private Crook appears to have fought at the front, gaining the Victory and British Medals.

Again, with his passing, there is little information surrounding Gordon, or George. A brief notification in the Shepton Mallet Journal stated that "*On March 31, at Royal Victoria Hospital Netley, Gordon Spencer, the dearly loved son of W and E Crook, [passed away] aged 21 years.*"

Gordon Spencer Crook lies at rest in the cemetery of his home town, Shepton Mallet.

Gordon's brother Walter is also buried in Shepton Mallet Cemetery – read his story, and that of third brother Bertie, in the next entry.

Name: Crook, Walter

Rank: Rifleman

Regiment: Rifle Brigade

Date of death: 30th October 1916

Age at time of death: 27

Cause of death: Unknown

Grave location: Shepton Mallet Burial Ground

Walter George Crook was born in 1900, one of thirteen children to William – a gardener – and Elizabeth Crook from Shepton Mallet in Somerset.

When he left school, Walter worked as a printer for the town's newspaper and, by the time of the 1911 census, he was living with his family in a six-roomed house in the middle of the town.

Walter moved on from the Shepton Mallet Journal and found employment at the Hare and Hounds Hotel in the town. War was coming, however, and he enlisted in the 22nd (Wessex and Welsh) Battalion of the Rifle Brigade.

Rifleman Crook was stationed with his battalion in Salonica, Greece, and it was while he was here that he suffered a cerebral tumour. He was invalided home, and treated in the Royal Victoria Hospital in Netley, Hampshire. Sadly, he lost his fight, passing away on 30th October 1916, aged just 27 years old.

Walter George Crook lies at rest in the cemetery of his home town of Shepton Mallet.

Walter's brother, Bertie, also gave his life in the Great War. The local newspaper had given a touching report on his death in April 1916.

> *Bertie Crook left school at the age of 13, and went into service with Mrs Dickinson at Whitstone, as a stable lad. He was there a year and then, on account of Mrs Dickinson giving up horses and leaving the town, they recommended him to Lord Derby's stables at Newmarket, under the Hon. G Lambton. Small as he was,*

Bertie Crook undertook the railway journey alone, with a label in his buttonhole. He served five years apprenticeship, which expired at the beginning of October [1915]. He then tried to join the Royal Field Artillery, but not being tall enough he joined a West country regiment on the 20th October, and left Tidworth Barracks for France in the early part of January. He was in his 21st year, having been born on the 29th July. 1895.

The Hon. George Lambton writes "I was terribly shocked and grieved to hear of the death of your boy... Mrs Lambton and I send our deepest sympathy... I always liked your boy so much when he was in my stable; and I felt sure that with his quiet and courageous character he would make a good soldier. I shall have a plate put up in the stable in memento of his glorious death."

Shepton Mallet Journal: Friday 21st April 1916

Lance Corporal Bertram Stanley Crook is buried at the 13th London Graveyard in Lavantie, France.

A third brother, Gordon, is also buried in Shepton Mallet Cemetery – read his story in the previous article.

Name: Cummings, Henry

Rank: Serjeant

Regiment: Royal Army Service Corps

Date of death: 6th April 1915

Age at time of death: 38

Cause of death: Meningitis

Grave location: Wembdon Road Cemetery, Bridgwater

Henry Cummings was born in Wembdon, near Bridgwater in Somerset in 1876. The son of agricultural labourer John and his wife Jane, Henry was one of six children.

When he left school, Henry followed his father into agricultural labouring, as his older siblings had done before him. Jane had died when Henry had just reached his teens, so he continued to live with his widowed father, and was recorded there as late as the 1911 census.

On 4th August 1912, he married Sarah Palmer in Wembdon Parish Church; Henry was 36 by this point, and his new wife was 30. The couple may not have thought they could have children, as they went on to adopt a girl, Edith, who was six years old when they had married.

From a military perspective, it appears that Henry had initially tried to enlist in 1908. Based on his service records, it seems that he was not accepted at that point, but when war broke out, things were a different matter. He joined the Army Service Corps on 6th January 1915, attaining the rank of Sergeant.

Henry's service was to be cruelly short, at just 85 days. Hospitalised in Rugby, Sergeant Cummings passed away from cerebrospinal meningitis on 6th April 1915. He was 38 years old.

Henry Cummings was brought back to Bridgwater for burial and lies at rest in the Wembdon Road Cemetery there.

In September 1915, Sarah gave birth to a baby girl, Irene. Henry was never to see his little girl, and, tragically, may not have known he was to be a father.

Name: Currey, Joscelin

Rank: Lance Corporal

Regiment: Somerset Light Infantry

Date of death: 28th June 1915

Age at time of death: 18

Cause of death: Meningitis

Grave location: St James' Cemetery, Taunton

Joscelin William Currey was born in the summer of 1897, one of six children to Job Arthur Currey and his wife, Eliza Jane. Job was a shoe smith and brought his young family up in his home town of Taunton, Somerset.

When Joscelin left school, he worked as an errand boy, before becoming an apprentice with the local foundry of Messrs. Rudman, Lancey and Co. But with war on the horizon, things were about to change.

Along with his older brothers, Joscelin enlisted in the army, joining the 3/5th Reserve Battalion of the Somerset Light Infantry in August 1914. Initially based on Salisbury Plain, he was soon transferred to Bath, and attained the position of Lance Corporal.

It was in Bath that he fell ill and was admitted to hospital with cerebrospinal meningitis. Sadly, Joscelin was to succumb to this condition, and he passed away on 28th June 1915. He was just 18 years of age.

Joscelin William Currey was laid to rest in the St James' Cemetery of his home town of Taunton.

The newspaper report of Lance Corporal Currey's funeral confirmed that one of his brothers was a prisoner of war in Germany, while another was in the Royal Field Artillery. Joscelin was the only one of the three to die during the conflict.

Joscelin's name is spelt variously as Jocelyn and Joslin across the documents relating to him, and his surname is also spelt Curry. For the purposes of this post, I have chosen to use the spelling cited on the Commonwealth War Graves Commission records.

Name: Curtis, Charles

Rank: Private

Regiment: Royal Army Medical Corps

Date of death: 3rd July 1918

Age at time of death: 23

Cause of death: Rheumatic fever

Grave location: St Matthew's Churchyard, Wookey

Charles Curtis was born in Wells, Somerset, in January 1894, one of fifteen children to Charles and Mary Jane Curtis. Charles Sr worked as a gardener in the Wells area, and, after leaving school, Charles Jr started work as a mill hand for the local paper mill (this would have been either St Cuthbert's Mill in Wells, or the Wookey Hole Mill in the nearby village).

Charles enlisted in October 1915, joining the Royal Army Medical Corps. He was posted to France a month later and, while specifics of his military service are not readily apparent, Private Curtis was awarded the Victory Medal, the British Medal and the 1915 Star.

Charles was admitted to hospital on 1st November 1917 with an inflamed cervical gland (reported as Trench Fever), for which he underwent an operation. He remained hospitalised at Whalley Range for more than two months, and was passed for active service, having apparently recovered.

Private Curtis was suddenly taken ill again on 1st July, and his family telegrammed. His mother and one of his sisters boarded a train for the hospital – again in Whalley – but they had not gone far when word came that he succumbed to rheumatic fever. He was 24 years old.

Charles Curtis Jr lies at rest in the graveyard of St Matthew's Church in the village of Wookey, Somerset.

A newspaper report of his funeral confirms he was one of five brothers who entered military service during the Great War. Given that seven of the brothers served, Charles was the only one to die as a result of the war.

Name: Davidge, Alfred

Rank: Leading Seaman

Regiment: Royal Navy

Date of death: 17th March 1917

Age at time of death: 32

Cause of death: Rheumatic fever

Grave location: St James' Cemetery, Taunton

Alfred Ernest Davidge was born on 22nd July 1882, one of six children to Richard and Ermina. Richard was a boilermaker from Bristol but brought his family up in the Wiltshire town of Swindon.

Alfred was keen on adventure and sought out a life on the open seas. In August 1898, at the age of sixteen, he joined the Royal Navy. After serving two years at the rank of Boy, he officially enlisted for a term of twelve years.

Starting as an Ordinary Seaman, Alfred had worked his way up to Leading Seaman by 1905. He continued in this role until 7th June 1909, when he was knocked back a rank for misconduct. He evidently realised the error of his ways, however, as, just over a year later, he was promoted again.

Leading Seaman Davidge's term of service came to an end in July 1912, and, having been assigned to seventeen vessels during that time, he became part of the Royal Naval Reserve.

Back on home soil, Alfred set up home in Taunton. He found work as a labourer and, in October 1913, married local lady Louisa Pomeroy. The couple went on to have a daughter, Hilda.

Storm clouds were gathering over Europe by now, and Alfred was soon recalled to the Royal Navy. He took up his previous role, and, after a period of training at HMS Vivid in Plymouth, he was assigned to HMS Suffolk.

Leading Seaman Davidge spent eighteen months aboard HMS Suffolk, before being transferred to HMS Columbella in November 1916. His time there was short, however, as he became unwell.

Admitted to the Royal Infirmary in Glasgow with influenza, Leading Seaman Davidge sadly succumbed to the condition on 17th March 1917. He was 34 years old.

Alfred Ernest Davidge was brought back to Taunton for burial. He lies at rest in the St James' Cemetery in the town.

Name: Dawbin, William

Rank: Trooper

Regiment: Wellington Mounted Rifles

Date of death: 22nd August 1915

Age at time of death: 27

Cause of death: Died of wounds

Grave location: St Andrew's Churchyard, Compton Dundon

William Joseph Dawbin was born on 23rd April 1888, in Yeovil, Somerset. He was the oldest of three children to William and Julianna Dawbin, a farming family.

In 1897, when William Jr was 9 years old, the family emigrated to New Zealand, settling in the town of Feilding, 100 miles (150km) north of Wellington.

William enlisted in 1905, joining the Wellington Mounted Rifles for a five-year term of service, and being promoted to the rank of Corporal. He re-enlisted on 14th August 1914, and the troop departed New Zealand for Europe a month later.

Trooper Dawbin arrived in Alexandria, Egypt on 3rd December, from where they travelled to Cairo for training. Initially planning on becoming involved in the defence of the Suez Canal, on 14th April 1915, William and his battalion landed in Gallipoli, to support the invasion there.

History knows that the fighting in this battle was some of the fiercest of the Great War. History also tells us that this campaign resulted in huge losses for the Anzac troops, including the Wellington Mounted Rifles. Sadly, Trooper Dawbin was not to escape injury.

On 27th May 1915, he received a gunshot wound to the back, fracturing his spine. He was evacuated by hospital ship back to Egypt, and, suffering from paralysis, was shipped back to England ten days later.

Trooper Dawbin was admitted to the Netley Hospital in Southampton, but his wounds appeared too severe; he died there on 22nd August 1915. He was 27 years old.

William Joseph Dawbin lies at peace in the quiet churchyard of St Andrew's, in the village of Compton Dundon, Somerset, not far from extended family in Butleigh.

Name: Diamond, William

Rank: Private

Regiment: Hampshire Regiment

Date of death: 15th August 1917

Age at time of death: 29

Cause of death: Illness

Grave location: St Mary the Virgin Churchyard, Litton

William Diamond was born in around 1888. Documentation relating to his life is tantalisingly absent. From what *does* remain, the following can be identified.

William was one of ten children, whose mother was Maryann (or Mary Ann) Diamond. His father had passed away by the time of the 1911 census, by which point Maryann was living with six of her children, including William, in the village of Litton, on the north side of the Somerset Mendips.

When war broke out, William enlisted, and was assigned to the 15th Battalion of the Hampshire Regiment. Again, there is little documentation to confirm his military service; sadly, the next time Private Diamond appears in the records is to confirm his passing.

The local newspaper reported on his funeral:

> *The funeral took place on Sunday afternoon, at Litton, his native place, of Private W Diamond, 28 [sic], late of the Hampshire Regiment, who died in hospital in Northampton after a serious illness, after serving some seven months at the front.*
>
> *Among the chief mourners was a younger brother in khaki (an elder one is now serving in India) and several officers of the AOF, of which deceased was a member.*
>
> *Shepton Mallet Journal: Friday 24th August 1917*

Private William Diamond passed away on 15th August 1917, at the age of 29 years old. He lies at rest in the churchyard of St Mary the Virgin, in Litton, Somerset.

Name: Dibble, Charles

Rank: Private

Regiment: Oxfordshire & Buckinghamshire Light Infantry

Date of death: 7th May 1921

Age at time of death: 31

Cause of death: Exhaustion, sarcoma of the rectum

Grave location: St John's Cemetery, Bridgwater

Charles Lang Dibble was born in 1890, one of nine children to Evan and Eliza Dibble from Bridgwater in Somerset. Evan was a labourer in a brickyard, and clay must have run through the family's veins, as Charles found employment as a kiln hand in a local tile maker when he left school.

By the 1911 census, Charles was boarding with William Rainey and his family in Bridgwater; whether there was a connection before he moved in or not, I don't know, but the following year he married one of William's daughters, Constance. The young couple wed on Christmas Day 1912 and went on to have one child, Charles, who was born in 1915.

Full details of Charles' military service are not available. However, when he enlisted, he initially joined the Somerset Light Infantry, before transferring to the Devonshire Regiment and finally the Oxfordshire and Buckinghamshire Light Infantry. During his service, he was awarded the Victory and British Medals, but there is little further information about Private Dibble.

Charles survived the war, but his pension records confirm that he passed away on 7th May 1921; the cause of death was noted as exhaustion and sarcoma of the rectum. He was 31 years old.

Charles Lang Dibble lies at rest in St John's Cemetery in his home town of Bridgwater.

Name: Doble, Charles

Rank: Private

Regiment: Royal Sussex Regiment

Date of death: 13th December 1916

Age at time of death: 32

Cause of death: Died of wounds

Grave location: St James' Cemetery, Taunton

Charles Doble – also known as Charlie – was born 12th September 1884, the second of seven children to James and Mary Ann Doble from Dunkeswell in Devon. James was a carpenter, but on leaving school, Charles initially found work as an errand boy, before becoming employed as a porter at the Taunton and Somerset Hospital.

The 1911 census found Charles in the village of Cotford St Luke, working as an attendant at the Somerset and Bath Asylum. Housing more than 800 patients at the time, it is reasonable to assume that his duties would have been wide and varied.

Details of Charles' military service are scarce. He enlisted in the Hertfordshire Regiment as a Private in April 1916, but soon transferred over to the 13th Battalion of the Royal Sussex Regiment.

In the spring of that year, Charles married Ethel Willmott; presumably this was before he was sent abroad, because he was soon on the Western Front.

His battalion was caught up in the Battle of the Boar's Head, during which the Royal Sussex Regiment succeeded in capturing a section of the German front line trench *and* second line trench, before being pushed back because of mounting casualties and a lack of ammunition.

It seems likely that Private Doble was one of those injured on what became known as *The Day Sussex Died*, as he was evacuated back to England for treatment. Admitted to a Military Hospital in Stourbridge, sadly his wounds proved too much for Charles to bear; he passed away on 13th December 1916, at the age of 32 years old.

Charles Doble's body was brought back to Taunton, and he was buried in the St James' Cemetery in the town.

Name: Drew, Gilbert

Rank: Private

Regiment: Somerset Light Infantry

Date of death: 1st July 1917

Age at time of death: 19

Cause of death: Influenza

Grave location: St Michael's Churchyard, Dinder

Gilbert Victor Drew was born in Dinder, Somerset in 1898, the youngest of eight children of James and Theresa Drew, a groom/coachman and a laundress.

Gilbert initially enlisted in the West Somerset Yeomanry on 11th December 1915, serving on the Home Front.

Private Drew then transferred to the 1st Battalion of the Somerset Light Infantry and was shipped overseas as part of the British Expeditionary Force on 1st August 1916.

He first reported to a medic in mid-November 1916; his records pick up the story from there:

> First noticed he was passing a larger quantity of water than usual and was also feeling very thirsty.
>
> 2nd December 1916, caught influenza and was sent to England. Thirst has been great and urine very large in quantity since November. General condition good. Passes from 14 to 17 pints of urine each 24 hours – large quantity of sugar contained. No evidence of other disease. No improvement since admission.
>
> Result of AS[?] Prolonged strain – especially during Somme offensive.
>
> Medical Records

Private Drew was discharged from the army on 3rd February 1917 as "*no longer physically fit for war service*" due to diabetes.

Gilbert Victor Drew died on 1st July 1917; he was just 19 years of age. He was buried in the graveyard of the Church of St Michael in his home village of Dinder, Somerset.

He was one of six villagers to fall during the Great War.

Name: Dummett, Harold

Rank: Guardsman

Regiment: Coldstream Guards

Date of death: 15th February 1919

Age at time of death: 19

Cause of death: Pleurisy and pneumonia

Grave location: All Saints' Churchyard, Kingsdon

Harold Joseph James Dummett was born in early 1900, one of ten children – and the eldest son – of Harry and Elizabeth of Kingsdon, Somerset.

Harold joined the Coldstream Guards, although there are no records to confirm the date of his enlistment. His battalion – the 5th – remained stationed in Windsor throughout the war; it is likely, therefore, that Guardsman Dummett never saw front line service.

His pension records give his mother as his next of kin, while the Register of Soldiers' Effects also name his father.

Guardsman Dummett passed away from pleurisy and pneumonia at the Military Hospital in Purfleet on 15th February 1919. He was 19 years of age.

Harold Joseph James Dummett lies at peace in the quiet All Saints' Churchyard in his home village of Kingsdon.

While Harold does not appear in the newspaper records, his parents do. In April 1937, the Taunton Courier reports that:

> *Mr and Mrs Harry Dummett celebrated their golden wedding...*
> *There was a happy family gathering of all their children and two*
> *grandsons.*

> *Taunton Courier and Weston Advertiser – 24th April 1937*

Name: Dyer, Charles

Rank: Private

Regiment: Canadian Infantry

Date of death: 30th May 1918

Age at time of death: 23

Cause of death: Pneumonia

Grave location: Milton Cemetery, Weston-super-Mare

Charles William Dyer was born on 12th May 1895, the youngest of seven children to Harry and Mary Dyer.

Harry was a farmer, who brought his family up in the village of Kewstoke, just to the north of Weston-super-Mare, Somerset. He seems to have been keen to try new things because he and Mary lived for a while in Australia, and their first two children were born there. They then moved back to the UK in around 1887, settling back in Somerset.

By the time of the 1911 census, Charles was 16 years old, and all of the family were helping out on the farm. He seemed to share his father's sense of adventure; in 1913, he emigrated to Canada, setting himself up as a farmhand in Winnipeg.

War was coming to Europe, however, and Charles joined up. He enlisted in October 1917, joining the Canadian Infantry. Leaving Canada on a troop ship on 19th February 1918, he arrived back in England on 4th March.

Private Dyer was soon installed at the Canadian Infantry camp at Bramshott in Hampshire. Within weeks of arriving in England, however, he had contracted influenza; this developed into pneumonia, and was admitted to the camp's Military Hospital on 22nd May. Sadly, a week later, Private Dyer was dead. He was just 23 years old.

Charles William Dyer was taken back to Weston-super-Mare and laid to rest in the Milton Cemetery there.

Name: Dyer, John

Rank: Private

Regiment: Somerset Light Infantry

Date of death: 9th July 1915

Age at time of death: 50

Cause of death: Unknown

Grave location: Milton Cemetery, Weston-super-Mare

John Frederick Dyer was born in Crediton, Devon, on 3rd July 1864. He was one of twelve children to William Dyer, a shoemaker, and his wife Sarah.

When he left school, John initially found work as a tanner – presumably helping with his father's business. He soon moved on from this, however, and worked as a labourer and then a stonemason.

In 1888, aged 24, he married a woman called Emily; they went on to have four children. By the time of the 1901 census, John was a fully-fledged mason, and the family had moved to Weston-super-Mare in Somerset.

From this point in, there is little information available relating to John's life. The 1911 census records him as living in the centre of Weston-super-Mare, in a six-room house with his wife, two of his children and his niece.

Storm clouds were on the horizon in Europe, but not much documentation records his military service. He was 50 years old when war was declared, and he was old enough to be exempt from volunteering or conscription. However, he did put his name forward, and enlisted at some point at the beginning of 1915.

Private Dyer joined the 4th Battalion of the Somerset Light Infantry. This was a primarily territorial force, that served in India and the Middle East, although there is no confirmation that he was anywhere outside of the UK during his time in the army.

In fact, Private Dyer's service was not destined to be a long one; the next available record shows that he died on 9th July 1915 at the 2nd Southern

General Hospital in Bristol. He had just turned 51 years old. Sadly, no details of the cause of death exist.

John Frederick Dyer's body was brought back to Somerset for burial. He lies at rest in the Milton Road Cemetery in his adopted home town of Weston-super-Mare.

Name: Dyke, Bernard

Rank: Private

Regiment: Devonshire Regiment

Date of death: 18th January 1918

Age at time of death: 20

Cause of death: Accidental shooting

Grave location: Wembdon Road Cemetery, Bridgwater

Bernard Dyke was born in 1897, the oldest of three children to Albert and Edith Dyke from Bridgwater, Somerset. Albert worked for a brewery, and the young family lived in a house on the main road west out of the town.

Bernard received a scholarship to attend Dr Morgan's School, a grammar school in the town, and he was a pupil there from autumn 1910 to spring 1913. He left at the age of 16 and became a merchant's clerk.

War was on the horizon, however, and Bernard joined up. Full details of his military service are not available, but he enlisted in the Devonshire Regiment. Private Dyke spent some time at the Tregantle Fort, near Plymouth, and it was here that he was caught up in an accident:

> It has transpired that a rather remarkable shooting fatality
> occurred at Tregantle rifle ranges, near Plymouth, on Friday,
> when Private Bernard Dyke, aged about 24, of the Devon
> Regiment, received a gunshot wound in the left side, and almost
> immediately expired.
>
> The soldier was acting as an observer for a Lewis gun section
> when he received the fatal injury, the section being at the time
> out of action awaiting the appearance of a moving target. On
> the deceased's left-hand side was a musketry party of nine
> carrying out an exercise, and when he received his injury only
> one or two rounds had been discharged by this party.
>
> When the first shot or so had been fired deceased suddenly
> shouted "Oh! Oh!" and dropped. An officer and NCOs ran to

assist him, but found that life was extinct. A military doctor was soon on the spot, and found the bullet had entered the deceased's left side below the ribs and made its exit at the top of his right arm.

As the musketry party was 80 degrees to the right of the firing party it is strange that a shot could have been fired so wide, but the explanation may be found to be in a ricochet or a soldier's erratic action.

Western Morning News: Monday 21st January 1918.

Private Bernard Dyke died on 18th January 1918, aged just 20 years old. He lies at rest in the Wembdon Road Cemetery in his home town of Bridgwater, a few minutes' walk from his family home.

Name: Edwards, Harry

Rank: Private

Regiment: Royal Warwickshire Regiment

Date of death: 24th July 1917

Age at time of death: 32

Cause of death: Tetanus

Grave Location: St Lawrence's Churchyard, Lydeard St Lawrence

Henry Charles Edwards was born in 1883, the eldest of four children for Joseph and Elizabeth.

Joseph was an agricultural labourer, and Henry (or Harry) followed his father in the farming life, continuing in the role after Joseph died, and up until at least the 1911 census.

I was unable to find much regarding Harry's military service. He signed up with the Royal Warwickshire Regiment, and subsequently transferred to the Somerset Light Infantry.

He died from tetanus on 24th July 1917, aged 34. His pension records give his mother, Elizabeth, as his beneficiary.

Private Henry Edwards lies at rest in the churchyard of Lydeard St Lawrence, Somerset.

Name: Edwards, Ralph

Rank: Corporal

Regiment: Labour Corps and Gloucestershire Regiment

Date of death: 11th March 1919

Age at time of death: 35

Cause of death: Unknown

Grave location: Milton Cemetery, Weston-super-Mare

Ralph Henry Edwards was born in December 1883, the oldest of six children to Charles and Emma. Charles was a house painter from Somerset and raised his family in the coastal town of Weston-super-Mare.

When he left school, Ralph followed in his father's footsteps, taking over the business when Charles passed away in 1909. By the time of the census two years later, Ralph was living with his mother Emma, his two younger brothers and Emma's brother Harry. Harry was also a house painter, while Ralph's siblings were working as grocer's assistants. The family were living in a five-room, semi-detached house within walking distance of the town centre.

War was on the horizon, and Ralph was keen to do his part. Full details of his service are no longer available, but what is certain is that he enlisted in the Gloucestershire Regiment and was assigned to the 8th (Service) Battalion. Initially formed in Bristol, the battalion spent the first year of the war on home soil, before being sent to France in July 1915.

By the middle of the war, Ralph had been promoted to the rank of Corporal. He transferred over to the Labour Corps and was attached to the 106th Prisoner of War Company. Initially, German POWs had been shipped to England, but by 1916 those with useful skills were retained in France and drafted into the Forestry Companies, Army Service Corps and Royal Engineers. Corporal Edwards' role would have been to oversee such men. (Whether this was in France or back in England is unclear.)

At this point, Ralph's trail goes cold. He served out the war, passing away back at home on 11th March 1919, although the cause of his death has been lost to time. He was 35 years of age.

Ralph Henry Edwards lies at rest in the Milton Cemetery in his home town of Weston-super-Mare.

Name: Embleton, Charles

Rank: Private

Regiment: Royal Army Ordnance Corps

Date of death: 20th July 1916

Age at time of death: 26

Cause of death: Tuberculosis

Grave location: Shepton Mallet Cemetery

Charles Embleton was born in Alexandria, Egypt, in 1891. One of five children, his father John was a captain in the army, and his wife, Sarah was based wherever he was.

Military service was obviously in Charles' blood. He joined up in 1908, and was assigned to the Army Ordnance Corps. After three years' service, he was moved back to the Reserves.

Charles had met Mary Cooper, a baker's daughter, from Farnham. They married in September 1911, and, two months later, Mary gave birth to their daughter, Florence. Her baptism records show that, by this time, Charles was working as a registry clerk for his former Corps.

When war broke out, Private Embleton was remobilised and by 14th August 1914, he was in France. His service abroad was brief, however. Within a fortnight he had been shipped back to England and there he stayed until he was medically discharged in March 1915.

While no cause for his dismissal is evident from his service records, his war pension document confirms that, when he passed away, it was from tuberculosis, contracted while on active service. It is reasonable to assume, therefore, that his lung condition was the cause for his initial discharge.

It seems that Charles and his family had relocated to the south west of England when his service was completed. It was here that he died – on 20th July 1916 – at the age of just 25 years old.

Charles Embleton lies at peace in Shepton Mallet Cemetery in Somerset.

Name: Fear, Alfred

Rank: Driver

Regiment: Royal Field Artillery

Date of death: 22nd October 1918

Age at time of death: 20

Cause of death: *"Infirmation of the brain"*

Grave location: Milton Cemetery, Weston-super-Mare

Alfred Fear was born towards the end of 1898, the youngest of nine children to Charles and Eliza Fear. Charles was a mason from Weston-super-Mare in Somerset, who raised his family in the town of his birth.

Sadly, given his youth, there is little documented about Alfred's early life. He was still at school at the time of the 1911 census and, while he would have found some sort of employment after leaving, there is no record of what that would have been.

Alfred's military service records are also sparse. He enlisted in the Royal Field Artillery and was assigned the role of Driver in the 321st Brigade. While dates cannot be confirmed, he would have enlisted before the spring of 1918.

The next two documents relating to Driver Fear are his Pension Ledger record and the Army Register of Personal Effects. These confirm that he passed away on 22nd October 1918 at the Norfolk War Hospital. The cause of death given was *infirmation of the brain*, (or possibly inflammation of the brain). He was just 20 years old.

Alfred Fear's body was brought back to Weston-super-Mare for burial. He lies at rest in the town's Milton Cemetery.

Name: Flower, William

Rank: Private

Regiment: Royal Field Artillery

Date of death: 8th November 1918

Age at time of death: 31

Cause of death: Unknown

Grave location: Milton Cemetery, Weston-super-Mare

William Alister Flower was born in 1887, one of five children to Joseph and Annie Flower. Joseph was a platelayer for the local railway and brought the family up in Weston-super-Mare, in his home county of Somerset.

When he left school, William worked as an errand boy for a local greengrocer; he stuck with it, and, by the time of the 1911 census, he was employed as a van driver for the grocer.

War was on the horizon and, while William enlisted in the army, it is difficult to get a complete handle on his military service. There are a number of servicemen with similar names, but the documentation that is available is not easy to directly connect them with the gravestone in the Weston-super-Mare cemetery.

What *is* clear is that William enlisted as a Private in the Army Service Corps at some point before May 1918. He was assigned to the Motor Transport division (this was likely on the back of his van-driving experience). His time seems to have been spent on home soil, although he was awarded both the Victory and British Medals for his service.

At some point, he had married a woman called Mabel. Exact details again are unclear – ancestry.com confirms the marriage of a William Flower and Mabel Richardson in December 1909, but as this took place in Northamptonshire, it is unlikely to be the Somerset Flowers researched here.

Details of Private Flower's passing are also scarce. He died on 8th November 1918, in the Military Hospital in Croydon, Surrey, but the is no information as to the cause of his death. He was just 31 years old.

William Alister Flower's body was brought back to Somerset; he lies at rest in the family grave, in the Milton Cemetery of his home town.

While I was researching William Flower, I was taken by the note of the accidental death of the first name on the family grave.

Edward Thomas Flower was two years William's senior who, after leaving school, had gone on to be an errand boy for a local butcher.

Edward had decided to follow in his father's footsteps and join the railways, leaving his home town in 1905 to work in Cornwall. After initially working as an engine cleaner, he progressed to be a fireman, helping to stoke the engine with coal. The local newspaper of the time picked up the story of the accident:

> At the moment of the accident, a goods train was standing in the Redruth station, shunting having been temporarily suspended to admit the passage of the down motor rail car.
>
> It appears that the flap of one of the cattle trucks in the goods train... had been allowed to remain down, and the folding doors above it had been insecurely fastened, with the result that as the motor rail car ran into the station the doors of the truck suddenly flew open outward and one of them struck deceased on the side of the face and head, inflicting terrible injuries.
>
> There was a very extensive fracture of the skull, the whole of the left side of the face was driven in and there was also a formidable wound at the back of the head, death occurring within a few moments.
>
> It appears that the rail motor was not proceeding at a greater rate than some five or six miles an hour, according to the statement made at the inquest by the driver, and the latter noticed that when the doors of the goods truck swung open they struck one of the handles on the fore part of the car. He applied the brake immediately, but did not know that Flower had been struck until afterwards.
>
> Weston Mercury: Saturday 7th October 1905

The inquest found that there had been some neglect on the part of the porter and guard in not ensuring that the goods truck's doors had been secured, and it seems that this was something that had been highlighted previously.

Edward had shortly been due to marry, leaving a fiancée, as well as a family, bereft. He was just 20 years old.

His body was brought back to Weston-super-Mare and was the first to be buried in the family grave.

Name: Fowler, James

Rank: Private

Regiment: Royal Army Medical Corps

Date of death: 2nd November 1918

Age at time of death: 46

Cause of death: Influenza and bronchial pneumonia

Grave location: Street Cemetery

Thomas James Buckley Fowler – known as James – was born in 1872, the eldest of eleven children to Tom and Ellen Fowler.

Much of his early life is lost to time, but we do know that James married Emily Ann Gregory on 26th December 1898 and the couple went on to have four children – Wilfred, Harold, Violet and Ivy.

On his marriage certificate James lists himself as a shoemaker and, given the family were living in the Somerset town of Street, it is likely that he was employed at the Clark's factory there. By 1911, however, the family had moved to Glamorgan, where he had taken work as a timber man in the coalmine in the village of Nelson.

Private Fowler enlisted when war broke out, joining the 10th Battalion of the Welch Regiment in October 1914. During his time with the regiment, he was promoted, first to Lance Corporal and then to Acting Sergeant. He transferred to the Royal Army Medical Corps just under a year later. In November 1915, he was admitted to hospital with enteritis, which led to him being shipped back to England for treatment. Once he had recovered, Private Fowler was enlisted in the Provisional Company of the RAMC, transferring again to the 7th Company in 1916. He then operated on home soil for the next few years.

James was admitted to the Royal Military Hospital in Bristol on 28th October 1918 with influenza and bronchial pneumonia. He sadly passed away a few days later, on 2nd November 1918. He was 46 years old.

James Fowler lies at rest in the cemetery in Street, Somerset.

Name: Frampton, Henry

Rank: Private

Regiment: Royal Defence Corps

Date of death: 26th October 1919

Age at time of death: 37

Cause of death: Dyspepsia and debility

Grave location: St John's Cemetery, Bridgwater

Arthur Henry "Harry" Frampton was born in 1882, the oldest of six children to Henry and Alice. Henry Sr worked as a clerk and cashier in a shoe factory in Bridgwater, while Harry and his brothers also initially followed that line of work.

In the autumn of 1908, Harry married Emma Jane Lee, who was originally from Crediton in Devon. The couple went on to have two children, Rose and John, and, by the time of the next census, the family were living in a small house in the middle of Bridgwater. Harry, by this time, was working as a general labourer.

War broke out, and Harry was quick to enlist. Initially assigned to the Somerset Light Infantry in December 1914, Private Frampton was transferred to the Royal Defence Corps after two years' service.

He was part of the army's territorial force, and it seems likely that his transfer to the RDC may have been on medical grounds. He had been admitted to Castlemount Military Hospital (in Dover) a couple of times, suffering from "*rheumatism and debility*".

Private Frampton's later medical report stated that he was a frail man, with an accentuated heartbeat, which gave rise to fainting. He had no appetite and suffered from insomnia, and, according to the report, was "*quite unfit to perform the duties of a soldier*".

Ultimately, this led to Harry being medically discharged from the army, and he was demobbed on 10th March 1917, after just over two years' service.

Little is known about Harry after his discharge from the army. His pension record confirms that he passed away on 26th October 1919, having suffered from dyspepsia (indigestion) and debility. He was 37 years old.

Harry Frampton lies at rest in the St John's Cemetery in his home town of Bridgwater, Somerset.

Name: Francis, Leonard

Rank: Sapper

Regiment: Royal Engineers

Date of death: 3rd May 1915

Age at time of death: 19

Cause of death: Wounded in action, tetanus

Grave location: Shepton Mallet Burial Ground

Leonard George Francis (who was known by his middle name) was born in October 1895. He was one of fourteen children to Jonas and Eleanor (or Ellenora) Francis, and his father worked on the railways as a plate layer or ganger.

George followed his father into manual labour, and, by the time of the 1911 census, aged 15, he was already listed as a mason.

He seems to have enlisted fairly early on in the war, and by January 1915 had joined his troop – the 2nd Wessex Field Company of the Royal Engineers – on the front line.

Sadly, Sapper Francis' time in the army was to be brief. He was caught up in the fighting at Ypres, and he was injured at Hill 60 on 27th April. He was moved to a local hospital for treatment.

It seems that messages crossed in the communication with George's family. They received a letter confirming that he was recovering in hospital after receiving a wound to the body, but not to worry. A day or so later his postcard confirming his arrival in France was received, but by this time he had been shipped back to England for treatment.

His parents received a telegram to confirm this, and his father and brother set out to visit him. By the time they had reached the hospital, however, he had sadly passed from a tetanus infection. In his pocket was a piece of shell, a sad souvenir of his frontline action.

Leonard George Francis died at Netley Hospital on the 3rd May 1915. He was just 19 years old.

He lies at rest in the cemetery of his home town, Shepton Mallet in Somerset.

Name: Fry, Clarence

Rank: Private

Regiment: Wiltshire Regiment

Date of death: 5th November 1918

Age at time of death: 20

Cause of death: Died of wounds

Grave location: Wembdon Road Cemetery, Bridgwater

Clarence Vivian Clements Fry was born in November 1898 to William and Rosa Fry. William was a 'provisions merchant clerk', who went on to become a 'cheese and provision dealer', or grocer. Sadly, Rosa passed away in 1904, at the tender age of 31, leaving Clarence without a mother at just six years old.

William remarried in 1908, and he and new wife Amy had a daughter, also called Amy, a year later. By the 1911 census, the family of four were living in a three storey Victorian Terraced house to the south of Bridgwater town centre.

Sadly, little of Clarence's military career remains documented. Initially joining the Royal Army Service Corps, Private Fry soon transferred over to the Duke of Edinburgh's Wiltshire Regiment.

The 1st Battalion fought in some of the key battles on the Western Front, including Mons, Ypres, Messines and Vimy Ridge. As his enlistment date isn't known, it's impossible to say whether Private Fry was involved in these conflicts or not.

What *is* likely is that Private Fry was involved in the Battle of the Selle, which took place near the towns of Cambrai and Valenciennes in northern France in October 1918. Clarence was certainly injured at this point and was evacuated to England for treatment.

Admitted to the Cambridge Military Hospital in Aldershot, it seems that his injuries were too severe, and he succumbed to them on 5th November 1918, just a week before the Armistice was signed. Private Fry was just 19 years old.

Clarence Vivian Clements Fry lies at rest in the Wembdon Road Cemetery in his home town of Bridgwater in Somerset.

Name: Gane, Edward

Rank: Private

Regiment: Wiltshire Regiment

Date of death: 24th November 1918

Age at time of death: 19

Cause of death: Influenza

Grave location: St Mary's Churchyard, Ditcheat

Edward Lionel Gane was born in 1899 and was one of eight children. Known as Lionel, he was the son of Edwin and Joanna Gane, and lived in the quiet Somerset village of Ditcheat. Edwin began life as a pig dealer, but by the time of the 1911 census, had changed direction and become an insurance agent.

Joanna passed away in 1915, and this may have been the impetus Lionel needed to find his way in the world. He enlisted in the Wiltshire Regiment, joining the 3rd (Reserve) Battalion of the Duke of Edinburgh's brigade.

The battalion – a depot and training unit – were initially based in Devizes, before moving to Dorset and then Kent. While there is no confirmation of when Private Gane enlisted, it would have been by September 1917, which is when the battalion became part of the Thames & Medway Garrison.

The end of the war marked another ending for the Gane family. Edwin passed away on Armistice Day – 11th November – and further tragedy was to follow, as Private Gane contracted influenza and died less than two weeks later.

Edward Lionel Gane died in a Military Hospital in Malling, Kent, on 24th November 1918. He was just 19 years old. He lies at rest in the graveyard of St Mary's Church in his home village of Ditcheat.

Name: Gardner, William

Rank: Serjeant

Regiment: Gloucestershire Regiment

Date of death: 14th July 1921

Age at time of death: 45

Cause of death: Unknown

Grave location: Wells Cemetery

William Gardner was born in Cirencester, Gloucestershire, in around 1877. While I have been unable to totally confirm this, his parents seem to have been William and Sarah Carpenter; William Sr was an agricultural labourer, and both he and his wife were from Cirencester.

It has been difficult to track down William's early life, because of the potential variations of his surname and the number of William Gardner's in the Gloucestershire area.

The first time I can definitively identify him is on the 1911 census; he was living in Cheltenham and working as gardener. The census shows that he had been married for 16 years and had one child. However, William's wife is not recorded on the census; instead, a Lily Marie Denley is boarding with him, as is her daughter, Irina May Gardner Denley.

William's military life also needs a little piecing together. His gravestone confirms that he was a Serjeant in the Gloucestershire Regiment, and it seems that he enlisted towards the end of the 1800s, as he is recorded as having served in South Africa.

Serjeant Gardner re-enlisted (or was called back up) when the Great War broke out; at the age of 39, he was sent to France, collecting the Victory Medal, the British Medal and the 1915 Star for his service. At some point, however, he transferred back to England, joining the 440th Agricultural Coy. Labour Corps.

While there is no evidence of why William transferred, his later records certainly seem to suggest there were some issues going on in his life. When he was demobbed in February 1919, this seems to have been for medical reasons; his pension records show that he was suffering from neurasthenia (or shell shock), and that this was directly attributable to his war service.

William's suffering evidently continued; a further record shows that he was admitted to an asylum in March 1921; it is likely that this is where he died, just four months later. While there is no cause of death, William passed away on 14th July 1921, at the age of 45 years old. Given where he is buried, it is likely that he was treated at Somerset and Bath Pauper Lunatic Asylum, not far from Wells.

William Gardner lies at peace in the cemetery in Wells, Somerset.

Name: Gillard, Sydney

Rank: Private

Regiment: Gloucestershire Regiment

Date of death: 23rd January 1919

Age at time of death: 30

Cause of death: Died of wounds

Grave location: Othery Cemetery

Sydney Gillard was born in October 1888, one of eight children to Charles and Lily. Charles was a stonemason, and this is the trade that Sydney and his older brother Harry also followed.

When war broke out, he enlisted in the Gloucestershire Regiment; Private Gillard's troop, the 1/4th (City of Bristol) Battalion, were initially based in Swindon, before moving to Maldon in Essex. They were posted to France in March 1915, eventually being shipped to Italy in November 1917.

While Sydney's military records do not confirm when he enlisted or where he served, that he saw fighting is beyond any doubt because his war pension records confirm that he died from his wounds.

Sydney Gillard passed away on 23rd January 1919, at the age of 31. He lies at rest in the cemetery of his home village of Othery, Somerset.

Name: Gillson, Wilfred

Rank: Corporal

Regiment: Devonshire Regiment

Date of death: 10th November 1918

Age at time of death: 30

Cause of death: Unknown

Grave location: St John's Cemetery, Bridgwater

Wilfred Allen Gillson was born in 1888, the fourth of nine children – and one of eight boys – to George and Emma Gillson. George was a coachbuilder from Cornwall; Emma, whose maiden name was Allen, came from Derbyshire. The family were living in Torquay by the time Wilfred was born.

In 1895, George had moved the family to Bridgwater in Somerset, presumably as railway work had dried up in the coastal Devon town. By this time his oldest son, also called George, was working as a compositor, keying text for a printer. Wilfred was still at school, but his other two older siblings – William and Albert – were both working with their father, working on railway coaches.

Wilfred was also to follow in his father's employment, and the 1911 census found him living in Bristol, boarding with the Cridland family, earning his keep as a carriage painter.

He joined up within weeks of war breaking out, enlisting in the Worcestershire Regiment on 20th September 1914. Private Gillson readily proved his worth, and was promoted to Lance Corporal after three months, and Corporal within a year of enlisting.

Corporal Gillson's promotion coincided with his shipment abroad, and he served on the Western Front for eight months. Returning to England in March 1916, he subsequently transferred to the Devonshire Regiment, before being moved to the 4th Reserve Battalion in the spring of 1917.

Things were not right for Wilfred; he was reprimanded for neglecting his post on the night of the 26th May that year, before being medically discharged with neurasthenia in August.

The root of the matter is detailed in his discharge report; he was hospitalised at Neuve Chapelle in February 1916, suffering from shell shock, and it seems that he never really fully recovered.

Sadly, at this point Wilfred's trail goes cold. He passed away on 10th November 1918, aged 30 years old.

Wilfred Allen Gillson lies at rest in St John's Cemetery in Bridgwater, Somerset.

There are a couple of additional notes to Wilfred's life.

During the war, Wilfred's youngest brother, Thomas, fought with the Oxfordshire & Buckinghamshire Light Infantry. He was involved in the fighting in France but died from wounds on 10th June 1918. He was just 18 years old and is buried at Aire-sur-la-Lys, not far from Boulogne.

Given that Wilfred was one of eight brothers, all of whom would have been of fighting age during the war, it is lucky – although still a tragedy – that only he and Thomas died as a result of the conflict.

Sadly, Wilfred's mother, Emma, passed away in the autumn of 1914, at 57 years of age. It might be a blessing, however, that she was not alive to see two of her sons suffer so.

Name: Godden, James

Rank: Private

Regiment: Army Cyclist Corps

Date of death: 29th April 1917

Age at time of death: 37

Cause of death: Illness

Grave location: Wembdon Road Cemetery, Bridgwater

James Godden was born in the autumn of 1879. The youngest of six children to Charles and Mary Ann Godden, the family lived in Bridgwater, Somerset. Charles was a labourer and, while his older brothers followed in a similar vein, by the time of the 1901 census, aged 21, James was listed as a hairdresser.

James married Hester Addicott in 1906, and the couple had three children – Ruby, Leslie and Freda. Hairdressing may not have been that well paid; according to the 1911 census, the young family had four boarders, ranging from 17 to 60 in age.

War was on its way, and James enlisted at the end of 1914. Initially joining the Somerset Light Infantry, he was soon transferred to the Army Cyclist Corps. Sadly, full details of his military service are not readily available, but it seems likely that he was part of the company's First Line, who saw service overseas.

Private Godden served three years before being medically discharged from the army. His discharge records give a startling insight into his health:

Originated at Chiseldon Camp: April 12th 1917.

He is in a condition of violent excitement, talks without ceasing and suffers from insomnia. Refuses solid food, but will take a little milk. Not result of, but aggravated by, strain of ordinary military service.

Permanent total incapacity. Treatment in an asylum required.

Cause of discharge: Medically Unfit – Acute Mania

James Godden: WW1 Pension Records

James was admitted to the Somerset & Bath Asylum in the village of Codford, near Taunton. For good or bad, his time there was brief. Within a couple of weeks, he contracted bronchitis. Sadly, James was to succumb to this, and passed away on 29th April 1917. He was 27 years of age.

An additional twist in the tail came from the local newspaper report of his passing:

Somerset Athlete Killed

The death is reported of a former well-known athlete in the person of Mr James Godden, who before joining the Army carried on business as a hairdresser at Bridgwater. The deceased, who was 37 years of age, enlisted in December 1914, and was subsequently transferred to a cycle corps. His death occurred at a Somerset institution after a short illness. The deceased was well known throughout the West of England as a crack cyclist, and competed at big athletic meetings at Exeter, Plymouth, Bath and Bristol, in addition to local sports. He had won altogether over 400 prizes. He leaves a widow and three children.

Wells Journal: Friday 4th May 1917

James Godden lies at rest in the Wembdon Road Cemetery in his home town of Bridgwater, Somerset.

Name: Grabham, Thomas

Rank: Private

Regiment: West Somerset Yeomanry

Date of death: 28th March 1915

Age at time of death: 33

Cause of death: Perforated ulcer

Grave location: St Mary's Cemetery, Taunton

Thomas William Grabham was born in September 1883, one of six children to Thomas Richard Grabham and his wife Emma. Thomas Sr was a labourer and drayman for a brewery and the family lived in Taunton, Somerset.

When Thomas Jr left school, he found work as a grocer's porter, before he too found work in a brewery, working as a maltster. He married a local woman, Maria Rowsell, and the couple went on to have a son, who they named after Thomas' father.

Details of Thomas' military service are sketchy; he enlisted in the West Somerset Yeomanry, but there are no details of when this was.

Sadly, Private Grabham's period of service was short; his pension records show that he passed away from a perforated gastric ulcer on 28th March 1915. He was just 32 years old.

Thomas William Grabham lies at peace in St Mary's Cemetery in his home town of Taunton.

Sadly, the tragedy for the young Grabham family was not to end there. Maria, Thomas' widow, died just five months after her husband.

Young Thomas was just eight years old when his parents died; he seems to have been brought up by a Mrs Kate Barnes, possibly a maternal aunt. Here, however, the family's trail goes cold.

Name: Gulliford, William

Rank: Private

Regiment: Devonshire Regiment

Date of death: 23rd December 1917

Age at time of death: 40

Cause of death: Heart failure

Grave location: St Mary's Cemetery, Taunton

William Gulliford was born on 8th November 1877 in the village of Thurloxton, just to the north of Taunton, Somerset. William's father – also called William – was an agricultural labourer who, with his wife Charlotte, had nine children in total.

William Jr found work as a labourer for a brewery and, by 1899, had moved to Staffordshire, and met and married a local woman called Elsie Sutton. The couple settled down in Burton-on-Trent, and went on to have a daughter, also called Elsie.

War was coming, however, and, in August 1916, William enlisted. Initially assigned as a Private in the 14th Devonshire Regiment, he was soon moved to the Labour Corps, and within a couple of months was on the Western Front as part of the British Expeditionary Force.

In November 1917, Private Gulliford was shipped back to England, suffering from ill health. He was admitted to the Military Hospital in Taunton with heart failure, and sadly passed away from this a month later. He had just turned 40 years old.

William Gulliford lies at rest in St Mary's Cemetery in Taunton, Somerset.

Name: Hain, James

Rank: Lance Corporal

Regiment: Royal Engineers

Date of death: 13th June 1921

Age at time of death: 39

Cause of death: General paralysis of the insane

Grave location: St James' Cemetery, Taunton

James Frederick Hain was born on 5th November 1881 in the village of Holmer in Herefordshire. He was one of seven children to James and Catherine Hain and was more commonly known as Fred. On James Jr's birth certificate, his father was listed as a manure agent, although by the time of the 1891 census, the family had moved to London, where James Sr was now running a coffee house.

When he left school, James Jr started work as a French polisher, but he had a taste for adventure and joined the army. He served in South Africa during the Boer War campaign of 1899-1900, attaining the Cape Colony, Orange Free State and Transvaal Clasps.

In 1900 James returned home, finding work as a French polisher. The military life was in his blood by now, though, and in September, he re-enlisted. Initially joining the Royal Berkshire Regiment, he was soon transferred over to the Royal Engineers as a Sapper.

James had signed up for a period of eight years and, as part of his role as a wireman (maintaining and fitting telegraph cables), he was stationed abroad. On one particular trip, when his battalion was travelling from Plymouth to Limerick early in 1908, he was injured. According to the accident report: "*owing to bad weather on boat between Fishguard and Waterford he was thrown violently forward, striking his head against a girder.*" Treated in Limerick, "*the disability is of a slight nature, and in all probability will not interfere with his future efficiency as a soldier.*"

Sapper Hain's time with the service was nearly up, and he was put on reserve status in November 1908. By 1911, he was working as a linesman, and boarding in a house in Hayle, Cornwall.

War was on the horizon by now, and on 5th August 1914, James was called back into service. He saw action on the Western Front, adding the Victory and British Medals and the 1915 Star to his count. In October 1915, he was treated for shell shock, and evacuated back to England.

At the beginning of 1917, Lance Corporal Hain was transferred back to the Army Reserve, suffering from neuritis. His health was to suffer for the rest of his life.

In September 1917, having settled in Cornwall, James married Beatrice Opie, an innkeeper's daughter from the village of Wendron, Cornwall. The couple would go on to have a son, who they called Frederick, two years later.

Discharged from the Army, James put his engineering experience to good use, joining the General Post Office to work with telegraphs.

By this time, James' medical condition had been formally diagnosed as General Paralysis of the Insane. A degenerative disease, similar to Alzheimer's disease, it was associated with brisk reflexes and tremors (usually most obvious of the lips, tongue, and outstretched hands) and characterised by failing memory and general deterioration.

By August 1920, James was admitted to the Somerset and Bath Asylum in Cotford, because of his worsening condition. He was not to come out again, and passed away ten months later, on 13th June 1921. He was just 39 years old.

James Frederick Hain was buried in the St James' Cemetery in Taunton, Somerset.

Name: Hallett, Roberts

Rank: Private

Regiment: Royal Warwickshire Regiment

Date of death: 16th October 1918

Age at time of death: 18

Cause of death: Disease

Grave location: St Mary's Churchyard, Charlton Mackrell

Private Roberts Pretoria Hallett was born in the summer of 1900, to Frank – a shepherd from Charlton Adam in Somerset – and Emily, who came from the neighbouring village of Charlton Mackrell. Roberts (the correct spelling) was the youngest of eleven children.

Roberts was just twelve when his father died, and, when war came, he enlisted in Taunton, along with his brothers, Francis and William.

Private Hallett was assigned to the 5th Battalion Royal Warwickshire Regiment. While his records don't identify exactly when he saw battle, by the last year of the war the battalion would have been involved in the fighting in northern Italy. What we can say for certain is that he was shipped home at some point towards the end of the war. He was admitted to the No. 1 Northern General Hospital in Newcastle-upon-Tyne in October 1918. Private Hallett's records show that he died "*of disease*" on 16th October.

Roberts Pretoria Hallett lies at rest in the churchyard of St Mary's in his home village of Charlton Mackrell, Somerset.

The Great War was not kind to Emily Hallett: having lost her husband in 1912, her son William died while fighting in India in 1916 and that is where he was buried. Her other son Francis died in the Third Battle of Ypres in June 1917 and lies at rest in Belgium.

Roberts Hallett, therefore, is the only one of the three brothers to be buried local to her.

Name: Hann, Edwin

Rank: Private

Regiment: South African Infantry

Date of death: 23rd October 1918

Age at time of death: 18

Cause of death: Unknown

Grave location: Glastonbury Cemetery

Edwin Robert Hann was born in Johannesburg, South Africa, to Albert Edward and Jemima Jane Hann in around 1900.

Research has led me to numerous dead ends regarding Edwin's life. Hann's tombstone shows that he enlisted in the 2nd Regiment of the South African Infantry.

The 2nd Regiment served in numerous key battles on the Western Front, including Ypres, Passchendaele, Marrieres Wood and Messines. Their last major engagement was at Le Cateau in early October 1918. Given how soon afterwards Private Hann passed away, it seems possible that he was fatally wounded – or at least suffered trauma – during this battle.

His war pension records suggest that he died at a Military Hospital in Woking, Surrey. A little research suggests that, unless this was the medical wing of the local army barracks, then it is likely that Hann was treated at the former Brookwood Hospital (at the time known as Brookwood Asylum or the Surrey County Lunatic Asylum).

While I can find nothing concrete to confirm this, other Brookwood records suggest that fellow patients were either suffering the effects of shell shock or mustard gas. It is reasonable to assume, therefore, that Private Hann passed away as an indirect result of the fighting on the front, rather than a direct one.

A second mystery arises around his burial, however.

Born in South Africa, fighting on the Western Front, treated and passing in Surrey. How did Edwin Hann come to be buried in a cemetery in Glastonbury?

Again, I can only surmise why this poor teenager was buried so far from home. Hann is a fairly common name in Somerset and, from a bit of research on Ancestry.co.uk, at the turn of the last century there are a large number of Hanns in and around Glastonbury and Shepton Mallet, and in particular a lot of Alberts and Edwards (like Private Hann's father). The assumption can only be, therefore, that Edwin came to be buried close to where his father's family lived.

Edwin Robert Hann died aged just 18 years old. He lies at rest in the cemetery in Glastonbury, Somerset.

Name: Harriss, John

Rank: Stoker Petty Officer

Regiment: Royal Navy

Date of death: 7th June 1916

Age at time of death: 38

Cause of death: Pneumonia

Grave location: Milton Cemetery, Weston-super-Mare

John Thomas Harriss was born on 22nd February 1878, one of seven children to George and Mary. George was a jeweller, who moved the family from London to Weston-super-Mare when John was three or four years old.

Following in his father's footsteps was not something John was going to do, and the move to the coast seemed to have sparked an interest in the sea. He enlisted for twelve years' service in the Royal Navy in March 1900, working as a stoker.

After initial training at HMS Pembroke in Chatham, Kent, Stoker 2nd Class Harriss was assigned to HMS Terpsichore and, over the length of his service, he worked on a further ten vessels. During this time, he was promoted a couple of times, reaching the role of Leading Stoker by 1911, while he was serving aboard HMS Magnificent.

With war imminent, when John completed his period of service, his term was extended until the end of hostilities. He had, by the beginning of 1914, attained the rank of Stoker Petty Officer, and was assigned to HMS Russell.

After the start of the war, this ship was assigned to the Grand Fleet and worked on the Northern Patrol, and in November 1914, she bombarded German-occupied Zeebrugge. The following year, HMS Russell was sent to the Mediterranean to support the Dardanelles Campaign, though she did not see extensive use there.

On 27th April 1916 HMS Russell was sailing off Malta when she struck two mines laid by a German U-boat. Most of her crew survived the sinking, though 125 souls lost their lives. Stoker Petty Officer Harriss was one of the survivors; his service records note that he was *"commended for [the] great coolness shown on the occasion of the loss of HMS Russell"*.

Brought back to the UK, John contracted pneumonia, and spent time at home with his family, in Weston-super-Mare. It was here, sadly, that he was to succumb to the lung condition, and he passed away on 7th June 1916. He was 38 years old.

John Thomas Harriss lies at rest in Milton Cemetery in Weston-super-Mare.

Name: Hartnell, Walter

Rank: Private

Regiment: Machine Gun Corps

Date of death: 15th April 1917

Age at time of death: 28

Cause of death: Unknown

Grave location: Evercreech Cemetery, Evercreech

Walter Ernest Hartnell was born in 1888 to William and Jane Hartnell in Charlton Musgrove, on the outskirts of Wincanton in Somerset.

One of eight children, it appears he could have been a bit of a tearaway in his youth; in October 1905, the Shepton Mallet Journal reports on a "*Hobbledehoy Nuisance*" in Evercreech, when a Walter Hartnell was caught with nine of his friends causing a disturbance close to the church.

> *They were shouting, racing after each other up and down the road, using obscene language, and smoking cigarettes. This continued till 7.15, about half an hour.*

> *Shepton Mallet Journal – Friday 20th October 1905*

Hartnell was fined 5/- and 2/6 costs or would face ten days in prison.

Things looked up for Walter and, by the time his call to enlist came, he was working on the railways. He joined the Somerset Light Infantry and the Machine Gun Corps (MGC), while his brother Fred fought in the Royal Artillery.

The MGC was a particularly brutal part of the armed forces. Of the 170,500 officers and men who served in the corps, 62,049 became casualties, including 12,498 killed, earning it the nickname 'the Suicide Club'.

Details of Private Hartnell's death are sketchy; his company saw action at Ypres and Arras. However, records suggest that he died in Colchester; the Military Hospital there was used to dealing with troops straight from the front. It is likely that he was injured at Ypres and shipped back home to recuperate but died of his injuries.

This is all conjecture on my part, of course, but either way, Private Walter Hartnell lies at peace in a quiet cemetery at Evercreech in Somerset.

Name: Harvey, Tom

Rank: Serjeant

Regiment: Royal Defence Corps

Date of death: 1st July 1917

Age at time of death: 46

Cause of death: Heart attack

Grave location: Milton Cemetery, Weston-super-Mare

Tom Harvey was born in the spring of 1871, one of four children to John and Caroline. John was a *fly driver*, hiring out a pony and trap for a fee, while his wife brought in extra money working as a laundress. The family lived in Weston-super-Mare, on the Somerset coast, in a town house they shared with another family, the Painters.

Details of Tom's early life is a bit sketchy. The 1891 census lists him as a Private in the Royal Marine Light Infantry, with his address as the Royal Naval Hospital in East Stonehouse, Plymouth, where he was 'receiving treatment'. Sadly, none of his military records survive, so there is nothing to confirm his dates of service.

In 1894, demobbed and working as a cab driver in his home town, Tom married a woman called Sarah. Little other information exists about her, but what *is* known is that she worked as a dressmaker to supplement her husband's income, and the couple did not go on to have any children. The couple lived in Hopkins Street, near the centre of Weston-super-Mare, and initially took in boarders to help finances.

By the time war broke out in 1914, Tom was in his forties. Called back into service, he joined the 261st Company of the Royal Defence Corps and, with the role of Serjeant, he would have had men under his command. The 261st was part of Southern Command, which provided a territorial defence force, or Home Guard, and a lot of his time was spent in Birmingham.

It was while he was home on leave that Tom fell ill. The local media picked up the story:

The death occurred on Sunday under sudden circumstances of Sergeant Tom Harvey, Royal Defence Corps... The deceased was proceeding to his residence... when he fell, and was only able to give his address and to state that he was suffering from chronic indigestion before he expired. Prior to joining up as a National Volunteer, the deceased has been engaged as an omnibus driver.

Western Daily Press: Tuesday 3rd July 1917

Tom Harvey was 46 years old when he died. He was laid to rest in the Milton Cemetery in his home town of Weston-super-Mare.

Name: Hatcher, Harold

Rank: Second Lieutenant

Regiment: Royal Air Force

Date of death: 30th July 1918

Age at time of death: 23

Cause of death: Flying accident

Grave location: St Mary's Cemetery, Taunton

Harold Blake Hatcher was born on 11th February 1895, one of nine children to Robert Hatcher and his wife Ellen. Robert was a draper and brought his family up in his home town of Taunton in Somerset. At least one of his children followed him into the cloth business, and, after he died in 1908, this seems to have fallen to Harold's older brothers, Arthur and Ernest.

After leaving school, Harold became a dental student. Initially studying with Kendrick's in his home town, he was about to begin training at Guy's Hospital in London when war broke out.

Harold joined up in May 1915 and was initially assigned as a Lance Corporal to the 6th Battalion of the Somerset Light Infantry, before transferring to the Middlesex Regiment.

In November 1917, he was badly injured while fighting at Bourlon Woods, as part of the Battle of Cambrai. It was while he was recuperating that he transferred again, this time to the fledgling Royal Air Force.

Second Lieutenant Hatcher gained his wings in June 1918, and soon became a flying instructor. It was while he was working at RAF Fairlop in North West London, that an incident occurred. A local newspaper picked up the story:

> Many in Taunton have learnt with sincere regret of the
> accidental death whilst flying of Lieutenant Harold Blake Hatcher
> of the Royal Air Force, third son of the late Mr Robert Hatcher of
> Taunton, and of Mrs Hatcher, now of Bristol.
>
> The accident in which he met his death on Monday was a triple

fatality, two other airmen being killed at the same time, Second Lieutenant Laurie Bell, of Bournemouth, and Flight Sergeant AR Bean, of Burslem.

At the inquest... it was stated in evidence that while Lieutenant Hatcher and Sergeant Bean were flying at a height of about 500ft, Second Lieutenant Bell, who was flying a single-seater, dived from a position some 700 feet higher, his machine striking and cutting clean through the double-seater, which folded its wings, hovered a few seconds, and then crashed to the earth. The three men were instantaneously killed.

A verdict of Accidental Death was returned.

Taunton Courier and Western Advertiser: Wednesday 7th August 1918

Further witness testimony described how the Sopwith Camel, piloted by Bell, cut the AVRO airplane in two. Hatcher fell out of the wrecked two-seater as the Camel's wings slowly folded into a V and fluttered free following the fuselage to the ground. All three airmen lost their lives. Bean was found in a sitting position, still strapped in the front half of the AVRO's fuselage, his instructor's body was found unmarked thirty yards away in the grass where it had fallen. The wingless Camel crashed close by, and Bell was found to have almost every bone in his body broken.

The accident took place on 30th July 1918. Second Lieutenant Hatcher was just 23 years old.

Harold Blake Hatcher lies at rest in St Mary's Cemetery in his home town of Taunton, Somerset.

Name: Hawkins, Ernest

Rank: Lance Corporal

Regiment: The Cameronians (Scottish Rifles)

Date of death: 2nd July 1918

Age at time of death: 31

Cause of death: Unknown

Grave location: St Mary's Cemetery, Taunton

Ernest Frederick Hawkins was born in Street, Somerset, in 1884. He was the youngest of six children to Charles Hawkins and his wife Elizabeth. Both of Ernest's parents were shoemakers in the Clark's factory in the town, and this was the trade Elizabeth continued in after her husband's death in 1887.

Ernest's life has some mysteries about it and there is a sense that he spent time trying to escape from something. In August 1904, he enlisted in the army, joining the Scottish Rifles (also known as the Cameronians). He did this under an assumed name, preferring to be called James Fisher.

"James" gave his next of kin as his parents, listing them as George and Annie in South Acton (even though these were not his actual parents' names, and that his father had passed away 17 years previously).

His enlistment papers give an interesting insight into the young man. He was listed as 22 years old, 5ft 4ins (1.62m) tall, with brown eyes, black hair and a sallow complexion. His arms were adorned with a number of tattoos, including Buffalo Bill on his upper right arm and a ship surrounded by flags on his upper left.

Private Fisher served for a year on home soil, before being shipped out to India. He returned to the UK in October 1907 and transferred to the Army Reserve.

Ernest returned to Somerset, and it was here that he met Sarah Jane Manning. The couple married in a registry office in Bristol, and went on to have two children, Hubert and Iris.

War broke out, and Private Fisher was remobilised. By August 1914 he was promoted to Lance Corporal and sent to France as part of the British Expeditionary Force. Here he became caught up in a number of the key battles of the conflict.

On 24th July 1916, during the British attacks on High Wood at the Somme, he was wounded in the right arm, and invalided back to England for treatment. Admitted to the War Hospital in Guildford, Surrey, it was confirmed that he had received a gunshot wound to his right arm, which had resulted in a compound fracture of the humerus, radius and ulna. Sadly for Ernest, the only option was a full amputation of his right arm.

After some time to recover, Ernest was transferred to the Pavilion Military Hospital in Brighton where he was fitted for an artificial limb. He spent three months in the Brighton facility, before being moved to the Queen Mary's Convalescent Home in Roehampton to recuperate. He was eventually discharged – from the hospital *and* the army – on 10th March 1917 and returned to his wife and family in Somerset.

There is little further documented information about Ernest. He and Sarah went on to have a further child – Leslie – in 1917. Sadly, where Ernest had been a toddler when his father had died, Leslie was consigned to be a babe-in-arms when Ernest passed away.

Ernest Frederick Hawkins – also known as James Fisher – died in Swindon on 2nd July 1918, at the age of 34. He lies at rest in St Mary's Cemetery in his adopted home town of Taunton, Somerset.

Ernest's gravestone also commemorates his brother Frank Hawkins. Frank was nine years older than Ernest, and, like his younger brother, had decided that the military life was for him.

Frank enlisted in the Royal Navy in November 1894 and was assigned a Boy 2nd Class on HMS Impregnable – the training ship based in Chatham, Kent. Over the period of his twelve years' service, Frank rose through the ranks to Able Seaman. When his term was up, he joined the Royal Fleet Reserve for a further five years.

When war came, Able Seaman Hawkins was immediately called back into action. He was assigned to HMS Goliath, serving off German East Africa and the Dardanelles. On the night of the 12th May 1915, the ship was guarding the water off Gallipoli, when it was struck by three Ottoman torpedoes.

The resulting explosions caused the ship to sink quickly, and 570 souls – out of a total complement of 750 crew – were lost.

Able Seaman Hawkins was one of those lost and was subsequently commemorated on his brother's gravestone.

Name: Hawkins, Francis

Rank: Lance Corporal

Regiment: Rifle Brigade

Date of death: 23rd November 1918

Age at time of death: 23

Cause of death: Influenza and pneumonia

Grave location: St Mary's Cemetery, Taunton

Francis Moreton Hawkins was born in Cottingham, Northamptonshire on 15th July 1895. He was the eldest of eight children to Francis and Louisa Hawkins. Francis Sr was a butcher and, by 1905, he had moved the family to Taunton, where he set up a shop on the main shopping street in the town.

When Francis left school, he became a clerk for the business; he went on to take civil service exams, gaining employment in the General Post Office and then Customs & Excise. War was looming, however, taking him in a different direction.

Sadly, a lot of Francis' military records no longer exist. What the records do tell us, though, is that he initially enrolled with the Somerset Territorials in October 1914, transferring first to the Civil Service Rifles and then the Rifle Brigade. He served his term in the army, rising to the rank of Lance Corporal.

When the war came to a close, Lance Corporal Hawkins was placed on furlough while he waited to be demobbed and returned home on 19th November 1918. Feeling unwell, he took straight to his bed, and, three days later, was admitted to the Military Hospital in Taunton with influenza and pneumonia.

Tragically, these were to get the better of him; Francis passed away at the hospital on 23rd November 1918. He was just 23 years old.

Francis Moreton Hawkins lies at rest in St Mary's Cemetery in his home town of Taunton.

Name: Hawkins, Francis

Rank: Sapper

Regiment: Royal Engineers

Date of death: 17th February 1915

Age at time of death: 19

Cause of death: Spinal meningitis

Grave location: Wembdon Road Cemetery, Bridgwater

Francis Ralph Hawkins was born in Somerset in March 1895 and was one of twelve children to Charles and Jane Hawkins. Charles was a police sergeant and the family lived in Bishop's Lydeard, a village to the west of Taunton.

By the time of the 1911 census, Charles had retired from police work, and was operating as a licenced victualler in nearby Bridgwater. While Jane was supporting her husband running the business, Francis was apprenticed to a local clothier.

When war broke out, Francis was quick to enlist – he joined the Royal Engineers and was appointed a Sapper. He wasn't with the company for that long, however, as by February he had been admitted to the Red Cross Hospital in Christchurch, Dorset, with a fever.

Sadly, he was not to recover; Sapper Hawkins passed away from spinal meningitis on 17th February 1915. He was just 19 years of age.

Francis Ralph Hawkins lies at rest in the Wembdon Road Cemetery, Bridgwater.

Name: Haye, Samuel

Rank: Gunner

Regiment: Royal Marine Artillery

Date of death: 6th July 1919

Age at time of death: 38

Cause of death: Unknown

Grave Location: St Michael & All Angel's Churchyard, Milverton

Samuel James Hayes was born in the Somerset village of Milverton in May 1879. He was the eldest son of James and Harriet.

James was an agricultural labourer, but Samuel wanted more than this; he enlisted in the Royal Marine Artillery in February 1897, three months before his 18th birthday.

The 1901 census finds Gunner Hayes in the Eastney Barracks in Portsmouth, while ten years later, he was on board HMS Swiftsure in the Mediterranean.

In May 1912, he married Annie Thorne, also from Milverton, in his home village. Two years later, just before Christmas 1914, their first – and only – child, Lionel, was born.

I have struggled to find anything specific relating to Gunner Hayes' wartime service. He certainly continued to serve, and by the time of his death had clocked up more than twenty years' service in the Royal Marine Artillery.

Samuel passed away on 6th July 1919, at the age of 38. One record I have located suggests that he died in a Military Hospital in Malta, but whether he passed there or in the UK, he was buried back in Somerset.

Gunner Samuel James Hayes lies at rest in St Michael & All Angel's Churchyard in Milverton.

Name: Heard, Arthur

Rank: Serjeant

Regiment: Royal Engineers

Date of death: 14th April 1918

Age at time of death: 30

Cause of death: Brain tumour

Grave location: Shepton Mallet Burial Ground

Arthur Reginald Heard was born in 1887, the youngest son to Herbert and Emily. Herbert was a local surveyor and land agent, and the family lived in the middle of Shepton Mallet in Somerset, two doors up from the town's Baptist Church and within sight of the Magistrate's Court.

In 1908, aged 21, Arthur made the journey across the Atlantic to Argentina, settling in Buenos Aires and working for the Pacific Railway Company. When war broke out, however, he immediately returned to England, where he enlisted in the army and was assigned to the Royal Engineers.

Sapper Heard was shipped out to France and was quickly promoted, first to Corporal, then to Serjeant. In November 1917, Arthur was caught up in a shell impact on the front and was buried. He was quickly dug out, and not severely hurt.

On 25th March 1918, Serjeant Heard was due to return home on leave but was taken ill. Back in England, he was hospitalised in Birmingham, where meningitis was confirmed. He seemed to recover – even going out for tea with his sister-in-law when she visited him – and was transferred to recuperate in Saltash, Cornwall.

Within days of arriving, he collapsed with a fit, and passed away within half an hour. Subsequent examination confirmed that Arthur had died from a brain tumour. He was just 30 years old.

Arthur Reginald Heard lies at rest in the cemetery of his home town, Shepton Mallet.

Name: Hector, Ernest

Rank: Private

Regiment: Machine Gun Corps

Date of death: 9th May 1920

Age at time of death: 45

Cause of death: Unknown

Grave location: St Peter's Churchyard, North Wootton

Ernest Edward Hector was born in 1875, one of six children – all boys – to Thomas and Mary Hector. Thomas was a farm labourer, and this was a trade that Ernest and his brothers all went on to follow.

Ernest was keen for a better life, however, and enlisted in the Somerset Light Infantry in May 1896, aged 21. After initial training and service in England, Private Hector was off to the East Indies, arriving there just after Christmas 1897.

Six years abroad followed, after which Ernest returned to England to serve another four years. He completed the 12 years of his military career in May 1908.

By this point, Ernest had married Eliza Humphries, a young lady seven years his junior, who came from his home village of North Wootton in Somerset. The couple went on to have six children and, by the time of the 1911 census, Ernest had settled his family in West Pennard, near Glastonbury, and was working as a farm labourer.

Ernest's service during the Great War remains tantalisingly hidden. Given that he was 39 when hostilities broke out, it is unlikely that he was called up again straight away; his gravestone confirms that he was assigned to the Machine Gun Corps (Infantry), but research on his service number provides little other detail.

There is nothing in the media of the time reporting on his death or funeral either, so no concrete cause of death can be confirmed. All that is known is that Private Hector died on 9th May 1920, aged 45 years old.

Ernest Edward Hector is buried in the graveyard of St Peter's Church in North Wootton.

Name: Henderson, William

Rank: Private

Regiment: Royal Warwickshire Regiment

Date of death: 24th August 1917

Age at time of death: 18

Cause of death: Drowned

Grave location: Milton Cemetery, Weston-super-Mare

William Henry Henderson was born in Weston-super-Mare in December 1898. The oldest of four children, his parents were tailor Herbert Henderson and his wife Fanny.

As with a lot of servicemen born around 1900, there is little documentation around William's early life. When war broke out, he was 15 years old, and seems to have been eager to do his bit. Few military records for him survive, but he joined the Royal Warwickshire Regiment and was given the role of Private in the 5th (Reserve) Battalion.

Part of William's training seems to have taken place in Northumberland, and he was based near the coastal town of Blyth. On 24th August 1917, he was one of 600 men taken on a route march from the camp to the coast. The Somerset Standard took up the story of that day's events:

> *Lieutenant Colonel Frank Martin Chatterley, the officer in command, said that he... allowed the men 20 minutes to cool, and after taking all necessary precautions gave orders for them to enter the sea.*

> *The witness inquired from a boy the state of the tide, and was told that it was low ebb; he expected it to rise shortly. The witness undressed, bathed and came out of the water, and was dressing when he was told that some of the men were in difficulties.*

> *Somerset Standard: Friday 31st August 1917*

The Morpeth Herald added to this: *"The soldiers had not been in the water long when some of them got into difficulties and were washed out seawards, in spite of their struggles. A number of comrades rushed to their assistance until at the fatal spot 13 men were seen struggling and evidently drowning. Soldiers formed a human chain by joining hands and wading as far they could into the fast-ebbing tide. They succeeded in saving 5 of their comrades, three of whom were very exhausted, when they got ashore that they were immediately rushed off by car."*

Nine soldiers, including Private Henderson, drowned that day, despite the commended attempts by Reverend Verschoyle, the Army Chaplain, to save their lives.

Some of the survivors told the inquest that they were from the Midlands; they could not swim, and one had never seen the sea before. The inquest was told that there were terrific currents and shifting sands in that particular spot that day, and the conditions seemed to have changed after the soldiers had entered the water. Chatterley said that he had had men bathing at that spot before and had also seen civilians bathing there before.

The other eight servicemen who perished that day were Privates Thomas Forley, Henry Southern, Fred Shale, George Beavan, Gordon Noy, William Blann, Lieutenant Kenneth Brown and Sergeant Riley. Private Henderson was just 18 years old.

William's body was brought back to Weston-super-Mare for burial. He lies at rest in the Milton Cemetery in the town.

Name: Hobbs, Fred

Rank: Private

Regiment: Somerset Light Infantry

Date of death: 12th June 1920

Age at time of death: 29

Cause of death: Unknown

Grave location: St John's Cemetery, Bridgwater

Occasionally I have found that some people are destined to remain hidden. No matter how much research you try and do, details stay lost, and the name on a gravestone will remain just that.

Private Fred Hobbs is one of those people.

He was born in around 1891; he enlisted in the 1st/5th Battalion of the Somerset Light Infantry. Private Hobbs' service records are not available, but he was awarded the Victory and British Medals for his actions.

His pension record gives Mrs Ellen Louisa Hobbs as his next of kin; there is no confirmation of whether this was his mother or his wife – research has uncovered nothing to identify either.

Private Hobbs does not appear in the contemporary media – this would seem to suggest nothing out of the ordinary about his passing.

All we know for certain is that Fred Hobbs passed away on 12th June 1920, aged 29 years old. He lies at rest in St John's Cemetery in Bridgwater, Somerset.

Name: Hobbs, Frederick

Rank: Private

Regiment: Devonshire Regiment

Date of death: 25th November 1916

Age at time of death: 29

Cause of death: Unknown

Grave location: St John's Cemetery, Bridgwater

Frederick Hobbs was born in December 1886, the fourth of ten children to William and Martha Hobbs, from Bridgwater in Somerset. William was a mason, and all of his children seemed to be good with their hands. Frederick went on to become a plumber's apprentice, while his siblings worked as a mason, a dressmaker and a carpenter.

The 1911 census found him living in Polden Street, Bridgwater with his mother and youngest sibling, Florrie. William, however, was living round the corner in Bath Road, with three of his other children, Clara, Tom and George. Both of Frederick's parents are listed as married, which adds to the confusion of them being in separate houses.

Frederick enlisted within weeks of war being declared; he joined the 10th (Service) Battalion of the Devonshire Regiment and, after a year on home soil, his troop was shipped to France. This wasn't the end of the journey for Private Hobbs, however, as within a couple of months, he was sent on as part of the Mediterranean Expeditionary Force, finally arriving in Salonica, Greece, in November 1915.

Private Hobbs had only been serving for a month when he was admitted to the Hospital Ship Asturias in Alexandria, with lacerations to his cheeks and eyelids. The initial report seemed to suggest the wounds were as a result of gunshot, although a more detailed report later confirmed that the injuries were caused by barbed wire.

While in hospital, Frederick's urine was found to include a high level of sugar. He also confirmed having lost a lot of weight in recent months but could not confirm when this had begun. He was diagnosed with diabetes and was evacuated back to England for treatment for both his injuries and his illness.

The damage to his left eye healed, but he was left with significant ptosis (drooping of the eyelid). When it came to his diabetes, specialists back in England determined that, while it could not be put down to Private Hobbs' service, it had definitely been aggravated by it. He was deemed no longer fit for military service and furloughed in June 1916, with a report confirming this three months later.

Sadly, whether Frederick's life returned to normal is not recorded. It seems likely, however, that the diabetes got the better of him, and he passed away on 25th November 1916, aged just 29 years old.

Frederick Hobbs lies at rest in St John's Cemetery in his home town of Bridgwater, Somerset.

Frederick's younger brother Herbert Hobbs also fought in the Great War. He enrolled in the Royal Marines Light Infantry and fought on the Western Front. Caught up in the Battle of Gavrelle Windmill, he was one of 335 Royal Marines to be killed in that skirmish. He lies buried at the Arras Memorial in Northern France.

Name: Hockey, Wilfred

Rank: Private

Regiment: Royal Marine Light Infantry

Date of death: 25th March 1915

Age at time of death: 23

Cause of death: Meningitis

Grave location: St Matthew's Churchyard, Wookey

Wilfred James Hockey was born in September 1892, the sixth of nine children to William and Mary. William was the village butcher, but Wilfred followed his older brother Oliver into the gardening business.

Military records for Wilfred are difficult to locate, but it appears that there is a reason for this.

He enlisted in February 1915, joining the Royal Marine Light Infantry. His initial service took him to Crystal Palace in South London – then a naval training base.

Returning home on leave on 12th March, Private Hockey fell ill on his first evening at home. Quickly diagnosed with 'spotted fever' (or meningitis), he sadly passed away on 25th March. He was just 23 years of age.

Wilfred Hockey lies at rest in the graveyard of St Matthew's Church in his home village of Wookey, in Somerset.

Name: Hoskins, Sidney

Rank: Driver

Regiment: Royal Engineers

Date of death: 5th November 1917

Age at time of death: 26

Cause of death: Meningitis

Grave location: Shepton Mallet Burial Ground

Sidney Victor Hoskins was born in February 1892, one of eleven children to Sidney and Elizabeth Hoskins from Shepton Mallet in Somerset. Sidney Sr worked as a quarryman and labourer in local factories.

Sidney was keen to make a life for himself, enlisting in the army in 1909. He served two years as a driver for the Royal Engineers, before being put on the reserve list. By the time of the 1911 census, he was listed as a packer on the railway. In November of that year, Sidney married Ada Lambert, also of Shepton Mallet.

While working on the line in April 1913, Sidney had an accident, suffering a fractured skull. He wasn't able to carry out any hard labour from that point on.

War broke out and Sidney was remobilised; just a month after Ada gave birth to their one and only child, a daughter they named Ada.

New baby notwithstanding, Driver Hoskins was shipped to France as part of the British Expeditionary Force. After two months he was sent down the line after suffering a fit and was subsequently treated for pleurisy in Nantes. In November 1914, he returned to England and was ultimately discharged on medical grounds in February 1915.

During his time in France, he had also developed tuberculosis, and eventually spent three months in a sanitorium in Taunton, Somerset, to recover.

The condition continued to haunt Sidney, however, and he succumbed to the illness on 5th November 1917. He was 25 years of age.

Sidney Victor Hoskins lies at rest in the cemetery of his home town of Shepton Mallet.

Sidney's younger brother, William Napier Hoskins, was also involved in the Great War. He had enlisted in the Somerset Light Infantry and was based in India. Injured in fighting in the Persian Gulf, he was invalided back to India to recover. He was well enough to return to the fray, and was shipped to Mesopotamia, where he was again injured. He died of his wounds in Kut-al Amarah, Iraq, in 1915, aged just 20 years old.

The boys' older brother Charles had also died in 1895, aged just six years old. While Sidney Sr and Elizabeth had had a family of eight girls, they were to outlive all three of their sons.

Name: Howard, William

Rank: Gunner

Regiment: Royal Garrison Artillery

Date of death: 15th January 1919

Age at time of death: 31

Cause of death: Enteritis

Grave location: St James' Cemetery, Taunton

William Arnold Howard was born in Cumbria towards the end of 1887. He was the youngest of two children, the son of gospel minister Edwin Howard and his wife Alethea. Edwin's role took him across the country; by the time William was four, the family were settled in Worksop, Nottinghamshire; ten years later, they were based in Taunton, Somerset.

William's older sister became a music teacher and was presumably inspired by her father's calling. William, however, took a different route, and, by the time of the 1911 census, was listed as a physical culture expert.

He had, by this time, met and married a woman called Alice, and the couple had two children, Edna and Marjorie. The census found the young couple living in a three-roomed house in the middle of Taunton.

War was on the horizon, and William enlisted as a Gunner in the Royal Garrison Artillery. His battalion – the 3rd/4th Siege Reserve Brigade – were those manning large scale weaponry, although, as part of the reserve, Gunner Howard was based in England for the duration of the conflict.

William was awarded the Victory and British Medals for his service but once the Armistice was declared it seems that he fell ill. He was admitted to the Military Hospital in Taunton with exhaustion following a bout of enteritis and succumbed to this on 15th January 1919. He was 31 years old.

William Arnold Howard lies at rest in the St James' Cemetery in Taunton, Somerset.

Name: Howe, Alfred

Rank: Private

Regiment: Gloucestershire Regiment

Date of death: 6th April 1916

Age at time of death: 31

Cause of death: Unknown

Grave location: Milton Cemetery, Weston-super-Mare

In the Milton Cemetery in Weston-super-Mare is a gravestone to Alfred Harry Howe. He seems destined, sadly, to be one of those servicemen whose stories are lost to time. The stone confirms that he died on 6th April 1916 and that he was a Private in the Gloucestershire Regiment. Further research adds that he was assigned to the 3rd/4th Battalion.

The UK Army Register of Soldiers' Effects gives his father's name as William. It also confirms that he was not eligible for a war gratuity, as he had insufficient service; given the date of his death, it is likely, therefore, that he enlisted on or after October 1915.

Beyond this information, however, there is little documentation to confirm exactly who Alfred was. As there is no date or place of birth, it is difficult to get an exact match. There are at least three William/Alfred matches in the Somerset/Bristol area, but nothing to connect them to the headstone in Weston-super-Mare, and nothing to even confirm that Alfred was from the South West.

There is nothing in any contemporary newspapers to suggest that Private Howe's passing was anything out of the ordinary.

Sadly, therefore, he remains a name lost to history. Alfred Harry Howe, whoever he was, and however he died, lies at rest in a Somerset cemetery.

Name: Humphries, Thomas

Rank: Driver

Regiment: Royal Horse Artillery

Date of death: 8th April 1919

Age at time of death: 21

Cause of death: Unknown

Grave location: St Peter's Churchyard, North Wootton

Thomas George Edward Humphries was born in November 1897, one of six children to George and Annie Humphries, from North Wootton in Somerset. George was a farm labourer and had been married to his wife for 19 years before her untimely death at the age of 40.

When war came, Thomas was just 16 years old. He enlisted quickly though, joining the Royal Horse Artillery as early as the summer of 1915. Driver Humphries joined the 120 Brigade of the Royal Field Artillery, which was one of the many Howitzer brigades moving the large, long-barrelled field guns along the front line.

Given the high use of horses during the war, and that Thomas was a Driver, it is likely that his role would have been guiding the animals in his care – this may also account for why his gravestone gives his troop as the Royal Horse Artillery. Little remains of Thomas' service records; he was awarded the Victory and British Medals as well as the 1915 Star, so would have been in the thick of the fighting and seen action on the Western Front.

When it comes to his passing, again details are scant. His pension records simply state that he died of 'disease', and he passed in the Military Hospital in Southwark, South London. Again, given when he died and the lack of any contemporary media report on his passing, it seems likely that the cause was a lung condition – influenza, pneumonia or tuberculosis – but that is a presumption on my part.

Whatever the cause, Driver Humphries died on 8th April 1919, aged just 21 years old.

Thomas George Edward Humphries lies at rest in the quiet graveyard of St Peter's Church in his home village of North Wootton.

Name: Hunt, Robert

Rank: Private

Regiment: Royal Army Medical Corps

Date of death: 4th November 1918

Age at time of death: 24

Cause of death: Influenza and pneumonia

Grave location: Somerton Cemetery

Robert Edward Nichols Hunt was born in Somerton, Somerset in 1894. One of five children to Charles and Rose Hunt, his father was a bootmaker.

By the 1911 census, however, things had taken a different turn; Charles and two of his sons were working for a brewer, Rose was working as a shop assistant in Boots, and the youngest of the family, Kate, was apprenticed to a dressmaker.

It was against this backdrop that war came, and, within a year, Robert had enlisted in the Royal Army Medical Corps. His sign-up documents confirm that he was short-sighted, although this was corrected with glasses, and he was deemed fit for active service.

Sent to the Western Front in October 1915, Private Hunt definitely found himself in the thick of the action.

In August 1916, he was supporting the fighting at High Wood on the Somme, when a gas shell exploded. He fell and, when he woke, he remembered little of what happened. Robert had inhaled a lot of gas, however, and was left coughing with difficulty breathing. He was transferred to England by train and ship to recover, arriving back on the 2nd September.

There is no record of Robert having gone back to the front. The impact of the gas appears to have been severe and long-lasting. At the end of October 1918, he was admitted to the Becket House Auxiliary Hospital in St Albans with influenza and bronchial pneumonia. Sadly, this was to be a battle he would not recover from, and he passed away on 4th November 1918. He was 24 years old.

Robert Edward Nichols Hunt lies at rest in the cemetery of his home town, Somerton.

Name: Hussey, Frank

Rank: Sapper

Regiment: Royal Engineers

Date of death: 26th May 1920

Age at time of death: 49

Cause of death: Tuberculosis

Grave location: Milton Cemetery, Weston-super-Mare

Frank Hussey was born in the autumn of 1870, one of eight children to William and Ann Hussey. William was a mason and raised his family in Weston-super-Mare in his home county of Somerset. When he left school, Frank found employment as a general labourer, initially in Somerset, but then in South Wales with his older brother Samuel.

By 1889, Frank had moved back to Somerset, where he married Elizabeth Webber in December. Work was obviously more available in South Wales, however, as the couple moved back to Glamorgan, and had their first four children – Beatrice, William, Edith and Hubert – there.

The turn of the century saw the Hussey family return to Somerset. Frank, by now, was working as a bricklayer. They settled in a small house near the centre of Weston. Life continued, with building work helping to support the family. Frank and Elizabeth had two more children – James and Marion – and, by the time of the 1911 census, the couple lived with their five youngest children in a two-up-two-down house on the then outskirts of the town.

Storm clouds were gathering over in Europe, and Frank was more than willing to do his bit for King and Country. Having already been a volunteer with the Royal Engineers, he formally enlisted with the regiment on 5th May 1915.

Sapper Hussey was assigned to the 2nd (Wessex) Field Company, which was a territorial force. He was mobilised for fourteen months, before being discharged from the army as he was no longer physically fit for war service. Unfortunately, his military records give no further indication as to his ailment or condition.

Frank's trail goes cold for a few years. Released from service in July 1916, the next identifiable record is from four years later. This confirms that he died from tuberculosis on 26th May 1920, aged 49 years old. Given the debilitating effect of the condition, it seems likely that Sapper Hussey contracted it during the war, and this is what had led to his dismissal.

Frank Hussey had died at home, and it was in the Milton Cemetery in Weston-super-Mare that he was laid to rest.

Name: Hutchinson, Ernest

Rank: Lieutenant

Regiment: Royal Naval Reserve

Date of death: 10th January 1920

Age at time of death: 42

Cause of death: Drowned

Grave location: Milton Cemetery, Weston-super-Mare

Ernest Henry Hutchinson was born in January 1878, one of four children to Dorothy Hutchinson, from Blyth, Northumberland. Details of Ernest's father are sketchy and, by the time of the 1891 census, Dorothy seems to have been widowed and remarried, as her surname was now Alexander.

By this time Ernest was at school, and boarding with his aunt and uncle, but his siblings were all living with Dorothy and listed as 'step-children'. Dorothy gave her employment as 'housewife; husband at sea', and it seems that this was likely her first husband's job and, in fact, it would turn out to be her eldest son's as well.

Ernest disappears from the census records for a while but had readily taken to a life at sea. Over the next few years, he became certified as a *Second Mate of a Foreign-Going Ship* (1897), *First Mate of a Foreign-Going Ship* (1899) and *Master of a Foreign-Going Ship* (1904).

When war broke out, Ernest was seconded into the Merchant Navy. Sadly, his military records no longer exist, but during his time he attained the rank of Lieutenant. Ernest survived the war and was retained as part of the Royal Naval Reserve, while continuing with his own sailing work.

At some point, Ernest married a woman called Emma Jane; documentation on the couple is scarce, so the date of the marriage is lost to time. The couple settled, however, in Weston-super-Mare, Somerset, but do not appear to have had any children.

Ernest's maritime career continued after the war. One of his commissions was as First Mate aboard the SS Treveal. This was a new vessel in 1919, making its maiden voyage from Glasgow to the Middle East. It then sailed on to Calcutta and was on its way back to Dundee by the beginning of 1920.

A local Cornish newspaper took up the story:

> The terrible toll of 36 lives were levied by the wreck of the St Ives steamer Treveal, off the Dorset Coast on Saturday morning. The crew totalled 43, only seven surviving.
>
> The Treveal, 5,200 tons, one of the Hain fleet of steamers, was caught by a fierce gale during Friday night and was firmly wedged on the Kimmeridge Ledge, near St Alban's Head.
>
> A Portland tug and Swanage lifeboat came to her assistance, but were unable to lend any practical aid, and on Saturday morning the Treveal was abandoned in favour of the ship's boats. The latter were soon capsized and only seven of the crew succeeded in reaching the shore.
>
> West Briton and Cornwall Advertiser: Monday 12th January 1920.

The report went into much more detail about the tragedy, including "*a warm tribute to the vicar of a parish nearby, the Revd. Pearce, who stood up to his neck helping to pull the men in. The vicar tried for an hour to resuscitate the First Mate [Ernest Hutchinson], but without success.*"

Another newspaper gave further information about Ernest's funeral, and the impact of the shipwreck on his widow:

> There was a simple but affecting scene in Weston-super-Mare Cemetery on Saturday afternoon, when the body of Chief Officer EH Hutchinson, one of the 35 victims in the wreck of the SS Treveal... was laid to rest.
>
> It will be recollected that... the first tidings of his tragic fate reached the widow... through the columns of a Sunday newspaper. Only on the previous morning she had received a letter notifying the date on which the Treveal was due to reach Dundee – whither the major portion of her cargo has been consigned from Calcutta – asking him to meet her there.
>
> Western Daily Press: Monday 19th January 1920

Ernest Henry Hutchinson drowned at the age of 42 years old. He was buried in the Milton Cemetery in his adopted home town of Weston-super-Mare in Somerset.

Name: Jenkins, Herbert

Rank: Private

Regiment: Royal Marine Light Infantry

Date of death: 24th August 1919

Age at time of death: 27

Cause of death: Disease

Grave location: St Mary's Churchyard, Yatton

Herbert Jenkins was born in 1891, the youngest of five children to George and Amelia Jenkins. George was a domestic gardener, and the family lived in the Somerset village of Yatton next to the Prince of Orange public house. Amelia helped make ends meet, by working as a seamstress and upholsterer.

Amelia passed away in 1909, and it was around his time that Herbert felt the calling of military service. He enlisted as a Private in the Royal Marines Light Infantry on 17th September 1909.

Sadly, little documentation remains about Private Jenkins' naval service, although the 1911 census gives his location as the Stonehouse Barracks in Devon.

Herbert's family life held a series of highs and lows. His father George died in 1915, and he went on to marry Blanche Elvins, a bootmaker's daughter from Bristol, the following year. Sadly, however, she passed away in December 1918, and Herbert was again alone.

By this time, the Great War was over, although Private Jenkins was still serving. He was assigned to HMS Warspite, which had fought, and been damaged, in the Battle of Jutland. While there is no evidence Herbert had been on board during the skirmish, this is the last vessel on which he served.

As with his military career, details of Herbert's passing are lost to time. All that is known is that he died in Bristol on 24th August 1919 and that the cause was 'disease'. He was just 27 years of age.

Herbert's next of kin was his sister Jennie; she brought him back to his home town of Yatton to be buried in the graveyard of St Mary's Church.

Name: Jones, Arthur

Rank: Serjeant

Regiment: Somerset Light Infantry

Date of death: 27th January 1919

Age at time of death: 47

Cause of death: Influenza and pneumonia

Grave location: St Mary's Cemetery, Taunton

Arthur Henry Jones was born in 1874, the oldest of five children to James and Kate Jones. James worked as a coachman and travelling seems to have been his thing.

Born in Wiltshire, he met and married Kate in Somerset, and this is where Arthur was born; by 1879, the young family had moved to Hampshire, and within a year they had relocated again, this time to Folkestone in Kent. Three years later, by the time James and Kate's youngest two children were born, they were back in Wiltshire again, having competed their tour of the south of England.

Sadly, tragedy was to strike the Jones family, when Kate passed away in 1888, at the tender age of 31 years old. James had a family of boys to bring up, however, and he married again, this time to a Miriam Millard. The couple went on to have two children, giving Arthur a half-brother and half-sister.

At this point, Arthur falls off the radar. It may well be that he chose to take up a military career early on – if he was serving overseas, it is possible that the census documentation no longer exists. Twelve years' service would certainly seem to account for his absence between 1881 and the next time his name appears on records.

These records relate to Arthur's marriage to Fanny Hill. The couple were married by Banns in May 1906, marrying in Westbury, Wiltshire. They went on to have four children – Arthur, Kathleen, Gladys and Percival – between 1907 and 1911.

Again, at this point, Arthur falls off the radar. His service records no longer exist, but what evidence remains confirms that he enlisted in the Somerset Light Infantry and was assigned to the 7th (Service) Battalion. Initially formed in Taunton, they shipped out to France in July 1915, although there is no documentation to confirm when or if Arthur was involved.

Sadly, the only other reference to Serjeant Jones is his final pension record. This confirms that he succumbed to a combination of influenza and pneumonia on 27th January 1919. He was 44 years old.

Arthur Henry Jones lies at rest in St Mary's Cemetery in Taunton, Somerset.

Name: Kick, Harry

Rank: Ordinary Seaman

Regiment: Royal Navy

Date of death: 17th September 1918

Age at time of death: 18

Cause of death: Pneumonia

Grave location: Holy Cross Churchyard, Middlezoy

Harry Kick was born in August 1900, the oldest of six children to George and Georgina Kick from the small village of Middlezoy in Somerset. George was an agricultural labourer, while his wife helped with the dairy side of Jones Farm, where he worked.

Details of Harry's military service are scarce, but, based on his age, it is likely to have been the second half of the war when he enlisted. He joined the Royal Navy and was assigned to HMS Osea, a naval base in Essex.

Sadly, there is little evidence of Harry's time in the navy. His pension records confirm that he passed away on 17th September 1918, having been suffering from pneumonia. He was just 18 years old when he died.

Harry Kick lies at peace in the churchyard of Holy Cross Church in his home village of Middlezoy, Somerset.

Name: Kiddle, Martin

Rank: Private

Regiment: Royal Defence Corps

Date of death: 5th March 1917

Age at time of death: 46

Cause of death: Carcinoma of the liver

Grave location: Holy Trinity Churchyard, Street

Martin Kiddle was born in 1871, the oldest of four children to Joseph and Annie Kiddle. Joseph was a butcher in the Somerset town of Street, and the family lived above the shop on the High Street.

When Joseph died in 1886, Martin took on the role of shopman, before taking over the business entirely.

In 1895, aged 24, Martin married Eleanor Freeman, four years his senior from the nearby town of Ilminster. The young couple had five children and, by the time of the 1901 census, they were running the business as a family, employing an assistant in the shop and a domestic servant.

It is evident that Martin left the butchery business behind him, though. Ten years later, on the 1911 census, he is listed as a Stock Room Manager in a local rug factory.

Martin joined up when war broke out, initially serving in the Somerset Light Infantry, before transferring across to the Royal Defence Corps.

While there is no date for his transfer, it is likely to have been at some point in 1915. Private Kiddle's wife, Eleanor, passed away in May of that year, so it is reasonable to assume that he requested a transfer to support her before her death, or to support his children afterwards.

Sadly, however, Martin was also to succumb to illness. His pension ledger shows that he passed away on 5th March 1917, dying from carcinoma of the liver. He was 46 years old.

Martin Kiddle lies at rest in the graveyard of Holy Trinity Church in his home town of Street. The gravestone gives dedications to his father,

Joseph, and his brother, John, who had died at just over a year old.

Guardianship of Martin and Eleanor's five, now orphaned, children – Eleanor, Martin, John, Rachel and George – passed to Martin's mother, Annie.

Name: King, Harry

Rank: Cook's Mate

Regiment: Royal Navy

Date of death: 21st September 1918

Age at time of death: 27

Cause of death: Died of wounds

Grave location: Wells Cemetery

Harry George King was born in Somerset in December 1894, one of nine children to John and Sarah King. John worked as a cabinet maker in Wells, and Harry followed in a similar vein to his father, becoming an upholsterer.

When war broke out, Harry – who stood at 5'3" (1.6m) tall – enlisted in the Royal Navy as a Cook's Mate. He trained on HMS Victory I in Portsmouth, before transferring to the HMV Vernon, a land-based ship, also in Portsmouth.

While on leave in 1917, Harry married Alice Trickey, who had also been born in Wells.

Harry's first sea-going assignment was on the HMS Hermione, which was a guard ship off the Southampton coast. After two years on board, Cook's Mate King was transferred to another vessel.

The HMS Glatton was a monitor vessel requisitioned by the Royal Navy from the Norwegian fleet at the outbreak of the First World War. After a lengthy refit, she was finally ready for service in the autumn of 1918, and positioned in Dover in preparation for a future offensive across the Channel.

At 6:15 on the evening of 16 September, there was a small explosion in a 6-inch magazine below decks, which then ignited the cordite stored there. Flames shot through the roof of one of the turrets and started to spread. The fire was not able to be brought under control, and there were concerns that, if the ship's rear magazine exploded, the presence of the ammunition ship Gransha only 150 yards (140 m) away risked a massive explosion that would devastate Dover itself. The decision was taken to torpedo the Glatton, in the hope that the incoming flood water would quash the fire.

In the event, sixty men aboard the Glatton were killed outright, with another 124 men injured, of whom 19 died later of their injuries. This included Cook's Mate King.

While the incident wasn't reported in the media of the time, Harry's funeral was; it gives a little more insight into the tragedy:

> *News reached Wells... that 1st Class Cook's Mate Harry George King... was lying in a hospital at Dover suffering from severe burns caused through an internal explosion on the ship on which he was serving. His wife (...to whom he was married 12 months ago) and his sister at once proceeded to the hospital, where they arrived only a few minutes before he died.*
>
> *The unfortunate young man had sustained shocking injuries and was conscious for only two hours on Friday. He lost all his belongings in the explosion.*
>
> *Wells Journal: Friday 27th September 1918.*

Harry George King was only 27 years old when he died. He lies at rest in Wells Cemetery, Somerset.

Harry's widow, Alice, did not remarry; the couple had not had any children, and she passed away in their home town of Wells, in January 1974.

Name: Knight, Ronald

Rank: Flight Lieutenant

Regiment: Royal Naval Air Service

Date of death: 12th March 1917

Age at time of death: 22

Cause of death: Flying accident

Grave location: Wells Cemetery

Ronald Victor Knight was born in March 1894, the youngest of two children — both sons — to John Knight, an Ironmonger from London, and his Swiss wife, Marie.

Ronald was well educated — being taught at Wells and Bedford Grammar Schools in the UK and Neuchatel in Switzerland, not far from where his mother was born. After studying at Bristol University, he went to work at Guys Hospital in London, training as a dental student.

When war broke out, he volunteered at once, being enlisted in the 8th Battalion London Regiment. Lieutenant Knight went with his regiment to France and was involved in the Battle of Festubert and the fighting at Loos.

Returning home towards the end of 1915, Ronald married Gwendoline Dawkes, in a ceremony overseen by the Bishop of Bath & Wells.

Rather than returning to the front line, Lieutenant Knight accepted a commission to lead a section of the London Cyclist Corps, a position he held for a year or so. While in this service, Ronald and Gwendoline had their one and only child, a little girl they called Beryl.

In 1916, Ronald accepted a further move to the Royal Naval Air Service, becoming involved in flying as a Flight Lieutenant. It was while he was based at RNAS Cranwell that he was involved in the accident that led to his death.

An inquest was held into the incident, and evidence was taken:

> *Air Mechanic Charles Deboo [said] that the machine had been recently inspected, and that it was alright. He did not see the deceased flying, but saw the machine come down, nose first, in*

corkscrew fashion. He saw it at a height of 400ft. He went to the machine after it had fallen and found the officer was dead. The machine struck the ground and smashed up, but he could not say how the accident happened.

Charles Barrett, air mechanic, said he saw the accident. The deceased seemed as if he was going to turn towards the wind to land, and, as he turned, he banked, but he never righted himself. He nose-dived and spun round to the earth. He thought he lost control as he was turning, or the wind might have caught him. The machine was smashed, except for the tail.

The jury returned a verdict that deceased accidentally met his death while flying.

Retford and Workshop Herald and North Notts Advertiser: Tuesday 20th March 1917

Flight Lieutenant Knight died in an aeroplane crash on 12th March 1917. He was 22 years old.

Ronald Victor Knight lies at rest in Wells Cemetery, Somerset.

Name: Labdon, Hubert

Rank: Private

Regiment: Machine Gun Corps

Date of death: 22nd December 1919

Age at time of death: 23

Cause of death: Heart failure

Grave location: All Saints' Churchyard, Ashcott

Hubert Wilfred Labdon was born in the spring of 1896, to Alfred and Elizabeth Labdon, bakers in Ashcott, Somerset. One of five children, with two older brothers and two older sisters, he lost is mother at a very early age; Elizabeth died in 1901.

Hubert had left home by the time he was fifteen but had not gone far – the 1911 census found him learning a trade from Edgar and Betsy Vining, farmers in the village.

When war came, Hubert enlisted – he joined up in February 1916, aged 19 years and five months. Private Labdon was initially assigned to the Somerset Light Infantry, but he must have quickly shown aptitude, because he was soon transferred to the Machine Gun Corps. After initial training, he found himself on a ship to France, arriving in Camiers, to the south of Boulogne, on 25th September 1916.

Private Labdon's military records survive and are quite detailed – after an early mishap, where he was docked two days' pay for losing part of his kit *'by neglect'*, he also spent time in hospital in June 1917.

By August of that year, he was based permanently at Camiers, where he was acting as a stretcher bearer. This was a role he continued to execute until he was demobbed at the end of the war.

His records show Hubert was granted two periods of leave; it was on the second of these, in November 1918, that he married Eva May Acreman. She was two years his senior, a farmer's daughter from Ashcott as well, although the couple married in Ealing, London.

By mid-December, Private Labdon was back in France, and here he stayed until February 1919, when his unit was finally demobilised. On returning to England, the young couple moved back to Ashcott, to be close to his family.

Sadly, Hubert seems to have succumbed to illness as many of his returning colleagues did. The local newspaper gave details of his passing:

> The deceased, who was only 23, was recently married. He had served his country during the late war, part time as stretcher bearer. He had suffered from trench fever, which considerably injured his constitution and left him with a weak heart, which, no doubt, was the cause of death.
>
> He had left his home for a short walk, and having been away rather longer than usual [a] search was made for him, and he was found sitting in an unconscious state. He died in a short time after reaching his home.
>
> Deceased was of a very quiet and inoffensive disposition, and was much respected.
>
> Central Somerset Gazette: Friday 2nd January 1920

While the end result was the same, Private Labdon's military records adds the cause of death as 'heart failure following influenza and acute diarrhoea'.

Hubert Wilfred Labdon lies at peace in the graveyard of All Saints' Church, in his home village of Ashcott in Somerset.

Eva remained in Somerset after her husband's death. In 1930, she married William Langford, a baker, and the couple went on to have a daughter.

Name: Ladd, Alan

Rank: Private

Regiment: Royal Army Service Corps

Date of death: 14th October 1918

Age at time of death: 25

Cause of death: Pneumonia

Grave Location: Friends Burial Ground, Long Sutton

Alan Ladd was born in the summer of 1893 and was one of twins. His parents were plumber and gas fitter George Ladd and his wife Mary Ann, who was a midwife. The couple had eight children altogether, of whom Alan and his twin Arthur were the youngest.

George had been born in Exeter, Devon, and Mary Ann in Somerset, which is where they initially based their family. By 1887, however, they had moved to Berkshire, and were living in Knowl Hill, near Maidenhead, when their youngest four children were born.

The 1911 census found the family living in Dunster, Somerset, where everyone seemed to be bringing in a wage. George and Mary Ann had four of their children living with them, who were employed as an engine driver, grocer, baker's apprentice and, in Alan's case, a tailor's apprentice.

War broke out in 1914, and, in November 1915, Alan enlisted. He joined the Royal Army Service Corps as a Private, and his enlistment papers showed he stood 5ft 5ins (1.65m) tall and weighed in at 130lbs (59kg). He was stationed at the Corps' Remount Department in Swaythling, Southampton and thus his military service was completed on the Home Front.

Shortly after enlisting, on 16th April 1916, Alan married Ada Westlake. She lived in the village of Long Sutton, near Langport in Somerset, and the couple married at the Wesleyan Methodist Chapel in Somerton. They do not appear to have gone on to have any children.

Further details of Private Ladd's life are scant. What *can* be determined is that he was admitted to Netley Hospital in Southampton on 11th October 1918, having had symptoms of pneumonia for a few days. Sadly, his condition worsened, and Alan passed away just three days later, on 14th October 1918. He was just 25 years of age.

Alan Ladd was brought back to Long Sutton for burial. The war may have led him and Ada to adopt more of a Quaker way of life, as he lies at rest in the Friends Burial Ground on the outskirts of the town.

Name: Lake, Geoffrey

Rank: Private

Regiment: Inns of Court Officers Training Corps

Date of death: 10th November 1918

Age at time of death: 18

Cause of death: Influenza and pneumonia

Grave location: St Mary's Cemetery, Taunton

Geoffrey William Lake was born in London in 1900, the oldest of two children to George and Emma Lake. George was a bank clerk who soon got promotion to bank manager and, as a result, moved the family to the Somerset town of Taunton at some point between 1904 and 1911.

When he left school, Geoffrey found work at his father's bank and, with the war still being played out on the other side of the English Channel, he joined the Inns of Court Officers Training Corps in August 1918.

Sadly, this was to be the decision that saw Private Lake's undoing. Whilst training in Hertfordshire, he caught influenza, which then led to pneumonia. Admitted to the Military War Hospital in Napsbury, the illnesses got the better of him, and tragically he passed away on 10th November 1918. He was just 18 years of age.

Geoffrey William Lake was brought back to Taunton and lies at rest in St Mary's Cemetery in the town.

Name: Latcham, Arthur

Rank: Gunner

Regiment: Royal Horse Artillery

Date of death: 21st December 1915

Age at time of death: 26

Cause of death: Pneumonia

Grave location: Holy Trinity Churchyard, Street

Arthur James Latcham was born in 1889, the oldest of five children – all boys – to Walter and Matilda Latcham. The family lived in Street, Somerset, where Walter worked as a carpenter in the Clark's shoe factory.

Initially following his father into shoemaking, Arthur was quick to enlist when war broke out. Details of Gunner Latcham's military service are scarce, but documents confirm that he joined the Somerset Royal Horse Artillery on 8th October 1914. He did not see active service abroad but had been stationed on the east coast for his training.

While little remains of his service records, contemporary media of the day includes a lot of information about both his passing and his subsequent funeral:

> *On Sunday, December 5th, having a few hours' leave, he visited his parents at Street, and while at home complained that he was feeling unwell. On the following Wednesday, December 8th (which, by a coincidence, was his twenty-sixth birthday) Mr and Mrs Latcham received a post-card from him from Taunton [where the Somerset RHA was based] stating that he was very ill. They immediately engaged a motor car, and went to Taunton, where they found him in an extremely weak state, and on the point of collapse, he having had to walk to a hospital nearly a mile away three times a day for his medicine. Having obtained the captain's permission, they brought him home in the motor car, and at once put him under the care of Dr MacVicker. He was then found to be suffering from pneumonia and congestion of*

the lungs... In spite of the greatest care, and best of nursing,
however, he gradually grew worse, and never rallied.

Central Somerset Gazette: Friday 24th December 1915.

The following week's newspaper included nearly a whole column on Gunner Latcham's funeral, including two tributes, one from his captain and another from the local MP:

> *I am writing to tell you how very sorry all the officers of this*
> *battery are at your loss. Your son was the first member of the*
> *Somerset RHA to give his life for his country, and although he did*
> *not have the satisfaction of being killed in action, the honour is*
> *the same. I'm afraid the last few months he was in this battery*
> *were not very happy ones for him, owing to his trouble with his*
> *finger; but he bore the trouble and pain well. I had him with me*
> *for more than a year, so I can fully appreciate what a good*
> *fellow he was and how great your loss is.*
>
> *Captain M Clowes (Central Somerset Gazette: Friday 31st*
> *December 1915)*

> *I am very sorry indeed to learn of the sad loss you have suffered*
> *through the death of your son. I know that he was a fine fellow,*
> *an example of what an Englishman should be, and respected by*
> *all who knew him. I am sure you must feel proud to know that he*
> *has done all that a man can do, and has died serving his country.*
>
> *Ernest Jardine MP (Central Somerset Gazette: Friday 31st*
> *December 1915)*

Arthur James Latcham lies at rest in the graveyard of Holy Trinity Church in his home town of Street.

Arthur was the third son Walter and Matilda had lost. Their second-born, Herbert, passed when a little over a year old. Their third son, William, died a year before Arthur, when he was just 15 years old.

Name: Lavender, Arthur

Rank: Private

Regiment: Royal Army Medical Corps

Date of death: 7th May 1917

Age at time of death: 28

Cause of death: Pneumonia

Grave location: Milton Cemetery, Weston-super-Mare

Arthur Reginald Lavender was born in Bath on 17th January 1889, the second of two children to George Charles (or Charles George) Lavender and his wife, Elizabeth. George raised the family in Bath and seems to have been a jack of all trades, finding work where he could, as a porter in a warehouse according to the 1891 census and a stationary engine driver ten years later.

On 1st December 1907, at the age of just 18, Arthur married Kate Pearce, a painter's daughter from Weston-super-Mare. The young couple went on to have a son, Sidney, who was born the following year.

By 1911, Arthur was working in Weston-super-Mare as a warehouseman at a local laundry and, on the day of that year's census, was staying with his father-in-law. Kate, meanwhile, had taken Sidney to see her brother, Frank, who lived in Bristol.

War was coming to Europe, and, in November 1915, Arthur signed up, joining the Royal Army Medical Corps as a Private. After initial training – including a course on First Aid, he was sent overseas on 11th April 1916, where he was assigned to the 27th Casualty Clearing Station.

Private Lavender's time in the RAMC seems to have been a complicated one. He was admitted to a field hospital within a month of arriving in France with a double inguinal hernia, a condition that continued to dog him over the coming months.

Arthur was eventually shipped to England in March 1917 for an operation at the Metropolitan Hospital in London. The operation itself seemed to have been a success, but, while admitted, he contracted pneumonia, and it was this lung condition that was to end his life. Private Lavender passed away on 7th May 1917, aged just 28 years old.

Arthur Reginald Lavender was laid to rest in the Milton Cemetery in Weston-super-Mare.

Name: Lee, Arthur

Rank: Private

Regiment: Somerset Light Infantry

Date of death: 7th December 1914

Age at time of death: 19

Cause of death: Meningitis

Grave location: St Mary's Cemetery, Taunton

Arthur Henry Lee was born in April 1895 and was one of five children. His parents were Arthur and Hannah (or Annie) Lee, and the family lived in the Chard area of Somerset. Arthur Sr worked as a 'twist hand', operating the machines in a lace factory and, when his son left school, he too found work in the same factory.

There is little documented about Arthur's early life. When war broke out, however, he was quick to enlist, and joined the Somerset Light Infantry as a Private. He was assigned to the 5th (1st Reserve) Battalion and was stationed at Mansfield House.

Sadly, Private Lee's military service was not to be a long one. As happened with lots of young men from different parts of the country coming together in large numbers, illness and disease spread quickly in the military encampments.

Arthur was not immune to this and was admitted to the Military Hospital in Taunton with meningitis. He passed away on 7th December 1914, aged just 19 years old.

Arthur Henry Lee lies in St Mary's Cemetery in Taunton, Somerset.

Name: Lewis, Ernest

Rank: Private

Regiment: Somerset Light Infantry

Date of death: 27th October 1915

Age at time of death: 21

Cause of death: Gassed in France / Pneumonia and typhoid

Grave location: Wembdon Road Cemetery, Bridgwater

Ernest George Lewis was born in Bridgwater, Somerset, in the spring of 1895, one of fourteen children to labourer Frederick and his wife Harriett Rose. Two of his older brothers went to work for the local brickworks, but Ernest hauled coal to earn a living once he left school.

When war broke out, he was eager to do his part; he enlisted in the Somerset Light Infantry early on, serving as a Private in the 1st Battalion. His troop was to see some of the fiercest fighting in the conflict, including the Battles of Le Cateau, the Marne, the Aisne, and Messines within the first six months.

Private Lewis' troop was also involved in the Second Battle of Ypres in the spring of 1915, but it was later that year that his fate became sealed. At some point he was caught up in a German gas attack; he was evacuated home, but there is no confirmation whether he was hospitalised as a result (although it seems likely).

The gas was to damage his lungs to the extent that he would not recover. There are conflicting reports as to the cause of Private Lewis' passing, with one source identifying the gas in France, while another put it down to pneumonia and typhoid. (It seems probable that the attack ultimately resulted in Ernest catching pneumonia, although this is not clear.)

Either way, Private Lewis passed away at home on 27th October 1915. He was just 20 years old.

Ernest had eleven brothers, four of whom would have been old enough to be enlisted to fight. Ernest was the only one of the family to perish.

Ernest George Lewis lies at peace in the Wembdon Road Cemetery in his home town of Bridgwater.

Name: Llewellyn, Arthur

Rank: Lieutenant Colonel

Regiment: Somerset Light Infantry

Date of death: 27th April 1920

Age at time of death: 46

Cause of death: Sudden illness

Grave location: Holy Trinity Churchyard, Burrington

Arthur Llewellyn was born in the summer of 1873, one of four children to Evan and Mary Llewellyn. Originally from Wales, Evan was a Justice of the Peace in the Somerset village of Burrington, and the family lived in the comparative luxury of Langford Court, a mile or so from the village centre.

I use the term 'comparative luxury' with some sense of irony; according to the 1881 census, the family had a household staff of eight, including a governess, two nurses, housemaid, cook, kitchen maid, parlour maid and page.

Ambition was obviously what drove Evan; he was an army officer, who served initially in the Somerset Light Infantry. In 1885, he was elected MP for North Somerset, a position he held on and off for nearly twenty years. His military service continued, however, and he led the 2nd (Central African) Battalion, King's African Rifles in the Boer War.

Comfort ran in the Llewellyn family; according to the 1891 census, Arthur was staying with his maternal aunt, Rose Stewart. She also lived in Somerset, and, at the time the census was drawn up, she was recorded as a widow living on her own means, with her mother, mother-in-law, two nieces and Arthur, her nephew. She was not without help, however, as the house had a retinue of eight staff to support her.

Military life was an obvious draw for Arthur. He enlisted in the Somerset Light Infantry in October 1891 and, within a year, had been promoted to Second Lieutenant.

He had met and married Meriel Byrne, in 1895. The couple's marriage certificate confirms that he had been promoted to Captain in the militia, and his residence was Buckingham Palace Road, in south west London. They were married in Holy Trinity Church, Brompton, with Meriel's mother and Arthur's father acting as witnesses.

The couple went on to have five children, all girls, and they settled into a comfortable life. By 1901, Meriel had set up home in Worcestershire; Arthur does not appear on that year's census, which suggests that he may too have been fighting in South Africa.

Arthur's mother Mary passed away in 1906, at the tender age of 39. By 1911, he had been promoted to Lieutenant Colonel in the 3rd Somerset Light Infantry and was head of his household in Worcestershire. The family was, by this time, complete – Arthur and Meriel and their five children also had help running their home, with two nurses, a cook, parlour maid and housemaid to support them.

Evan passed away months before war was declared, at the age of 67. Lieutenant Colonel Llewellyn felt duty bound to re-enlist, and was given command of the 3rd Reserve Battalion, Somerset Light Infantry. He subsequently served as part of the Army Service Corps in France, before transferring to the Army Labour Corps in Nottingham.

According to the Evening Mail, on 27th April 1920, he *"was suddenly seized with illness in the street, and died as he was being conveyed to Nottingham Hospital. He was 46 years of age."*

Arthur was brought back to Burrington in Somerset, where he was buried alongside his parents in Holy Trinity Churchyard.

Sadly, Meriel passed away nine months after her husband; she too is buried in Holy Trinity Churchyard.

Arthur's estate passed to his brother, Owen, and totalled £12,023 15s 11d (approximately £530,000 in today's money).

As an aside to Arthur's illustrious story, another of his brothers is worthy of note. Hoel Llewellyn was two years older than Arthur.

Educated for the Royal Navy, he saw active service on the East Coast of Africa, 1888-90 with despatches. He also served as an Artillery Officer and commanded artillery in the Matabele War, where he was recommended for the Victoria Cross. He was promoted Captain in the British South Africa Police, and Justice of the Peace in Matabeleland in 1896.

Captain Llewellyn served throughout the South African War, commanding armoured trains north of Mafeking before transferring to the South African Constabulary in 1901. Hoel was eventually created a Companion of the Distinguished Service Order for his service in South Africa.

He was wounded while serving with the Mediterranean Expeditionary Force in the Great War. Hoel was subsequently promoted to the rank of Colonel and appointed Provost-Marshal of Egypt and the British Mediterranean Expeditionary Force.

In 1908, he had been made Chief Constable of Wiltshire, a role he was to hold for 37 years. He was key to pioneering the use of police dogs and went on to become the oldest serving person to hold the Chief Constable role in the county.

Another aspect of the Llewellyn family is that Evan was obviously a source of political drive for the family; his great-great-grandson is David Cameron, UK Prime Minister from 2010 to 2016.

Name: Lloyd, Albert

Rank: Gunner

Regiment: Royal Garrison Artillery

Date of death: 25th January 1919

Age at time of death: 25

Cause of death: Suicide

Grave location: Milton Cemetery, Weston-super-Mare

Albert Edward Prankard Lloyd was born in Somerset on 25th September 1893, in the Somerset village of Kewstoke (now a suburb of Weston-super-Mare). He was one of eight children to Jabez and Charity Lloyd. Jabez was initially a mason, but later went on to find work as a miner in South Wales. Charity worked as a laundress to help bring in extra money.

When Albert left school, he found employment as a labourer, remaining at home with Charity, with Jabez working away, and three of his sisters working as housemaids or laundresses. By 1911, however, he had moved to Wales with his father to work as a miner; steady employment that brought in a little more money because of the risks involved.

War, however, was on the horizon, and Albert enlisted before hostilities broke out. Enlisting on 12th January 1914, his military records show him as standing 5ft 7ins (1.7m) tall and weighing in at 166lbs (75.3kg). He joined the Royal Garrison Artillery and, over the next five years, served three tours of duty in France, totalling just over three years on the Western Front.

Gunner Lloyd's military service was not without incident, however. In November 1914 he was admitted to hospital for a week, suffering from shock. In April 1917, a shell exploded close to him, and he was again found to be suffering from shock. His records note that, following the injury, he had had suicidal thoughts, and wished he was dead.

Just a month later, back on the battlefield, Albert received a gunshot wound to his right thigh. Nine months later, he was admitted to the Hermitage General Hospital in Higham, Kent for three weeks. (The ailment is a mystery, with just the term *SCT Toe* to identify it.)

When the Armistice came, Gunner Lloyd remained in France, finally returning home on 13th January 1919 ready to be demobbed. While not clear in his records, it seems that the initial 'shock' he had suffered from in 1914 had continued throughout the war.

One of the last comments on Albert's service records is stark. "*Found dead on Great Western Railway near Weston-super-Mare. 25.01.19*". Frustratingly, there is no other documentary evidence to expand on this curt phrase, no contemporary newspapers seem to have reported on the event, and nothing more than a scribbled police report was provided for the inquest (again, of which nothing remains).

It seems that the effects of five years of conflict proved too much for Gunner Lloyd; he committed suicide at the age of just 25 years old.

Albert Edward Prankard Lloyd lies at peace at last in the Milton Cemetery in his home town of Weston-super-Mare.

Name: Lucas, Henry

Rank: Stoker 1st Class

Regiment: Royal Navy

Date of death: 23rd March 1920

Age at time of death: 31

Cause of death: Tuberculosis

Grave location: St Margaret's Churchyard, Tintinhull

Henry Luke Lucas was born in September 1888, in the Somerset village of Tintinhull. His father Luke worked as an agricultural labourer, while his mother, Ellen was a glovemaker. Henry had three siblings – Kate, Beatrice and Edwin – and two half-siblings – Martha and Eli – from Ellen's previous marriage (she was widowed in 1880).

Henry married Gertrude Woodman in 1909 having set himself up as a groomsman in the village. Henry Jr was born the following year and the young couple went on to have three further children, Ellen (born in 1913), Edwin (born in 1915, who sadly died shortly afterwards), and a further son, called Edwin, born in 1916.

The 1910s proved a tragic decade for the Lucas family. Henry's father Luke had passed away in 1912, and his mother Ellen had also died four years later.

It may well have been the death of his parents or the promise of continuous paid employment that spurred Henry into enlisting; he joined the Royal Navy on 26th July 1916 as a stoker.

Initial training was carried out on HMS Vivid II in Devonport, and Stoker Lucas was then assigned to HMS Liverpool for an eight-month tour of the Adriatic. While on this tour, Henry was promoted to Stoker 1st Class.

Returning to England, Stoker Lucas was assigned to HMS Egmont II, an accommodation vessel based in Chatham. His move here may have been due to health reasons; within a few weeks Henry was transferred back to HMS Vivid II, from where he was invalided out of service on medical grounds.

The reason for Henry's discharge from the Royal Navy was tuberculosis; the local newspaper gave more details when it reported on his funeral:

> The death has occurred of Henry Lucas (31) from tuberculosis, which he contracted while serving as a stoker in the Navy. Deceased served abroad during the period of the war and was in Eastern waters when he contracted the disease. He was removed to hospital at Malta, where he remained until his discharge. [This differs from his service records.] In health Lucas was a fearless man, and he maintained this spirit all through his trying illness.
>
> Western Chronicle: Friday 2nd April 1920

Henry Luke Lucas died on 23rd March 1920; he was 31 years old. He lies at rest in the grounds of St Margaret's Church in his home village of Tintinhull in Somerset.

Name: Maio, Manuel

Rank: Trabalhador

Regiment: Corpo de Lenhadores Portugueses

Date of death: 7th October 1918

Age at time of death: Unknown

Cause of death: Unknown

Grave location: St Mary's Cemetery, Taunton

In a quiet corner of the St Mary's Cemetery in Taunton, Somerset, sit a pair of headstones.

Both are adorned with the word Portugal and have the word *Trabalhador* (translated as *Worker*) and the phrase *Corpo de Lenhadores Portugueses* (or *Portuguese Forestry Corps*) inscribed on them.

During the Great War, vast quantities of timber were required by the army in France. Initially imports from Canada provided most of what was needed but, as the war progressed, ships were required for other essential supplies, so imports of timber fell dramatically.

In 1916, the British Government asked the country's oldest ally, Portugal, to send workers to assist with the war effort. Soon both the Portuguese Forestry Corps and Canadian Forestry Corps had teams working all across the United Kingdom, totalling many thousands of men.

This side of the war effort was not without its casualties, and those serving were accorded Commonwealth War Graves.

There is no information readily available for Manuel Ferreira Maio. He would have come to England from Portugal at some point in 1916, but the only record of him is that of his passing.

He died on 7th October 1918, although the cause of his death and the age at which he passed are lost to time.

Manuel Ferreira Maio lies at rest in St Mary's Cemetery in Taunton, Somerset.

Name: Manning, William

Rank: Air Mechanic 2nd Class

Regiment: Royal Flying Corps

Date of death: 8th July 1916

Age at time of death: 25

Cause of death: Flying accident

Grave location: Wembdon Road Cemetery, Bridgwater

William Charles Manning – known as Willie – was born in Bridgwater in 1890, one of ten children to Samuel and Emily Manning. Samuel was a cabinet maker, and at least three of his sons, Willie included, went into the family business.

There is little information available on Willie's life, but he married Nellie Dodden, also from Bridgwater, in November 1915. Sadly, this was around the time that Nellie's father passed away; tragedy for Nellie was still close by.

Willie's military records are minimal, although details of his passing can be determined from the subsequent newspaper report.

He had enlisted in the Royal Flying Corps around October 1915, certainly around the time he and Nellie married. He was an air mechanic, something his woodworking skills probably drew him to and was based at Manston Airfield in Kent.

On 8th July 1916, Willie was a passenger in a flight piloted by Lieutenant Bidie. It seems that Bidie was turning the plane while at low altitude, while attempting to land. The plane crashed, and both Bidie and Willie were killed. Air Mechanic Manning was just 25 years old.

William Charles Manning lies at rest in the Wembdon Road Cemetery in his home town of Bridgwater, Somerset.

Name: Matthews, Albert

Rank: Boy 2nd Class

Regiment: Royal Navy

Date of death: 27th October 1918

Age at time of death: 17

Cause of death: Influenza and pneumonia

Grave location: St Margaret's Churchyard, Tintinhull

Albert Edward Matthews was born in October 1901 in the Somerset village of Tintinhull. His father James was a glove maker, and he and his wife Mary had three children in all, Percival, born in 1897, Clementina, born in 1898, and Albert, the youngest.

Sadly, Clementina died in 1909, aged just 11 years old. Percival also passed away six years later, aged just 17. James and Mary must have been distraught when Albert announced his decision to do his bit for King and Country.

He enlisted almost as soon as he was able to, joining the Royal Navy on 14th September 1918, and you can almost sense his enthusiasm to get involved before missing out on the glory of military service.

Boy Matthews was assigned to HMS Impregnable, the ship based in Devonport, Plymouth, where he was to receive his training. Standing at 5ft 8ins (1.73m) tall, with brown hair, brown eyes and a fair complexion, he was recorded as having a very good character and satisfactory ability.

Sadly, however, Albert was not destined to meet his full potential. Shortly after beginning his training, he contracted influenza and pneumonia, succumbing to the disease on 27th October 1918.

He had just turned 17 years old.

Albert Edward Matthews lies at rest in the graveyard of St Margaret's Church in his home village of Tintinhull.

The story of this family continued to be tragic. By the time of Albert's death, the Spanish Flu pandemic was sweeping the world and his tiny part of Somerset was in no way immune.

Just four days after Albert Matthews passed away, his mother, Mary, also fell victim to the illness.

In the space of just nine years, poor James Matthews had buried all three of his children and his wife. A newspaper reported on Mary's funeral, recognising the "*very heavy trials*" he had undergone.

The same paper, reports that the influenza pandemic is fizzling out:

> *A large number of parishioners have been attacked with "flu",*
> *but the epidemic is now on the wane. The school has been closed*
> *for the last fortnight.*
>
> *Western Chronicle: Friday 8th November 1918*

Name: Mattick, Harold

Rank: Corporal

Regiment: Royal Engineers

Date of death: 24th July 1917

Age at time of death: 22

Cause of death: Lung condition

Grave location: Milton Cemetery, Weston-super-Mare

Harold Mattick was born in the spring of 1895, the youngest of four children to Walter and Augusta. Walter was a harness maker and brought the family up in his home town of Weston-super-Mare, Somerset.

When he left school, Harold found work as a plumber. He seemed to have sought a life of adventure, however, and, in 1908, aged just 14, enlisted in the Wessex Division of the Royal Engineers as a Bugler. He served for five years, fulfilling his duties at the same time as carrying out his plumbing work.

When war broke out, Harold immediately re-enlisted. As a Sapper, he was assigned to the 1st/2nd (Wessex) Field Company. After initial training, he was sent to the front as part of the British Expeditionary Force just before Christmas in 1914.

Sapper Mattick was caught up in some of the fiercest fighting on the Western Front, including the First and Second Battles of Ypres. On 30th September 1915, at Loos, he received a gunshot wound in his right leg, which fractured his tibia. The Germans were also using gas to attack the Allied front lines, which also affected Harold.

Medically evacuated to England for treatment on 9th October, his condition was such that he was discharged from the army on health grounds six months later, on 30th March 1916.

Sadly, while Harold's leg healed, the injuries he sustained in the gas attack were too severe for him to recover from. He died at home from a lung condition on 24th July 1917, aged just 22 years old.

Harold Mattick was laid to rest in the Milton Cemetery of his home town, Weston-super-Mare.

Name: Mayers, Robert

Rank: Private

Regiment: Bedfordshire Regiment

Date of death: 2nd May 1921

Age at time of death: 34

Cause of death: Tuberculosis

Grave location: St Mary's Cemetery, Taunton

Robert William Mayers – also known as Bob – was born in 1888, one of nine children to Charles and Louisa Mayers from Taunton in Somerset. Charles was a solicitor's clerk, whose work changed direction in the 1890s, and who became a general labourer.

When Robert left school, he became a carpenter, while his older brother became a motor mechanic, and other siblings became messengers, collar machinists and housemaids.

With war on the horizon, Robert enlisted. His complete service records no longer exist, but he enrolled in the Bedfordshire regiment and joined the 3rd Garrison Battalion. While there is no evidence of Private Mayers' time in the army, it is likely that he saw some service in India and Burma during and after the Great War.

Robert returned to England after being demobbed, but, having survived the war, was suffering from tuberculosis. Sadly, the condition was to get the better of him, and he passed away at his parents' home on 2nd May 1921. He was 34 years old.

Robert William Mayers lies at rest in St Mary's Cemetery in Taunton, Somerset.

Name: McDonald, Peter

Rank: Private

Regiment: Royal Army Service Corps

Date of death: 21st January 1916

Age at time of death: 34

Cause of death: Accidental shooting

Grave location: Milton Cemetery, Weston-super-Mare

Peter McDonald was born in Tullamore, King's County (now Offaly County), Ireland, on 28th May 1893 and was one of eight children to Michael and Mary McDonald. Michael had been in the army, and this seems to have been the route that Peter wanted to follow as well.

When he left school, however, he found work as a domestic servant at St Stanislaus College in his home town. War, by this time, was on the horizon, and so Peter was called on to other things.

Unfortunately, a lot of the documentation around Peter's military service is no longer available. He enlisted in the Royal Army Service Corps; while an exact date for his enrolment is not available, this would appear to have been at some point in the first year of the conflict.

Private McDonald was assigned to the 341st Mechanical Transport Company. This was formed in May 1915 and was designated an Ammunition Park (which was in essence a fleet of lorries and a workshop for maintaining them). While full details of his time with the RASC is not available, Peter certainly came to be based in Weston-super-Mare, Somerset.

> *Considerable sensation was created at Weston-super-Mare on Friday evening, by a rumour which prevailed that a member of the Army Service Corps billeted in the town had been shot and another man wounded.*
>
> *Inquiries revealed the fact that the rumour had some foundation, and it appears that some half-dozen members of the corps were*

attending their motor-bicycles in a shed at headquarters in Beach Road, when Lance Corporal Goldsmith produced an automatic Colt pistol, which he handed to Private McDonald for inspection.

In the course of the examination the weapon went off, and Goldsmith was shot in the leg. He at once took the revolver from McDonald, observing that he was unaware that it was loaded, and was apparently in the act of unloading it when it was again discharged, the bullet entering the lower part of McDonald's abdomen, severing the main arteries.

Medical aid was at once procured. The unfortunate man died as the result of internal haemorrhage about an hour later.

Goldsmith was removed to hospital, but his injuries are not regarded as serious.

Somerset Standard: Friday 28th January 1916

Private Peter McDonald had passed away from a gunshot wound at the age of just 20 years old. His body was laid to rest in the Milton Cemetery in Weston-super-Mare, where he had met his fatal accident.

Private McDonald's pension record gives his cause of death as *"explosion"*, something of a misinterpretation of the evening's events.

Name: Mees, Henry

Rank: Private

Regiment: Labour Corps

Date of death: 10th November 1918

Age at time of death: 30

Cause of death: Influenza

Grave location: Shepton Mallet Burial Ground

Henry Edward Mees was born in Shepton Mallet, in June 1888. Henry was one of six children and lived in Somerset with his father – Frederick and his mother Emma. Frederick was a gardener who worked as a groundsman for the local cemetery.

After leaving school, Henry found work as a clerk for a local auctioneer. Of his two brothers, the elder had found a trade in carpentry, while his younger sibling helped his father.

Henry's service records are scant; he enlisted in the Labour Corps, although there is no confirmation of when this happened. Private Mees joined the 615th Home Service Employment Company and was based in England.

The HSE Companies categorised the employment of the men serving with them, whether they were cooks, caretakers, clerks, policemen, butchers or telephone operators, and used the men to the best of their skills. It is likely, therefore, that Private Mees continued in his clerk role, albeit in a different line of work from auctioneering.

Sadly, few further details of Henry's life remain documented. He is listed as having been admitted to the War Hospital in Bath, and he died from influenza on 10th November 1918. He was 30 years old.

Henry Edward Mees lies at rest in the cemetery of his home town, Shepton Mallet, where his grave would sadly have been tended by his father as part of his day-to-day job.

Name: Millard, George

Rank: Engine Room Artificer 4th Class

Regiment: Royal Navy

Date of death: 26th January 1918

Age at time of death: 21

Cause of death: Tuberculosis

Grave location: Wembdon Road Cemetery, Bridgwater

George Edmund Millard was born in 1887, one of seven children to Edmund and Annie Millard, from Bridgwater, Somerset. Edmund was an engineer by trade, something George's elder brother followed him into.

Sadly, little of George's life remains documented. He enlisted in the Royal Navy, in January 1915, working as an Engine Room Artificer (or engineer). Stationed in Kent, his initial training was at HMS Pembroke II base on the Isle of Sheppey.

Artificer Millard spent nine months on HMS Dido, which formed part of the Royal Navy's force based in Harwich. At start of 1916, he was transferred back to HMS Pembroke II. This may have been for health reasons, as he was subsequently discharged with tuberculosis in April.

George's records finish there, and it is likely that he succumbed to his lung condition after an 18-month fight. He died at home in Bridgwater on 26th January 1918, aged 21 years old.

George Edmund Millard lies at rest in the family grave at the Wembdon Road Cemetery in his home town of Bridgwater.

Name: Millard, Walter

Rank: Private

Regiment: Machine Gun Corps

Date of death: 7th November 1918

Age at time of death: 31

Cause of death: Pneumonia

Grave Location: St Lawrence's Churchyard, Westbury-sub-Mendip

Walter John Millard was born in the summer of 1887, the youngest of nine children to Robert and Elizabeth. Robert was a farmer and brought his family up in the village of Wedmore, Somerset. Walter followed in his father's footsteps, and by the time of the 1911 census, was listed as a farm labourer in Wedmore, working for a William Millard, who presumably was a cousin of the family.

In March 1915, Walter married Jessy Masters, daughter of a grocer in nearby Wells. The couple set up home in the neighbouring village of Wookey but would later make their home in Westbury-sub-Mendip.

In December 1915, aged 28, Walter was called up, and assigned to the Reserve Machine Gun Corps. He was not formally mobilised for almost three years when, in October 1918, he was shipped to Rugeley, Staffordshire, for training.

During this time, Private Millard was taken ill, and was admitted to the Military Hospital at Cannock Chase within weeks with influenza. His health deteriorated and, on 7th November 1918, he died from pneumonia. He was 31 years of age.

Had it not been for the quirk of fate of having been mobilised a month before the war ended, tragically, this would likely not be a story that needed to be told.

Walter John Millard was brought back to Somerset and lies at rest in the graveyard of St Lawrence Church in Westbury-sub-Mendip.

Name: Moody, Thomas

Rank: Private

Regiment: North Somerset Yeomanry

Date of death: 27th April 1919

Age at time of death: 28

Cause of death: Tuberculosis

Grave location: Evercreech Cemetery, Evercreech

Thomas Edward Moody was born in 1890, the second of five children for Thomas and Emily.

By the start of the war, "Little Tommy Moody" was working with his father in the quarries around Shepton Mallet and was the eldest son living at home.

He joined the North Somerset Yeomanry and was shipped out to France, where he was badly injured. An article in the Shepton Mallet Journal, included after his funeral, says as much about the life of this young man as it does about the Edwardian approach to military matters:

> *DEATH AND FUNERAL OF A SOLDIER – The death has taken place of Thomas Edward Moody, son of Thomas Moody, of Stoney Stratton, Evercreech, at the age of 18, and who as a 1914 man, joined the North Somerset Yeomanry and went out to France. He was badly wounded, resulting in the loss of an eye, and after some time in hospital and a short leave at home, he was sent back to rejoin his regiment, the 3rd Reserve Cavalry, in France. This was about two years ago. He spent his last leave home at Christmas. After a time in hospital at Devonport, he was removed to Bath early last month, discharged from the army as incurable, and there he died on May 5th, the cause of death being consumption of the brain. The funeral, on Saturday afternoon last, was of military character. The corpse, brought from Bath the day before, was borne from the deceased's home at Stratton on a hand bier, attended by a bearer party of eight men from Taunton Military Barracks, to the Parish Church, where*

the first portion of the service was taken. The Union Jack
enshrouded the coffin, on and around which a number of floral
tributes rested. Sixty members of the Evercreech Branch of the
Comrades of the Great War, and a couple of marines, joined the
funeral cortege at the home, and on leaving the Church lines up
on either side, as the body of their dead comrade was borne
hence on the shoulders of four of their number to the cemetery.
The vicar, Rev. RY Bonsey, officiated. The Last Post was sounded
by Bugler Tucker, of Shepton Mallet, and another bugler from
Taunton Barracks. "Little Tommy Moody", as he was familiarly
called amongst his chums, was a conspicuous member of the
Evercreech Football Club previous to the War.

Shepton Mallet Journal – 9th May 1919.

(It is interesting to know that the date of death in the article does not match that on the gravestone. I would be inclined to believe the latter.)

Private Moody was obviously a fighter and a strong character – returning to the front after losing an eye, some time in hospital and a short leave – and you can guarantee he was missed in the village.

Thomas Edward Moody lies at rest in the cemetery of his home Evercreech Cemetery.

Name: Moore, Harry

Rank: 2nd Corporal

Regiment: Royal Engineers

Date of death: 28th August 1918

Age at time of death: 41

Cause of death: Illness

Grave location: St James' Cemetery, Taunton

Harry Moore was born in Tiverton, Devon, in early 1877. He was the fourth of eleven children to James Moore, a railway policeman, and his wife Ann.

By 1890, James had moved the family to Taunton, in Somerset (where his work was now listed as railway porter). Over the next decade, Harry was to encounter tragedy and happiness.

In 1894, his father died from Bright's disease (a kidney complaint), at the age of just 45 years old.

Three years later, Harry's mother died, from what appears to have been heart failure. Ann was 49 years of age.

On 13th November 1898, Harry married Alice Mary Larcombe, a dressmaker from Taunton. The young couple set up home together in the north of the town. They went on to have five children, although, sadly, only one would live to reach their 20s.

By now Harry had found employment as an insurance agent, but war was coming to Europe. His military records are lost to time, but he enlisted in the Royal Engineers and was assigned to G Depot Company. (The Depot Battalions received men who had returned from the Expeditionary Force and also those men who had enlisted for Tunnelling Companies, Special Companies and other specialist units.)

The next evidence we have of Corporal Moore is in the Army Register of Soldiers' Effects. This confirms that he had been admitted to the Southern General Hospital in Bristol with an illness, and that he subsequently passed away on 28th August 1918, at the age of 41.

Harry Moore was laid to rest in the St James' Cemetery in his home town of Taunton.

Name: Morgan, Henry

Rank: Private

Regiment: Australian Machine Gun Corps

Date of death: 8th May 1918

Age at time of death: 25

Cause of death: Died of wounds

Grave location: Wembdon Road Cemetery, Bridgwater

Henry Morgan was born in 1892 in Bridgwater, Somerset. He was the oldest of two children, both boys, to Charles Morgan and his wife Ellen. Charles managed the local collar works, making collars for shirts.

While Henry's younger brother, Herbert, followed his dad's business, according to the 1911 census, Henry was learning the farming trade. This was to stand him in good stead, and in 1912, he emigrated to Australia, to become a farmer.

Henry settled in Gunnedah, New South Wales, but was called up when war broke out. He enlisted in May 1916 and joined the Australian Machine Gun Corps. His troop left Australia on the ship Borda in November 1916, arriving in Plymouth two months later, and he finally reached France in March 1917.

Initially part of the 9th Machine Gun Battalion, Private Morgan transferred to the 3rd Machine Gun Corps in April 1918. Involved in the Allied defence of the German Spring Offensive, he was caught up in a gas attack and injured.

Wounded on 17th April 1918, Henry was evacuated back to England and admitted to the Voluntary Aid Detachment Hospital in Cheltenham. Sadly, Private Morgan was not to recover, and he died from his injuries on 8th May 1918. He was just 25 years old.

Henry Morgan lies at rest in the Wembdon Road Cemetery in his former home town of Bridgwater, Somerset.

Name: Morris, Ernest

Rank: Serjeant

Regiment: Rifle Brigade

Date of death: 28th June 1920

Age at time of death: 40

Cause of death: Unknown

Grave location: Langport Cemetery, Langport

Ernest George Morris was born in September 1879, one of six children to John and Eliza Morris. John was a carter for the railways, and this was a trade his son was to follow.

Ernest married Sarah Garrett in Bristol on Christmas Eve 1904, and the young couple went on to have two children, Charles and William.

Ernest's father died in 1907, and Ernest became head of the family. He moved them in with him in Bristol, and by the 1911 census, the household consisted of Ernest, his mother Eliza, his brothers Frank and William, sister Lily and his own son William.

The census also lists Ernest as a widow; I have not been able to track down any records of when Sarah died. Their eldest boy, Charles, passed very early on, however, so this is likely why Ernest set up home with his family.

By this time, Ernest was working as a carman in the Bristol Goods Yards, and it appears that he had a strong character. In September 1912, he was cautioned for "*smoking whilst on duty and refusal to give an undertaking to refrain from doing so in future.*" He cited his reason that the rulebook "*did not prohibit men from smoking when not with a load.*"

Ernest was suspended for two days and was only allowed back to work when he promised to follow instructions in the future. This, it seems he may not have done, as he was dismissed just three months later.

Ernest's military service records are hard to piece together. He enlisted in the Rifle Brigade as a Gunner, going on to achieve the rank of Serjeant. He was awarded the Victory and British medals – the standard awards for men involved in the Great War.

Serjeant Morris survived the war, but there is little information for him after that. He passed away on 28th June 1920, aged 40 years old, although there is no record of how he passed. His war pension was awarded to his mother, who was acting as guardian for his son William.

Ernest George Morris lies at rest in the cemetery of his home town of Langport.

Name: Morriss, Reginald

Rank: Private

Regiment: Royal Army Service Corps

Date of death: 3rd March 1919

Age at time of death: 33

Cause of death: Influenza and pneumonia

Grave location: Milton Cemetery, Weston-super-Mare

Reginald Benjamin James Morriss was born in the spring of 1886 and was the youngest of twelve children. His father, Thomas, was a bootmaker from Leeds, who had moved to Somerset and married Mary Ann Pennell. The couple brought their family up in her home town of Weston-super-Mare.

Thomas died in 1901, when Reginald was just 14 years old. Mary Ann, by this point, still had a lot of her family with her, including Reginald, three of his sisters, his brother-in-law and four nieces.

Reginald was about to leave school, and found work as a French polisher in Bristol, eventually moving in with his employer as a lodger. This may not have suited him, however, as, by the time he enlisted, he gave his trade as baker and confectioner, and he was living back with his mother in Weston-super-Mare.

Private Morriss was 30 when he joined up in 1916 and stood 5ft 7ins (1.7m) tall. He joined the Army Service Corps as a baker and was initially based in Aldershot. He was moved to Kent in September 1918, having been assigned to the 351st Horse Transport Company. The war was drawing to an end, but a new threat was on the horizon.

The following February, Private Morriss was admitted to St John's Hospital in Hastings, suffering from influenza and pneumonia. Sadly, he was to succumb to the lung conditions, and he passed away on 3rd March 1919. He was just 32 years old.

Reginald Benjamin James Morriss' body was brought back to Weston-super-Mare, and he was laid to rest in the Milton Cemetery in his home town.

Name: Neads, William

Rank: Lance Corporal

Regiment: Canadian Infantry

Date of death: 16th December 1917

Age at time of death: 24

Cause of death: Died of wounds

Grave location: St Andrew's Churchyard, Clevedon

William John Neads was born on 16th December 1892, the middle of three children to cab driver and groom William Neads and his wife Ellen. Both William Sr and Ellen were from Somerset, although William Jr and his brother Charles – who was eleven months older – were both born in the Monmouthshire village of Cwmcarn.

William's parents soon moved the family back to Clevedon in Somerset, and, when he left school, he found work as a farm labourer. He was eager to see more of the world, however, and in April 1913, he emigrated to Canada.

After working as a labourer there for a year or so, back in Europe war was declared. Keen to do his bit for King and Country, William enlisted in the 1st Battalion of the Canadian Infantry in January 1915. He soon found himself caught up on the front line.

In October 1916, he was involved in the Battle of the Somme – either at Le Transloy or The Battle of the Ancre Heights – and received a shrapnel wound to his left shoulder. Initially admitted to the Canadian General Hospital in Etaples, he was subsequently evacuated to England and the Northern General Hospital in Leeds. He spent three months recovering from his injuries and was back on the Western Front in January 1917.

Later that year, William – now a Lance Corporal – was involved in the fighting at the Second Battle of Passchendaele (part of the Third Battle of Ypres). He was wounded again, this time receiving a rather unceremonious gunshot wound to the right buttock. Treated at the scene, he was evacuated back to England and admitted to the Fusehill War Hospital in Carlisle on 17th November.

Sadly, despite treatment, Lance Corporal Neads' health deteriorated, and he passed away from his injuries on 16th December 1917, his 25th birthday.

William John Neads was brought back to his family's home of Clevedon, and buried in the clifftop churchyard of St Andrew's, overlooking the sea.

Tragically, William's father had died in May 1917, at the age of 51. While no details of his passing are recorded, it meant that Ellen had, in just over a year, seen her son wounded, her husband die, and her son wounded again and die as a result.

Name: Newington, Alfred

Rank: Second Lieutenant

Regiment: Somerset Yeomanry

Date of death: 4th May 1917

Age at time of death: 39

Cause of death: Tuberculosis

Grave location: St Bartholomew's Churchyard, Ubley

Alfred John Newington was born in 1878. The oldest of four children to Alfred and Minna Newington, Alfred Sr was a hosier, and the family lived in Brighton, Sussex.

Alfred Sr passed away in 1899, and by this time, his eldest son had followed his trade, becoming a gentleman's outfitter. By the time of the 1911 census, he was the only one of the siblings still living at home and was supporting Minna financially and in the family business along the coast in Worthing.

As with his early life, details of Alfred's military service are a little scarce. However, a newspaper report of his passing gives more detail:

DEATH OF LIEUTENANT NEWINGTON

We learn with regret that Lieutenant Alfred J Newington died at Nordrath [sic], Blagdon, Somerset, on Friday. He was the eldest son of the late Mr Alfred Newington and of Mrs Newington, of Somerset Villa, Richmond Road.

The death of Mr Newington Sr took place after an illness of a long duration, in July 1899, after he had been in business here for about sixteen years. He came hither from Brighton, and established himself as an outfitter at the corner of Warwick Street at the premises now occupied by Messrs. Kinch Brothers.

During his residence here, Mr AJ Newington, who assisted his father in the business, had an exciting experience in the summer of 1896. He and Mr Frederick Barnwell and a friend named Wadham went towards Lancing on a fishing expedition and the boat was capsized, and Mr Barnwell was drowned, whilst Mr Newington and Mr Wadham were in the water for an hour and a half, eventually reaching the shore in an exhausted condition.

In February 1897, Mr Newington went to South Africa, and when War broke out he became a trooper in the South Africa Light Horse. He was subsequently awarded the silver medal with six bars, bearing the names of Belmont, Laing's Nek, the Relief of Ladysmith, Orange Free State, Tugela Heights and Cape Colony.

When he came back to England, Mr Newington returned to the business and was a member of the Somerset Yeomanry, in which he advanced to the rank of Sergeant Major. His health failed about eight years ago, and he undertook a trip to the Baltic.

During the present War, he joined the Army Service Corps, and was attached to the Indian Cavalry Division in France, and it is only within a comparatively brief period that he was on leave at Worthing. His relatives will receive the sympathy of a wide circle of friends in the loss they have now sustained.

Worthing Gazette: Wednesday 9th May 1917

Second Lieutenant Newington had actually been admitted to the Nordrach Sanatorium near Blagdon in Somerset. This was a hospital that specialised in the treatment of tuberculosis, so it is safe to assume that this is the condition that affected him. He passed away on 4th May 1917, at the age of 39 years old.

Alfred John Newington wasn't taken back to Worthing for burial. Instead, he lies at rest in the quiet churchyard of St Bartholomew's in the village of Ubley, near Blagdon, in Somerset.

Name: Newman, William

Rank: Private

Regiment: Devonshire Regiment

Date of death: 29th October 1918

Age at time of death: 37

Cause of death: Unknown

Grave location: St Margaret's Churchyard, Tintinhull

William Newman was born in Dorset in 1880, the oldest of six children to George and Margaret Newman. George worked as an agricultural labourer and a carter, and, after leaving school, William followed suit.

William's life has been a challenge to piece together; however, I have managed to sketch together some information from a number of sources.

By the 1911 census, he was living with his now widowed father and three of his siblings. Listed as single, he was working as a labourer.

When William joined up, he enlisted in the Devonshire Regiment, before being transferred over to the Labour Corps. He was assigned to 652 Agriculture Company, serving on the Home Front, presumably somewhere close to home.

There are no details of Private Newman's death — contemporary newspapers do not highlight anything out of the ordinary or sudden about his passing. I can only assume, therefore, that he passed through natural causes, perhaps influenza or pneumonia.

He died on 29th October 1918, in the village of Martock, Somerset. He was 37 years old.

It appears that William did not marry — his war pension was allocated to his sisters Edith, Alice and Louisa and no spouse is mentioned (nor is his father).

William Newman lies at rest in the quiet churchyard of St Margaret's in the Somerset village of Tintinhull.

Name: Norris, Percy

Rank: Private

Regiment: Wiltshire Regiment

Date of death: 5th April 1918

Age at time of death: 24

Cause of death: Died of wounds

Grave location: Somerton Cemetery

Percy Norris was born in 1894, the youngest of eleven children to William and Julia Norris. William was the caretaker for the water works in Somerton, Somerset, and this is where the family lived.

By the time of the 1911 census, Percy's older brother Henry had joined his father at the water works. Julia had passed away five years before, and Percy and three of his siblings continued to live with William. At this point Percy was working as a gardener.

Private Norris' full military records are not readily available, but it is evident that he enlisted in the 7th Battalion of the Wiltshire Regiment. This was a service troop, formed in 1914, who saw service in France and the Balkans.

It seems that it was during one of the skirmishes that Private Norris was injured. While there is no confirmation of exactly when or where this happened, it is likely to have been at some point in the spring of 1918. Percy was shipped back the England for treatment, and admitted to the Red Cross Hospital in Bridgwater, Somerset.

Sadly, Private Norris did not recover from his injuries. He passed away on 5th April 1918, aged 24 years old.

Percy lies at rest in the cemetery of Somerton, his home town.

Percy's older brother Henry Norris also died in the Great War. Joining the Royal Naval Volunteer Reserves, Able Seaman Norris was also wounded on active duty, dying of his injuries in January 1918, aged 32. He is buried at the St Sever Cemetery in Rouen, France.

Name: Oaten, Henry

Rank: Private

Regiment: Devonshire Regiment

Date of death: 20th February 1917

Age at time of death: 40

Cause of death: Bronchitis

Grave location: St James' Cemetery, Taunton

Henry Oaten was born in 1876, the second youngest of seven children to Henry and Mary Ann Oaten. Henry Sr was an agricultural labourer, who raised his family in his home village of Pitminster, to the south of Taunton in Somerset.

When he left school, Henry Jr followed in his father's footsteps as a farm worker. Sadly, however, there is very little further documentation to expand on his life.

Henry married a woman called Emily; this is likely to have been at some point around 1900, although there is nothing to confirm an exact date. The couple went on to have four children – John, Albert, William and Howard.

When war broke out, Henry joined up. Again, dates for his military service are not available, but he enlisted in the Devonshire Regiment as a Private. He was assigned to the 13th (Works) Battalion, which was a territorial force, based in Plymouth.

Little further documentation exists in relation to Private Oaten. The next time he appears is on his pension record, which confirms that he passed away on 20th February 1917, having been suffering from bronchitis. He was just 40 years old.

Henry Oaten was brought back to Taunton and laid to rest in the St James' Cemetery in the town.

As an aside to this story, while researching Private Oaten, an additional piece of information about his father came to light. A record confirms that, on the 1st October 1851, at the age of just 16, Henry Oaten was admitted to gaol. Sadly, further details – including that of his crime and his sentence – are lost to time, but it adds an interesting footnote to his son's background.

Name: Packer, Francis

Rank: Private

Regiment: Machine Gun Corps

Date of death: 19th September 1917

Age at time of death: 33

Cause of death: Died from wounds

Grave location: St Andrew's Churchyard, Blagdon

Francis William George Packer was born in Bristol on 28th July 1884. The eldest of three children, he was the son of a grocer, Francis Packer Sr, and his wife, Eliza.

When Francis left school, he followed his father into the grocery business and married Kate Taverner on 1st September 1907. They had one child, a daughter called Dora, in 1909 and, by the time of the census two years later, Francis had moved his young family to Bath.

By the time he was called up, in December 1915, Francis had moved the family again, this time to the sleepy village of Blagdon, in the Somerset Mendips. He formally enlisted in the Machine Gun Corps of the Somerset Light Infantry in July 1916 and was sent to the front in January the following year.

Private Packer's battalion fought at Arras, and it was here that he was injured. On 1st May 1917, he received a gunshot wound to his right thigh, which fractured his femur. He was initially treated on site, before being shipped back to England, where he was admitted to King George's Hospital in London.

Sadly, it seems there were complications with his treatment, and Private Packer died from his wounds four months later, on 19th September 1917. He was 33 years old.

Francis William George Packer was brought back to his family in Blagdon and lies at rest in the churchyard of St Andrew's there.

The local paper reported on Francis' funeral, but what struck me is that there seems a glaring omission in the list of those who attended. It was obvious that he wanted a strictly private funeral, but:

> *The mourners were Mr FE Packer (father), Mr S Emery (brother-in-law), Mr SG Packer (uncle), Mr W Taverner (uncle), Mrs ES Packer (mother), Mrs E Emery (wife's sister), Amy Parker and Nellie Parker [his sisters-in-law], A Packer (aunt), Dolly Parker, Dolly Flower, Mr J Jones (uncle), Mr CJ Redwood, Mr J Nelson and Mr AH Bleacove.*

> *Western Daily Press: Wednesday 26th September 1917*

There is nothing in the report to suggest that Francis' widow attended the funeral.

Name: Packer, Herbert

Rank: Guardsman

Regiment: Coldstream Guards

Date of death: 3rd December 1916

Age at time of death: 26

Cause of death: Pneumonia

Grave location: St Andrew's Churchyard, Cheddar

Herbert Packer was born in December 1889, the youngest of nine children to Joseph and Ann Packer. Joseph was a railway carrier (or porter) and the family lived in Cheddar, Somerset.

The 1911 census found Herbert on his travels; he was working as a grocer's assistant, and boarding with a family in Abergavenny, South Wales. He was obviously keen to develop his skills, and soon moved to Barnstaple in Devon to work for the Lipton's grocery there.

In the autumn of 1914, Herbert married Lydia Snell, a dressmaker from Wales and the young couple lived together in the Devon town where he worked. He was very active in the community; he was a teacher at the local Wesleyan Sunday School, and active in the church choir having, according to a local newspaper, "*a capital voice.*"

Herbert enlisted in the spring of 1916 and had the honour of joining the Coldstream Guards. He did his training in London and was due back to Barnstaple on leave before starting his active service when he was taken ill. Admitted to the London Hospital with pneumonia, within a couple of weeks he had succumbed to the condition. Guardsman Packer died on 3rd December 1916, aged just 26 years old.

Herbert Packer lies at rest in St Andrew's Churchyard in his home town of Cheddar in Somerset.

Name: Painter, Ernest

Rank: Private

Regiment: Royal Army Veterinary Corps

Date of death: 15th April 1921

Age at time of death: 36

Cause of death: Sepsis

Grave location: St Andrew's Churchyard, Cheddar

Ernest Hart Painter was born in December 1884 one of eight children to Alfred and Elizabeth from Devon. Alfred moved the family to Cheddar, Somerset to work at a paper mill but sadly passed away when Ernest was only eleven years old.

The family rallied round Elizabeth, however, and, by the time of the 1901 census, she was living on the outskirts of the town with her six younger children. Elizabeth worked as a domestic cook; Ernest was an agricultural labourer; his two older sisters were shirt machinists; his 13-year-old brother Albert was listed as a gentleman's servant.

Ernest, by this point, seemed to have taken on the role of head of the family; he continued work as a farm labourer, while Elizabeth earned money as a housekeeper. Alfred became a mechanic for a car dealer and, at the 1911 census, the three of them lived with the youngest member of the family, Ernest's sister Emily, who had followed in her older sisters' footsteps as a machinist.

As with many of the fallen men and women of the Great War, a lot of Ernest's military service records have been lost to time. He enlisted in the Army Veterinary Corps in December 1915, his work as a farm labourer presumably having involved animals and livestock.

Private Painter must have been on the front line as, on 30th May 1918, he was shot in the ankle. Shipped back to England for treatment, he was eventually discharged from service on 19th November, a week after the Armistice. The ankle wound continued to give him trouble, however, and over the following couple of years, he had a number of operations on it.

Sadly, the last of these procedures resulted in an infection, and sepsis took hold. Private Painter passed away from blood poisoning on 15th April 1921. He was 36 years old.

Ernest Hart Painter lies at rest in the graveyard of St Andrew's Church in Cheddar, Somerset.

Name: Palmer, George

Rank: Second Lieutenant

Regiment: Rifle Brigade

Date of death: 28th October 1918

Age at time of death: 22

Cause of death: Pneumonia

Grave location: Wells Cemetery

George Henry Palmer is one of those names that has been a challenge to research and who risked being lost to time.

George and Henry are common names for the late Victorian era, so a simple search on Ancestry brought up too many options to confirm anything specific.

Given the ornate nature of his headstone, it seemed reasonable that his passing and funeral would have been recorded in contemporary media, and indeed it was; the only identifiable name was his own. (His parents "WR and A Palmer" are featured, as is his grandfather "Rev. J Palmer", but, again, this not enough to go on for research.)

The additional name on the gravestone, however – George's brother Albert – proved to be the key, though, identifying the following.

George Henry Palmer was born in May 1896, one of five children to William Richard Palmer and his wife Amy. William was a chemist's assistant, a job that seemed to move him around the country. William was born in Wells, Somerset, as was his wife and eldest son; George was born in Regents Park, London, while Albert, who was a year younger, was born back in Wells. By the time of the 1901 census (when George was 4 and Albert 3), the family were living in Leicester, and they remained so for the next ten years.

Details of George's military service comes primarily from the newspaper report of his funeral:

Deceased... was discharged from the Army through wounds received at Ypres in February, 1916, and had resumed his studies at Oxford and entered on a course of forestry, which he was following with great success.

He was well known in Wells, having spent a considerable time in the city and vicinity. He took a great interest in the Wells Volunteers, and was able to drill them in true Army style, having received his training in the Artist Rifles, and later gained his commission in the Rifle Brigade, where he was spoken highly of by his brother officers and men.

Mr Palmer was most thorough and painstaking in all his duties and studies. He was a Wyggestine [sic] scholar at the age of ten years in open competition, and later senior scholar at Wadham College Oxford.

Wells Journal: Friday 1st November 1918.

Second Lieutenant Palmer contracted pneumonia while up at Oxford, succumbing to the illness on 28th October 1918, just a fortnight before the end of the war. He was 22 years of age.

George Henry Palmer lies at rest in the cemetery of his home city of Wells.

Name: Palmer, Montague

Rank: Private

Regiment: Somerset Light Infantry

Date of death: 5th January 1919

Age at time of death: 32

Cause of death: Died from wounds

Grave location: Milton Cemetery, Weston-super-Mare

Montague Ashley Palmer was born in Weston-super-Mare, Somerset, in 1886, one of five children to Alfred and Martha. Montague's father was a postman in the town for 25 years, retiring through ill health in February 1898. Sadly, Alfred's retirement was not to last long, and he passed away that July aged 48, when his son was just 12 years old.

When he left school, Montague found work as a bus conductor and was now the oldest of Martha's children to still be living at home. He was obviously an ambitious and inventive young man; by the time of the 1911 census, he had started work for the Ordnance Survey, and had moved to Didcot in Berkshire where he was boarding with Frances Battison, a suiter and greengrocer.

At this point, details of Montague's life become a little hazier. At some point, he married a woman called Matilda, who either came from, or would go on to live in, Helston, Cornwall.

With war on the horizon, Montague enlisted – documented dates for this, again, are missing. He joined the 12th Battalion of the Somerset Light Infantry, which initially served in Egypt, before transferring to France in May 1918.

Where and for how long Private Palmer served is not clear, although he was definitely caught up in the fighting, and injured, towards the end of the war. Details of his wounds are not clear, but they were enough for him to be repatriated to England, and he was admitted to the Royal Hospital in Salford.

Private Palmer's injuries appear to have been too severe for him to survive; he passed away in hospital on 5th January 1919. He was just 32 years old.

Montague Ashley Palmer's body was brought back to Somerset, and he was laid to rest in the Milton Cemetery in Weston-super-Mare.

Name: Parsons, Hubert

Rank: Private

Regiment: Devonshire Regiment

Date of death: 27th March 1917

Age at time of death: 24

Cause of death: Unknown

Grave location: St Mary's Churchyard, Yatton

Hubert Stanley Parsons was born towards the end of 1892, the eldest of eight children to Frank and Emily Parsons. Frank was a burner, working in the lime kilns in his home village of Yatton, in Somerset. When he left school, Hubert followed in his father's footsteps, while his younger siblings found work in the local paper makers and bakers.

Sadly, a lot of Hubert's military records are lost to time. What *is* clear is that he enlisted on 22nd September 1915, joining the 10th Battalion of the Devonshire Regiment as a Private. He served on the Western Front, gaining the Victory and British Medals and the 1915 Star in the process.

In November 1915, Private Parsons' battalion was moved to Salonika, Greece, to help fight on the Serbian Front. Whether Hubert ever fought in the Balkans is not known; the next – and last – time he appears in documentation is in the Register of Soldiers' Effects. This confirms simply that he died in hospital on 27th March 1917. The cause and location are not known, but he was just 24 years of age.

Hubert Stanley Parsons lies at rest in the graveyard of St Mary's Church in Yatton, Somerset.

Name: Parsons, William

Rank: Lance Corporal

Regiment: Royal Army Service Corps

Date of death: 5th February 1916

Age at time of death: 25

Cause of death: Accidentally drowned

Grave location: St John's Cemetery, Bridgwater

William Edward Parsons was born in 1890, one of six children to John and Prudence Parsons. John found work in a number of fields, working as a blacksmith, porter, dock labourer and a hobbler (towing boats along the River Parrett) in his time. Throughout this, he lived with his family in the Somerset town of Bridgwater.

William found work as a collar cutter in a local shirt factory and went on to marry Matilda Mary Temblett on Christmas Day 1913. The young couple went on to have a son – Leslie William – who was born in February 1915. William was teetotal and played full back for the local rugby football club, Bridgwater Albion.

Sadly, Lance Corporal Parsons' military records are sparse; he had enlisted in the Royal Army Service Corps and was based in Fovant, to the west of Salisbury.

It was while he was on leave that William met his sad fate. On the evening of 5th February 1916, he had seen his parents and had set out to organise a football match in the town. He was walking over the town bridge, when a passer-by heard a splash. He saw a man in the water, who was crying for help, and then disappeared.

William's body was found in the river a fortnight later close to a local brickyard. He was just 25 years old.

William Edward Parsons lies at rest in St John's Cemetery in his home town of Bridgwater.

Name: Patch, James

Rank: Private

Regiment: Devonshire Regiment

Date of death: 26th March 1917

Age at time of death: 35

Cause of death: Fractured skull

Grave Location: Church of the Blessed Virgin Mary and All Saints, Meare

James Patch was born in 1882, the third of four children – all boys – to Albert and Jane. Albert was a farm labourer in the village of Meare, Somerset, and this is something that, once leaving school, the Patch boys also went into.

Albert passed away in 1904, so James stepped up and stayed living with his mother. By the time of the 1911 census, they were living near the Grape Vine Pub in Meare, both working as agricultural labourers, and had a John Lee boarding with them.

No firm details remain of James' military service, although it is evident he enlisted in the Devonshire Regiment and, from the Army Register of Soldiers' Effects, this can be narrowed down to the 7th Infantry Works Company.

While Private Patch's military records are sparse, his name crops up a lot in the newspapers around the time of his death, with headlines like *"Mysterious Death of Meare Soldier"*.

On the evening of the 25th March 1917, James was found lying across the tram tracks in Horfield, a suburb to the north of Bristol. He was in a semi-conscious state and was taken to the nearby barracks.

An inquest was held, and the story unfolded.

Witness statements confirmed that Private Patch was on a tram and had asked the conductress to let him know when they reached the barracks. The tram halted at the allotted stop, but, when nobody alighted, the driver started up again.

James apparently asked the conductress if that had been the stop for Horfield Barracks and, having confirmed that it was, and that he had wanted to get off there, she pressed the bell for the driver to pull up at the next stop. She then went up to the top deck of the tram, and it appear that James had decided he couldn't wait for the next stop and jumped off the moving tram.

It seems that James fell from the tram and hit his head when he landed; this was when a passer-by found him.

The morning after his fall, the camp doctor identified the extent of James' injury, and he was moved from the barracks to the Royal Infirmary in Bristol. Private Patch died an hour after being admitted, having suffered an extensive fracture of the skull. He was 35 years of age.

The inquest into his death returned a verdict of "*accidental death, due to a fall from a tram-car, caused by stepping from the car while in motion.*"

James Patch lies at rest in the ground of the Church of the Blessed Virgin Mary and All Saints in his home village of Meare in Somerset.

Name: Pavey, Roland

Rank: Private

Regiment: Machine Gun Corps

Date of death: 1st June 1920

Age at time of death: 29

Cause of death: Illness

Grave location: Milton Cemetery, Weston-super-Mare

Roland Adams Pavey was born in the summer of 1891, the youngest of three children to Anthony Pavey and his wife, Mary. Anthony was a painter, and both he and his wife were born in the Somerset town of Cheddar. Their life took them travelling, though, with their first child, Edward being born in Cheddar, while their middle child, Ada, was born in Oxford, and Roland born in Bath.

Anthony passed away in 1910, leaving Roland living with his widowed mother, earning a living as a draper's clerk. War was coming, however, and new opportunities lay in store.

Roland enlisted in the army in January 1915. Initially joining the North Somerset Yeomanry, he soon transferred across to the Cavalry Division of the Machine Gun Corps. Sadly, Private Pavey's military records are lost to time, but he definitely saw action on the Western Front, gaining the Victory and British Medals and the 1915 Star for his efforts.

The next record for Roland comes in the form of a newspaper article from South Wales:

SAD CASE OF NANTYGLO GIRL

Behind the untimely death of Mr Roland A Pavey, a popular young ex-Service man, and secretary of the Weston-super-Mare Federation of Discharged Soldiers and Sailors, lies a pathetic story of the double bereavement of a pretty Welsh girl, Miss Dorothy Morgan of Nantyglo.

Prior to the war, Miss Morgan was engaged to a compatriot of her own, who answered his country's call and, like so many thousands of others, made the great sacrifice. Time rolled on and the old wound was eventually healed. Then Miss Morgan went on a visit to Weston last year, and there met young Roland Pavey, just demobilised from the Army.

A mutual attraction soon ripened into affection, and the couple became engaged, and they were to have been married towards the end of the present month, but Fate intervened.

Pavey's long war service impaired his constitution, though how seriously was probably not realised until the damage was done. Returning from a Whitsuntide visit to Exeter, Mr Pavey was so ill that he was compelled to take to his bed. He rapidly became worse, and though his fiancée was hurriedly summoned, he passed away before she arrived at Weston.

Thus, within a short time, Miss Morgan has been twice bereaved as a result of the war.

Merthyr Express: Saturday 12th June 1920

Roland Adams Pavey was just 29 years old when he died. He was laid to rest in the Milton Cemetery in Weston-super-Mare, where his mother then lived.

Sadly, Dorothy Morgan is too common a name in South Wales to confirm much more information on her life. We are unlikely ever to discover if she ever found a lasting love.

Name: Payne, Percy

Rank: Private

Regiment: Royal Army Medical Corps

Date of death: 26th June 1918

Age at time of death: 21

Cause of death: Tuberculosis

Grave location: St Mary's Churchyard, Yatton

Percy Payne was born in the village of Kingston Seymour, between Weston-super-Mare and Yatton, Somerset. His parents were agricultural labourer Harry Payne and his wife, Elizabeth, and he had three brothers.

It seems that Percy's parents may well have separated by 1911; Elizabeth is listed as a widow in the 1911 census, but Harry appears to be alive and well and living in South Wales.

According to the census records, Elizabeth was working as a charwoman, while three of her children were working to help support the family. Percy's two older brothers were employed as a carter and a domestic servant, while Percy himself was working as an errand boy.

By the time war broke out, Percy has stepped up the ladder. His service records listed his trade as a groom, working in Congresbury, near Bristol. He enlisted in March 1916, at the age of 19 years and 8 months, and was assigned as a Private in the Northumberland Fusiliers. He spent most of that year training on home soil, before being shipped out to France at the end of December.

Illness seems to have dogged Private Payne; he returned to England after a couple of months and was transferred to the Labour Corps fairly soon afterwards. By September 1917 a further transfer was made, this time to the Royal Army Medical Corps, before he was finally discharged from military service on 21st January 1918, suffering from tuberculosis.

Sadly, the lung condition was to prove fatal, and Percy passed away on 26th June 1918. He was just 21 years old.

Percy Payne lies at rest in the graveyard of St Mary's Church in the village of Yatton, Somerset.

Name: Payne, Stanley

Rank: Major

Regiment: Royal Air Force

Date of death: 3rd March 1919

Age at time of death: 38

Cause of death: Influenza and pneumonia

Grave location: Milton Cemetery, Weston-super-Mare

Stanley James Payne was born towards the end of 1882, one of eleven children to Stephen and Elizabeth Payne. Stephen was a leather salesman from Essex, who had moved his family to Weston-super-Mare in Somerset in around 1880.

Stanley seems to have been drawn in to a military life from an early age. In January 1900, he enlisted as a Private in the Somerset Light Infantry, and the 1901 census listed him as living at the Raglan Barracks in Devonport, near Plymouth.

Military service took Private Payne to India, where he served for six years. His success and ambition were clear; in 1906 he was promoted first to Corporal and then to Sergeant. By 1911 – and now back in England – as a Lance Sergeant Stanley was working as a military clerk at the Royal Horse Artillery Barracks in Dorchester, although he was still attached to the Somerset Light Infantry.

Stanley's ambition and sense of adventure continued; by July 1912 he had made the transfer over to the newly formed Royal Flying Corps, as a Sergeant.

It was while he was based in Dorchester that he met Winifred Bell. She was the daughter of a local council worker, and the couple married in the town in September 1912. Stanley and Winifred went on to have a daughter, Doris, who was born in July 1914.

War had arrived in Europe, and on 7th October, the now Warrant Officer Payne was shipped to France. During his nine months on the Western

Front, he was mentioned in despatches and received the Croix de Guerre for his gallantry. The local newspaper also reported that he:

> ...had also the honour of being presented to the King on the occasion of His Majesty's last visit to the front, and at a home station had also been presented to Queen Mary.

> Western Daily Press: Saturday 8th March 1919

Returning to England on 1st June 1915, he was again promoted to Lieutenant and Quartermaster, although here his military records dry up. By this time, he had been in the armed forces for more than fifteen years, but his military records seem to confirm this as the last day of his service.

The next record for Stanley confirms his passing. Admitted to the Central Air Force Hospital in Hampstead with a combination of influenza and pneumonia, he died on 3rd March 1919. He was just 36 years of age.

Brought back to Weston-super-Mare, where his now widowed father was still living, Stanley James Payne was laid to rest in the Milton Cemetery in his home town.

Stanley's gravestone gives his rank as Major. While there is no documented evidence of any additional promotions after June 1915, the rank is the equivalent of Quartermaster in the Army Reserve. It seems likely, therefore, that the end date of his military service marked the start of his time in the reserves.

Name: Pearce, Stanley

Rank: Driver

Regiment: Royal Army Service Corps

Date of death: 10th November 1918

Age at time of death: 24

Cause of death: Malaria, influenza and pneumonia

Grave location: Wembdon Road Cemetery, Bridgwater

Stanley Arthur Robert Pearce was born in September 1895, the fourth of five children to Edwin and Rosetta Pearce from Bridgwater, Somerset. Edwin was a painter and sign-writer, and it was in the creative trades that his children followed.

Stanley's eldest brother Clifford became a gardener; his next oldest Edwin Jr was a mason's labourer, while his older sister Dorothy became a cardboard box maker. By the time of the 1911 census, when Stanley was 16, he was listed as a painter's errand boy, presumably helping out his father.

War was on the horizon, and Stanley was keen to do his bit. In October 1914, he enlisted, becoming a Driver in the Royal Army Service Corps. Assigned to the 662nd Heavy Transport Company, he was based in London. There was still time for visits home, however, and the local Bridgwater newspaper reported on an ASC football match in which Driver Pearce was involved in October 1915.

By this time, Stanley had met Flossie Vickery, from nearby North Petherton. The couple married the following year, and had two children, Ada and Geoffrey.

In 1916, Driver Pearce's battalion was shipped off to Salonica in Greece, as part of the British Expeditionary Force in the Balkans. While there, he contracted malaria and dysentery, and was evacuated back to England for treatment in September 1918.

Driver Pearce recovered well enough to enjoy a month's recuperation, but fell ill again, with a recurrence of malaria, combined with influenza and pneumonia. He was admitted to the Brook War Hospital in South East London, but sadly did not recover, and passed away on 10th November 1918, a day before the Armistice was signed. He was just 23 years old.

Stanley Arthur Robert Pearce lies at rest in the Wembdon Road Cemetery in his home town of Bridgwater.

Stanley's older sister Dorothy – the cardboard box maker – contracted influenza around the same time as her brother and, tragically, died just five days after him. The siblings were buried in a joint funeral at the cemetery.

Name: Pearn, William

Rank: Gunner

Regiment: Royal Field Artillery

Date of death: 19th October 1918

Age at time of death: 24

Cause of death: Pneumonia

Grave location: St John's Cemetery, Bridgwater

William Henry Pearn was born in January 1896, one of two children to Richard and Selina Pearn from Bridgwater in Somerset. Selina had been married previously, and had been widowed, and so William had a further four half-siblings. Richard was a lath renderer – a plasterer in today's terms – and he was not the only one of the household to be working. According to the 1901 census, Selina was a collar maker and William 's two older half-brothers were a landscape gardener and a bookshop assistant.

When William left school, he went to work for a local coal yard as a porter. The next census finds him living with his mother and his older brother, Wallace, who was a labourer in a brickyard. Richard is noticeable in his absence, but Selina is listed as having been married for 18 years.

Sadly, though, at this point William's trail goes cold. His military records are sparse, but we know that he enlisted as a Gunner in the Royal Field Artillery, although I have been unable to identify when he enrolled. The only other information I have been able to locate for him are his pension records, that confirm that he passed away from pneumonia on 19th October 1918. Gunner Pearn was just 24 years old.

William Henry Pearn lies at rest in St John's Cemetery in his home town of Bridgwater in Somerset.

Name: Percy, Albert

Rank: Private

Regiment: West Somerset Yeomanry

Date of death: 4th October 1914

Age at time of death: 25

Cause of death: Spinal Meningitis

Grave location: St Mary's Cemetery, Taunton

Albert Rudolph Percy was born in April 1889 in Taunton, Somerset. His parents were William Percy, a draper, and his wife, Elise, who had been born in Baden-Baden, Germany. Elise's background certainly influenced the naming of the couple's five children, all sons with middle names ranging from Rudolph and Frederick, to Leopold and Felix.

All but the eldest of William and Elise's children followed their father into the drapery business; after initially doing so when he left school, Albert's older brother Frederick took holy orders, a following he continued for the rest of his days.

On the outbreak of war in 1914, Albert volunteered for military service, leaving his father's business behind him. Enlisting in the West Somerset Yeomanry, he was shipped off to Colchester in Essex for training.

While taking two days' leave in September that year, Private Percy returned home, and, on the first evening complained of feeling unwell. A doctor was summoned and diagnosed spinal meningitis. Albert was swift to succumb to the illness, passing away on 4th October 1914. He was just 25 years old and likely one of the first from Taunton to die whilst on active service.

Albert Rudolph Percy lies at rest in St Mary's Cemetery in his home town of Taunton, Somerset.

Name: Percy, David

Rank: Private

Regiment: West Somerset Yeomanry

Date of death: 15th May 1915

Age at time of death: 19

Cause of death: "Chill"

Grave location: St James' Cemetery, Taunton

David Percy was born in 1896, one of ten children to Elizabeth Percy. By the time of the 1901 census – the first one on which David appeared – Elizabeth was widowed, so there is no record of who his or his siblings' father was.

Elizabeth, working to make ends meet, found employment as a cook at Taunton Boys' School, in her home town. The 1911 census shows her two youngest sons – David and his older brother Douglas – were living with her, as was a lodger, Owen Howe. David, by this time, had left school and found work as a labourer, while Douglas was employed as a carter.

David soon found a new job as a printer for Hammett & Co. in the town, but war was beckoning across the Channel. In October 1914 he enlisted, joining the West Somerset Yeomanry as a Private and was sent to Minehead for training.

The local newspaper picked up his story:

> He there caught a chill and was in hospital for some time. At Easter [1915] he was removed to the Taunton Hospital, and subsequently sent home.

> *Taunton Courier and Western Advertiser: 26th May 1915*

Sadly, after Private Percy's discharge home, he passed away from his 'chill', breathing his last on 15th May 1915. He was just 19 years old.

David Percy was buried in St James' Cemetery in his home town of Taunton.

Name: Perkins, Bertram

Rank: Captain

Regiment: Sherwood Foresters

Date of death: 14th June 1916

Age at time of death: 43

Cause of death: Enteric fever

Grave Location: St Matthew's Churchyard, Wookey

Bertram Falls Perkins was born in December 1872, the third of four children to Alfred and Mary Perkins. Alfred was a Colonel in the army and had met his wife while serving in Madras, India. He had retired by the time Alfred was born, and had brought his family back to England, where he set up as a Country Magistrate, living in the village of Wookey in Somerset.

Bertram was set for good things – by the time of the 1881 census, the family were living in Eastcott House, with a footman, cook, two ladies' maids, two house maid and a governess to look after them.

Bertram's military records are scant but can be pieced together from his funeral notice:

> The late Captain Bertram Perkins... joined the 1st Vol. Batt. of
> the Somerset Light Infantry as 2nd Lieutenant in February 1892,
> and, in November 1894, was transferred to his father's regiment,

the 3rd Batt. Welsh Regt. as Lieutenant... In October 1896 he went to South Africa and joined the Natal Mounted Police, in which he saw much active service... at the relief of Ladysmith and Dundee. Being stricken down with a very severe attack of enteric fever, he had to resign... and return home. As soon as he recovered his health he again retuned to South Africa as a Captain in the 3rd Battalion Welsh Regiment, where he saw much service...

Whilst at Vryburg, he was appointed Provost Marshal, and in recognition of his tact and energy in filling a very difficult position, was presented by the inhabitants of the district with a gold watch and an illuminated address. He was in possession of the Queen's Medal with four clasps and the King's Medal with two clasps. On his return home he took to farming... He retired from the Service in 1905, but on the outbreak of the present war was appointed as Captain to the 12th Battalion of the Sherwood Foresters. Unfortunately, his health, which had never been quite restored, broke down, and he was invalided out of the Regiment.

Wells Journal: Friday 16th June 1916

During the Great War, Captain Perkins' regiment had been the 12th (Service) Battalion for the Nottinghamshire and Derbyshire Regiment. His unit had been shipped out to France in August 1915, but it is likely that he saw little, if any, time on the Western Front. After being invalided out, he succumbed to his ongoing illness on 14th June 1916, aged 43.

Bertram Falls Perkins lies at rest in the graveyard of St Matthew's Church, in his home village of Wookey, near Wells in Somerset.

Name: Perrett, Frank

Rank: Private

Regiment: Dorsetshire Regiment

Date of death: 13th July 1918

Age at time of death: 39

Cause of death: Illness

Grave location: St John's Cemetery, Bridgwater

Frank Herbert Perrett was born in January 1880, the tenth of thirteen children. He was the son of Thomas and Thirza Perrett, bakers and grocers from Bridgwater in Somerset.

When he left school, Frank worked as a chemist's assistant, and boarded with the chemist – a Frank Sanguinetti – in Ealing, London.

In around 1908, having moved back to Somerset, he married Bessie Hutchings, who was also from the Bridgwater area. The couple went on to have a son, Douglas, who was born in 1910. A year later, the census sees him working as a commercial traveller for a chemist.

War was on the horizon and, although exact details of his military service are not available, it is evident that Frank enrolled in the Dorsetshire Regiment.

Assigned to the 6th Battalion, Private Perrett's troop would have been involved in the Battles of Ypres, Arras and Passchendaele, amongst others (although I have not been able to find confirmation of how involved he was in these skirmishes).

At some point, Private Perrett fell ill, and he was admitted to the Tidworth Military Hospital near Andover. Sadly, he succumbed to the condition, and he passed away on 13th July 1918. He was 39 years old.

Frank Herbert Perrett lies at peace in the St John's Cemetery in his home town of Bridgwater in Somerset.

Name: Perry, Walter

Rank: Private

Regiment: Royal Wiltshire Yeomanry

Date of death: 6th June 1917

Age at time of death: 42

Cause of death: Appendicitis

Grave location: Wembdon Road Cemetery, Bridgwater

Walter Perry was born in Bridgwater, Somerset, in 1874. He was one of ten children to James Perry, a general dealer, and his wife Hannah. After he had left school, Walter became a labourer; his older siblings had all become labourers or factory workers in the area.

In November 1899, Walter married Rebecca Cavill; their first child, Hilda, was born at the end of March the following year. By this time, Walter was working for a brewery, while his new wife was working at a shirt collar factory. The young couple went on to have two further children – Walter and Beatrice – before Rebecca tragically passed away in June 1906.

Walter married again in November 1908, this time to a Mary Ann Reed also from Somerset. The couple went on to have two children, Joseph and Edna, and the family lived together in the centre of Bridgwater.

The Great War was on the horizon. While details of Walter's military service are not readily available, it is unlikely he was called up when hostilities broke out – he turned 40 in 1914, and so was too old to qualify immediately.

Walter enlisted in the 2/1st Royal Wiltshire Yeomanry; he was based primarily in England, where his battalion acted as a training/reserve for the 1st Battalion, who were serving on the Western Front. It was while Private Perry was based in Essex, that he contracted appendicitis; he was admitted to the General Military Hospital in Colchester but passed away on 6th June 1917. He was 43 years old.

Walter Perry lies at peace in the Wembdon Road Cemetery in his home town of Bridgwater.

Name: Peters, Sydney

Rank: Serjeant

Regiment: West Somerset Yeomanry

Date of death: 15th August 1915

Age at time of death: 23

Cause of death: Sepsis

Grave location: Wembdon Road Cemetery, Bridgwater

Sydney Edward Peters was born at the end of 1891, the only child to farmers Edward and Annie Peters. The family lived in Bishop's Hull, near Taunton, where Edward also employed two members of staff to help with the household and his dairy herd.

Sydney went on to manage the neighbouring farm to his father and looked to be making a living with this. Keen on sport, he went on to captain the village cricket team, and took an interest in physical fitness.

War broke out and Sydney was quick to enlist. Joining the West Somerset Yeomanry, he was assigned to the 1st Battalion. Initially the regiment was based on home turf, and he spent a lot of that time in East Anglia. He must have made a positive commitment to the troop and was soon promoted to Serjeant.

In the early summer of 1915, he returned to Taunton, to help drill recruits at the Territorial Depot there. A short while after returning to Essex he fell ill, and before the battalion were due to be shipped overseas, Serjeant Peters went back to Somerset on leave.

By the time he reached home, however, he was severely ill, and very quickly died from what turned out to be blood poisoning. Serjeant Peters was just 23 years old.

Sydney Edward Peters was buried in St Mary's Cemetery in his home town of Taunton.

Name: Phillips, William

Rank: Private

Regiment: West Somerset Yeomanry

Date of death: 21st February 1915

Age at time of death: 20

Cause of death: Suicide by drowning

Grave location: St James' Cemetery, Taunton

William Phillips was born in 1895, the youngest of seven children to Frank and Emily Phillips. Frank was a joiner and carpenter and, while his young family initially grew up in his home village of Thurloxton, Somerset, he and Emily soon moved them to nearby Taunton, where there would be more work and more opportunities.

By the time of the 1911 census, the young family were all tied up with different jobs. While William had become an office boy for an accountant when he left school, his siblings all had different roles: one was a boiler cleaner, another a mason, a third a cellarman and the fourth a shop assistant. With Frank's own work, this meant that there were five wages coming into the home, albeit on a much smaller scale than we are used to these days.

War was coming, however, and, at the beginning of 1915, William enlisted in the West Somerset Yeomanry. Little information remains of his military service, but it *is* known that Private Phillips' experience as a clerk was made use of, and he worked in admin at the reserve depot in Minehead.

William had, by this time, got himself a lady friend, who worked at the hospital in Taunton, and, while they did not see each other a lot, they corresponded regularly.

His new-found freedom from the family home seemed to have led to William being a bit freer with his money than his parents would like, and it appears he may have run up debts. He reassured his mother that he did not want to worry them with any business he had. However, financial matters may well have played on his mind more than he would have liked to admit.

On Saturday 20th February 1915, Private Phillips travelled to Taunton to see his girlfriend; she was working, but he caught up with his sister instead, before returning to the base in Minehead that evening.

The following Tuesday morning, he received a letter from his girl and was last seen heading to breakfast in the hotel digs where he was billeted.

That afternoon, a local engineer was walking along the seafront, when he saw a body lying on the foreshore, about four feet (1.21m) from the high-water mark. The body – which was later identified as William – was wearing some clothing, but other bits were scattered around him. The police were called, and Private Phillips' body was taken to nearby Dunster.

The coroner confirmed William had drowned; the letter he had received was amongst his clothing, but there was nothing in it to suggest that anything was amiss. At the inquest, he suggested that "*he could hardly suppose at this time of year that the deceased had taken off his clothing in order to bathe. [His conclusion was that William] got into the water with intent to drown himself.*" [*Taunton Courier and Western Advertiser: Wednesday 3rd March 1915*]

The jury at the inquest returned the verdict of '*found drowned*'. Private Phillips was just 20 years old.

William's body was brought back to Taunton for burial. He lies at rest in the St James' Cemetery there.

Name: Pittard, Herbert

Rank: Private

Regiment: Devonshire Regiment

Date of death: 26th November 1918

Age at time of death: 22

Cause of death: Influenza and pneumonia

Grave location: Street Cemetery

Herbert Leonard Pittard was born in 1896, the youngest of two children — both boys — to Frederick and Lily Pittard. Frederick was a bootmaker, employed by the Clark's factory in the town.

Herbert's mother died in 1910, and by the time of the 1911 census, he was living with his father, brother and grandmother in Park Terrace, Glastonbury. All three of the household's men were bootmakers, all were working at the Clark's factory in Street.

Frederick Pittard was out to seek pastures new, emigrating to America in 1912. Herbert is recorded as having visited his brother a year later.

Herbert's military records are sparse; it seems that he enlisted in the Devonshire Regiment, joining the 3rd Battalion as a Private, before transferring to the Southern Command Labour Centre of the Labour Corps. When this happened, and for how long he enlisted, is not known, but he survived through to the Armistice in 1918.

A short notice in the Central Somerset Gazette (Friday 29 November 1918) confirmed that "*Mr Pittard, Park Terrace [Glastonbury], has just lost his younger son through the influenza epidemic. Private Bert Pittard died in Bath War Hospital from pneumonia subsequent to influenza at the age of 22.*"

Herbert Leonard Pittard died on 26th November 1918. He lies at rest in the cemetery in Street, Somerset.

Name: Poole, Arthur

Rank: Captain

Regiment: Gloucestershire Regiment

Date of death: 23rd November 1918

Age at time of death: 25

Cause of death: Influenza and pneumonia

Grave location: St Andrew's Churchyard, Clevedon

Arthur George Poole was born in Brislington, Somerset, in April 1893. His father, George, was a master builder, and with his mother, Rhoda, the family raised their five children in the Bristol suburb.

Arthur was obviously a bright lad; he attended the Bristol Grammar School, excelling at football, hockey and cricket. After finishing school, he joined a firm of Bristol solicitors and was also appointed secretary of the Bristol Law Society. He went on to continue his studies, when he was accepted to read law at Emmanuel College, Cambridge.

The war was on the horizon, and he was called upon to do his duty:

> *He joined Bristol's Own (12th Gloucester Regiment) in 1914, and was musketry officer at Chiseldon for some months before going to France in 1915, where he was attached to the 6th Gloucester Regiment.*
>
> *Within three months he had a severe attack of trench fever, and was home on sick leave for a few weeks. He was severely wounded in October 1917, and came back to England for good. Some months later he was mentioned in despatches. He spent a year in hospital, and although not discharged, was allowed to resume his law studies.*
>
> *Gloucestershire Echo: Saturday 14th December 1918*

While in hospital, Captain Poole contracted influenza, which then became pneumonia. Although recovering from his injuries, it was these conditions that were to get the better of him, and he passed away on 23rd November 1918, at the age of 25 years old.

Arthur George Poole was laid to rest in the pretty graveyard of St Andrew's Church in Clevedon, Somerset, where his parents now lived.

Name: Pople, Frederick

Rank: Stoker 2nd Class

Regiment: Royal Navy

Date of death: 11th February 1919

Age at time of death: 31

Cause of death: Pneumonia

Grave location: Glastonbury Cemetery

Frederick Richard Pople was the second of three children – all sons – of Frederick and Emma Pople, born in 1887 in Street, Somerset.

He married Beatrice Cox in 1910 and, by the following year the newlyweds had moved to South Wales, where Frederick found work on the railways. The couple had one child, Frederick Alonzo Pople, born in 1912.

Sadly, Beatrice passed away a couple of years later; Frederick married again, to Beatrice Salmon, in November 1914; the couple had a son, Edward George Salmon Pople, who was born on Valentine's Day 1918.

Frederick enlisted relatively late in the war – he was 30 when he signed up on 25th January 1918 and is likely to have missed the birth of his son.

He enrolled in the Royal Navy and his training took place at HMS Vivid II in Devonport. By March of that year, he was serving as a stoker on HMS Attentive III, part of the Dover patrol.

Stoker Pople continued to work on HMS Attentive after the conclusion of hostilities in November 1918. Sadly, he contracted pneumonia and passed away on 11th February 1919, leaving Beatrice with a son of less than a year old.

Frederick Richard Pople is buried in the cemetery of his home town, Glastonbury.

Name: Pow, Albert

Rank: Private

Regiment: Somerset Light Infantry

Date of death: 11th May 1917

Age at time of death: 30

Cause of death: Empyema and abscess of the axilla

Grave location: Wembdon Road Cemetery, Bridgwater

Albert Francis Pow was born in the autumn of 1886, one of five children to Albert and Annie Pow from Somerset. Albert Sr. was a farm labourer, but by the time he left school, Albert Jr. started work as a porter in the Singer sewing machine factory in Bridgwater.

Albert's father passed away in 1905, at the age of 51, and his son – who was by this time repairing the sewing machines – became head of the household.

He was obviously good at what he did, because by the time he married in 1913, he was able to support his wife Leonora as branch manager for the Singer store in the town. The young couple soon moved on, as, when war broke out, he was manager of the shop in Barnstaple.

War came calling, and while the date of his enlistment is absent from his records, Private Pow joined the 1st Battalion of the Somerset Light Infantry. Sent to the front, he quickly became ill, suffering from dysentery and trench foot, which led to him being hospitalised for nearly two months.

Returning to his troops, Private Pow's health remained unsteady, and he soon contracted trench fever. He was evacuated back to England for treatment and was admitted to the Canadian Red Cross Memorial Hospital in Taplow, Buckinghamshire.

Sadly, Albert was not to recover this time; he died at the hospital on 11th May 1917 as a result of empyema (pleuritis) and an abscess of the axilla (armpit). He was just 30 years old when he died.

Albert Francis Pow lies at rest in the Wembdon Road Cemetery in Bridgwater.

Albert left behind his widow, Leonora and their child Vanessa. Leonora was to be reunited with her late husband; she died in August 1986 and is buried with her beloved.

Name: Prince, Percy

Rank: Private

Regiment: Somerset Light Infantry

Date of death: 11th April 1918

Age at time of death: 30

Cause of death: Unknown

Grave location: St James' Cemetery, Taunton

Percy Prince was born in 1890, one of seven children to John and Eliza Prince. John was an agricultural labourer and coal merchant and brought his family up on the Somerset/Wiltshire border, near Bruton.

Percy followed in his father's line of work when he left school, eventually moving to Frome. He met and married a woman called Florence Stickler in July 1909, setting up home in Water Lane, to the south of the town centre.

War was soon beckoning, and Percy enlisted in the Somerset Light Infantry as a Private. Sadly, his service records are lost to time, and so details of his time in the army are not available. What we *do* know is that he was assigned to one of the depots, although which one is not clear.

Sadly, that is about the limit of information available about Private Prince. He died on 11th April 1918, at the Military Hospital in Taunton. There is nothing to confirm a cause of death, but he just was 28 years old.

Percy Prince was buried in St James' Cemetery in Taunton.

Name: Prout, Richard

Rank: Serjeant

Regiment: Somerset Light Infantry

Date of death: 13th February 1920

Age at time of death: 24

Cause of death: Asphyxia

Grave location: St Lawrence's Churchyard, Lydeard St Lawrence

Richard Edwin Prout was born in 1896, the second son of Frederick and Anna (Hannah) Prout. When his father died in 1908, his mother remarried and by the 1911 census, Richard and his family had moved to Lydeard St Lawrence, where he was a baker's boy.

He enlisted in June 1914, joining the Somerset Light Infantry and served throughout the war, receiving the Mons Star, Victory Medal and General Service Medals. After the war, he continued in the army, assigned to Taunton Barracks.

His death was unusual enough to be reported on in the local newspaper:

> *Sergt. Prout, it was stated at the Barracks yesterday, had been on*
> *leave for some days prior to his departure for Ireland, and had*
> *been spending his furlough at Crowcombe, where his parents live.*
> *On the evening of his death, he left home, after taking a hearty*
> *meal, to catch the 7.25 train to Taunton. He had to walk a mile to*
> *Crowcombe station, most of the way uphill. Early the following*
> *morning his dead body was discovered lying face downwards by*
> *the roadside, about 50 yards from the station. The body was*
> *removed to his home, and Dr. Frossard, of Bishop's Lydeard, was*
> *called in to make a post-mortem examination. The doctor has*
> *reported that death was due to asphyxia brought on by over*
> *exertion on a full stomach, and syncope, following pressure on the*
> *neck by the tightness of the collar of his outside jacket, the doctor*
> *adding that he had great difficulty in unfastening the collar.*

Western Daily Press – Friday 20th February 1920

A genuine case of someone going before their time. Having visited Lydeard St Lawrence, I recognise the hill he would have had to have climbed to reach the station, and it's steep enough in a car, let alone walking up it.

Serjeant Prout, the newspaper reported, was generally esteemed by his fellow company, and at his funeral he received full military honours.

Richard Edwin Prout lies peacefully in the churchyard of Lydeard St Lawrence.

Name: Pullen, Frederick

Rank: Second Lieutenant

Regiment: Royal Flying Corps

Date of death: 26th March 1918

Age at time of death: 18

Cause of death: Flying accident

Grave location: Shepton Mallet Burial Ground

Frederick John Edward Pullen was born in May 1899, the only son to Albert and Bessie Pullen from Shepton Mallet in Somerset. Albert worked at the local prison, acting as clerk, warden and school master to the inmates.

Little else survives to expand on Fred's military life; his gravestone confirms that he had enlisted in the Royal Flying Corps and, although no date can be attributed to this, it is likely to have been almost as soon as he turned 17.

A report of the funeral does give a little insight into the young man:

> ...before entering the service of his country, Lieutenant Pullen was in the Civil Service, and a letter from his late surveyor at Oxford, speaks in high terms of his character and abilities.
>
> He graduated to the rank of Service Pilot in February last, and was gazetted in March. By the Naval authorities he was considered a very good pilot, and was graded as Class A (exemplary).
>
> Shepton Mallet Journal: Friday 5th April 1918

Alongside the Edwardian trait of listing the chief mourners and floral tributes, the newspaper also gives an in-depth report of the cause of Second Lieutenant Pullen's demise:

> The brave young officer, who was at a war school [Manston Airfield, Kent], was engaged in 'stunting' or trick flying, absolutely necessary in warfare, when from some unknown cause, he fell into a field, and was instantly killed.

A farmer who was ploughing near the spot said he was not conscious of the presence of an aeroplane in the vicinity till this one seemed to drop from the clouds. It nose-dived, but righted on coming near the earth, and seemed to swoop up again, but before going far turned turtle and fell, upside down.

The poor lad was found crushed beneath his gun, and had met instantaneous death. Letters received from witnesses of the accident stated that people living in the neighbourhood hurried to the spot with remedies of all sorts, and were much saddened to find that nothing that they could do was of any avail.

Shepton Mallet Journal: Friday 5th April 1918

Second Lieutenant Pullen met his death in a flying accident on 26th March 1918. He was just 18 years old.

Frederick John Edward Pullen lies at rest in the cemetery of his home town of Shepton Mallet.

Name: Rapson, Frederick

Rank: Lance Serjeant

Regiment: Somerset Light Infantry

Date of death: 3rd March 1917

Age at time of death: 27

Cause of death: Pneumonia

Grave location: St James' Cemetery, Taunton

Frederick Ernest Rapson was born in the spring of 1888, one of nine children to Francis and Susan Rapson. Francis was a Serjeant in the 18th Hussars, and the family lived in Dulverton, a village on the edge of Exmoor.

Francis had served in the armed forces for 26 years but passed away after a short illness in February 1891. According to a local friend and supporter, he had been in charge of the local yeomanry in Dulverton for a number of years and had been *"in the prime and flower of life."* [West Somerset Free Press: Saturday 28th February 1891]

Susan was left widowed with nine children, the eldest of whom was only 13 years old. Frederick was only three at the time and had lost his father at a very early age.

In 1895, Susan married a Frederick Howard, who was a painter and carpenter. The family moved to Taunton in Somerset, and Frederick and Susan went on to have three children of their own.

On 6th February 1910, Frederick Rapson married Lucy Knight; by this time, he was working as a compositor for the local newspaper. The couple set up home in the middle of Taunton, and went on to have three children, Francis, Frederick and Ronald.

War was coming, and, while Frederick did not actively seek military service in the same way as his father had done, it was not something he was able to avoid. While his full military records are not available, it's clear that he enlisted in the Somerset Light Infantry at some point early on in the conflict.

Private Rapson was assigned to the 1st Battalion, who were based on the Western Front for the duration of the conflict. During his time there, he was awarded the Victory and British Medals, but not the 1915 Star, so that would narrow down his enlisting to some point in 1916.

While he was promoted to the role of Lance Serjeant, his service was to be a short one. At the start of 1917, he contracted pneumonia and was admitted to hospital. Sadly, the condition was to get the better of him, and he passed away on 3rd March 1917. He was just 27 years of age.

Frederick Ernest Rapson was buried in a quiet corner of St James' Cemetery in Taunton, Somerset.

Name: Rawle, Ernest

Rank: Private

Regiment: West Somerset Yeomanry

Date of death: 25th November 1919

Age at time of death: 21

Cause of death: Tuberculosis

Grave Location: St Lawrence's Churchyard, Lydeard St Lawrence

Ernest Charles Rawle was born in 1894, the fourth son of George Rawle, a sailor, and Louisa, his wife.

Ernest was still at school at the time of the 1911 census, and enlisted in the West Somerset Yeomanry, but enlisted in the army in April 1915. He served on the Home Front but was discharged as being unfit for war service on 22nd July 1916.

Private Rawle's discharge records confirm that he had pulmonary tuberculosis, which he had contracted a couple of months before. They go on to suggest that it was not a permanent condition but was likely to render him unfit for service for a number of months.

Eager to do his bit, Ernest's record show that he re-enlisted in August 1916, and that he was considered fit for military service by the November of that year.

His medical records continue further – he was admitted to a field hospital again in March 1917, again suffering from tuberculosis. He was moved back to base as he was "*a danger to his comrades.*"

His records after March 1917 are not available, but he passed way from TB in November 1919. He was just 21 years old.

Private Ernest Rawle lies at peace in the churchyard of Lydeard St Lawrence, alongside his two brothers, Stephen and William. Their stories can be read in the next two entries.

Name: Rawle, Stephen

Rank: Private

Regiment: West Somerset Yeomanry

Date of death: 5th September 1918

Age at time of death: 25

Cause of death: Unknown

Grave Location: St Lawrence's Churchyard, Lydeard St Lawrence

Stephen John Rawle was born in 1894, the second of four sons of George Rawle, a sailor, and Louisa, his wife.

By the time war broke out, Stephen was working as a groom in Wheddon Cross, just south of Minehead.

As the Great War loomed, he enlisted and Private Rawle served on the Home Front. His record shows that he stood at 5ft 9.5ins (1.76m) and was of good enough health to be enrolled for the Territorial Force. He was assigned to the West Somerset Yeomanry.

He was medically discharged from service on 29th March 1915, having served for one year and 31 days.

The records show no signs of injury or wounds, and newspapers of the period do not link him with any misadventure. I can only assume, therefore, that he died of natural causes, possibly linked to the Spanish Flu Pandemic. Stephen died on 5th September 1918. He was 25 years old.

Private Stephen John Rawle lies at rest in the churchyard of Lydeard St Lawrence, alongside two of his brothers, Ernest and William. Ernest's story can be read in the previous entry, William's in the next.

Name: Rawle, William

Rank: Private

Regiment: Somerset Light Infantry

Date of death: 11th June 1921

Age at time of death: 25

Cause of death: Unknown

Grave Location: St Lawrence's Churchyard, Lydeard St Lawrence

William Henry Rawle was born in 1894, the eldest child of George Rawle, a sailor, and Louisa, his wife.

At the time of the 1911 census, William was working as a carter on a farm not far from Porlock in Somerset.

He enlisted in August 1914, joining the Somerset Light Infantry and serving as part of the Expeditionary Force. After a couple of postings, Private Rawle was transferred to the Pioneer Depot in March 1916.

Six months later William was medically discharged as unfit for continued service. His notes highlight his distinguishing marks as 3 marks on his left arm, birth mark under his right nipple and gunshot wound to the left eye (which I am guessing is what led to his discharge).

William died on 11th June 1921, aged 27 years old. I have been unable to find anything specific relating to his death and it is likely, therefore, that no misadventure was involved.

Private William Henry Rawle lies at peace in the churchyard of Lydeard St Lawrence, alongside his brothers Stephen and Ernest. Their stories can be read in the previous two entries.

It should be noted that, by June 1921, Louisa Rawle had lost three of her four sons to the Great War. Her husband, George, had also passed away in 1915.

Louisa's other son – Edward – also served, enlisting in the Somerset Light Infantry and fighting in the Balkans. Private Edward Rawle survived the war, returning home in March 1919.

Name: Reed, Stephen

Rank: Lance Corporal

Regiment: Military Police Corps

Date of death: 27th April 1918

Age at time of death: 31

Cause of death: Tuberculosis

Grave location: Wembdon Road Cemetery, Bridgwater

Stephen Reed was born in August 1887, one of seven children to Stephen and Eliza Reed from Bridgwater, Somerset. Stephen Sr was a labourer, eventually working as a carter for the local council.

Stephen Jr sought bigger and better things, however. After initially working as a butcher, he enlisted in the army in January 1907. He served a term of three years in the Coldstream Guards, before being stood down to reserve status in 1910.

Stephen had by then, found his calling in life and joined the police force. Standing at 6ft 1in (1.84m) tall, he would have cut an imposing figure. By the time of the 1911 census, he was boarding at the barracks in Dorchester, where he was listed as a police constable.

In May 1913, Stephen, by now aged 25, married Emily Maud Bower, in their home town. By March of the following year, the young couple had settled back in Swanage, Dorset, and had had a child, Stephen George.

War was on the horizon, however, and Private Reed was re-mobilised in August 1914, finding himself overseas within weeks. He was quickly promoted to Lance Corporal, and, after a couple of years – including fighting at Mons and receiving a subsequent gunshot wound to his hand – was transferred to the Military Police Force.

In April 1918, Lance Corporal Reed contracted tuberculosis, and was ill enough to be evacuated back to England for treatment. He was admitted to the Royal Victoria Hospital in Netley, Hampshire, but passed away within a day of arriving. Sadly, his records show that a telegram was sent to Emily summoning her to the hospital, but, as this was dated the same day he passed away, it seems unlikely that she would have arrived in time.

Lance Corporal Reed died on 27th April 1918. He was 31 years old.

Stephen Reed lies at rest in the Wembdon Road Cemetery in his home town of Bridgwater.

A sad addition to Stephen's military records is a letter to his widow in September 1918, asking for acknowledgement of receipt of his belongings. The items in question boiled down to: *pair of braces; button stick; shaving brush; 2 boot brushes; comb; pipe lighter; handkerchief; pocket knife; safety razor; towel; flannel vest; waistcoat; identity disc; wrist strap; pair of scissors; tie clip; mirror; pipe; cigarette holder; 4 cap badges; card case; wallet and photos; wallet and correspondence; cigarette case; cigarettes; tobacco.*

We can assume that these items – especially the photographs and correspondence – gave some level of comfort to Emily but seeing her late husband's life summed up in a bagful of belongings must also have been heart-breaking.

Name: Richards, Alfred

Rank: Gunner

Regiment: Royal Horse Artillery

Date of death: 1st March 1919

Age at time of death: 28

Cause of death: Pneumonia

Grave location: Wells Cemetery

Alfred Henry Richards was born in 1891, the oldest of five children to William Henry Richards and his wife Jane. William (who was known as Henry) worked in the local paper mill, and this is a trade that his two sons – Alfred and Leslie – were to follow as well.

Paper making was a driving force in this part of Somerset during the Victorian era, employing a large number of people in Wells and the nearby village of Wookey, which is where Alfred and his siblings were born.

Details of Alfred's military service are sketchy. He enlisted as a Gunner in the Royal Horse Artillery, although when during the war this happened is unknown.

His troop – the 18th Brigade, 1st Somerset Royal Horse Artillery – was stationed in the UK for the first couple of years of the war, before serving in the Middle East. Again, I have not been able to confirm how much of this service Gunner Richards was involved in.

Alfred returned to Somerset after being demobbed, but within a few months of the end of the war, he succumbed to double pneumonia. He passed away on 1st March 1919, aged just 28 years old.

Alfred Henry Richards lies at rest in the cemetery in Wells, Somerset, not far from his home.

Name: Richards, Frank

Rank: Private

Regiment: Wiltshire Regiment

Date of death: 11th April 1917

Age at time of death: 27

Cause of death: Unknown

Grave location: Holy Trinity Churchyard, Long Sutton

Francis George Richards (or Frank) was born in 1889, the oldest of five children to William and Rhoda Richards. William was an agricultural labourer and the family lived in his home village of Long Sutton in Somerset.

Frank followed his father into agriculture, and, by the 1911 census, was working as a carter.

And that is where the trail of Private Richards goes cold.

What records do exist confirm that he enlisted in the Wiltshire Regiment, serving at its depot in Devizes. This suggests he was part of the 7th (Service) Battalion, raised through the Kitchener Scheme.

The battalion were shipped to France in September 1915, before being moved on to the Balkans, where they fought in the Battle of Horseshoe Hill and the Battles of Dorian. As there are no records of Private Richards' service, it is not possible to confirm how involved in the fighting in Europe he was, or whether he remained on the Home Front.

Frank's death also remains a mystery. All that can be said for sure is that he died in hospital on 11th April 1917, in a hospital in England. He was 27 years old. He does not appear to have married, and his pension was assigned to his father.

Frank George Richards lies at rest in the quiet graveyard of Holy Trinity Church in his home village of Long Sutton.

Name: Richards, Ossian

Rank: Corporal

Regiment: Royal Air Force

Date of death: 15th September 1919

Age at time of death: 21

Cause of death: Influenza

Grave location: Westonzoyland Cemetery

Ossian Emanuel Richards was born in Westonzoyland, Somerset, in December 1897. He was the youngest of two children and his parents – Emmanuel and Jane – were farmers in the area.

Ossian enlisted later in the war, joining the RAF in June 1918. While little detail of his service is available, he had been a fitter before joining up, so it may well have been on the mechanical side of things that he was involved.

After nine months' service, Ossian had been promoted to Corporal, and, with the war over, he was transferred to the RAF Reserves in March 1919.

Sadly, as with many young men of his generation, Corporal Richards succumbed to the flu pandemic that followed the war. He died on 15th September 1919, aged just 21 years old.

Ossian Emanuel Richards lies at rest in the cemetery of his home village of Westonzoyland.

Name: Ridge, Herbert

Rank: Sapper

Regiment: Royal Engineers

Date of death: 15th September 1919

Age at time of death: 31

Cause of death: Tuberculosis

Grave location: St Mary's Cemetery, Taunton

Herbert Gladstone Ridge was born in December 1886, the youngest of three children to Alfred and Sarah. Alfred was from Lancashire and had met and married his wife in Ireland, which is where Herbert's older siblings had been born.

Sarah had died when Herbert was only eleven years old. Alfred's skills were as a machine engineer, and, after his wife had passed away, he brought his family down to Somerset. Initially living with his father in Taunton, Herbert had found work as a piano tuner, and moved to a boarding house in Bristol to further his trade.

War was close, however, and, in July 1915, Herbert enlisted. Joining the Welsh Field Company of the Royal Engineers as a Sapper, he was quickly posted as part of the Mediterranean Expeditionary Force. He served nearly a year in Egypt, before being sent back to England in September 1916.

By this point, Sapper Ridge was suffering from a bout of tuberculosis, and had been sent back to England for treatment. The condition refused to clear up, however, and he was eventually discharged from the army on medical grounds three months after returning home.

Details of Herbert's life after the army are sparse. It can be assumed, however, that he remained dogged by tuberculosis, and this is what eventually killed him. He passed away on 15th September 1919, aged just 31 years old.

Herbert Gladstone Ridge lies at rest in St Mary's Cemetery in his adopted home town of Taunton in Somerset.

Name: Roberts, Robert

Rank: Company Quartermaster Sergeant

Regiment: Canadian Forestry Corps

Date of death: 6th February 1919

Age at time of death: 33

Cause of death: Influenza and pneumonia

Grave location: Wembdon Road Cemetery, Bridgwater

Robert Roberts was born in Liverpool in November 1887 the youngest of two children to Robert and Alice Roberts.

The New World beckoned for the Roberts family, and they set sail for Canada when Robert Jr was just 4 years old. The family settled in the city of Regina, Saskatchewan.

Little is recorded about Robert Jr until October 1911, when he married a Quebecois woman called Edna Webber. The young couple went on to have two children, a daughter, One, and a son, George.

In April 1916, he enlisted in the Canadian Expeditionary Force. His trade was noted as a lumberman, and his record notes that Robert had already served as part of the 95th Saskatchewan Rifles.

Joining the 224th Battalion, Robert was shipped to England in May 1916. He transferred to the Canadian Forestry Corps in November, reaching the rank of Staff Sergeant, and was assigned to the company's Base Depot in Sunningdale, near Windsor.

When the war ended, demobilisation was still a way off for a lot of soldiers, particularly those from the Commonwealth. Robert was transferred to Stirling and was appointed Quartermaster Sergeant (responsible for supplies and stores) for 121st Company.

On 28th January 1919, Robert was admitted to the Royal Infirmary in Stirling with influenza and double pneumonia. Sadly, he passed away just over a week later, breathing his last on 6th February 1919. He was 33 years old.

Robert Roberts lies at peace in the Wembdon Road Cemetery in Bridgwater, Somerset.

There is no evident connection between Robert and Bridgwater, so why this was chosen as his place of rest is a mystery. It is likely that there was some sort of family connection, but that cannot be definitely established.

Name: Roberts, Roland

Rank: Private

Regiment: Coldstream Guards

Date of death: 10th November 1918

Age at time of death: 22

Cause of death: Influenza and pneumonia

Grave location: Wembdon Road Cemetery, Bridgwater

Roland Roberts was born in September 1896, one of three children – all boys – to Albert and Minnie Roberts.

Minnie, who was originally from Yeovil, had married Walter Shury, a Londoner, in 1874, and the couple had six children together. Walter then went on to have four children with Alice Norwood, and the couple married in 1898. Minnie, meanwhile, had met Albert Roberts, who was from Dundalk in Ireland, and, while no marriage seems to be confirmed, the couple had three boys, including Roland. (It is pure speculation, but as Minnie's maiden was also Roberts, this might have provided a good enough cover for any divorce or re-marriage.)

Albert had been a Band Sergeant in the 4th Hussars and continued that passion by becoming a music teacher. Travel was also definitely in his blood: the couple's first child, Willie, was born in South London, Roland was born in Somerset, and his younger sibling, Glencoe, was born in Penzance, Cornwall. Albert's musical success led him to become bandmaster for the Penzance Town Band. Sadly, it was not all positive for him; in 1901, Minnie passed away, and in the same year, Willie also died, at the tender age of six.

It was the military that drew Roland in, and, in 1910, aged just 14 years old, he enlisted in the Coldstream Guards. According to the following year's census, he was stationed at the Ramillies Barracks in Aldershot, and held the rank of Boy.

Differing from the naval rank of the same name, lads of 14 or over could serve in any regiment as musicians, drummers, tailors, shoemakers, artificers or clerks, and all were ranked as boys. It seems likely, therefore, that his father's enthusiasm for music served him well.

When war broke out, he was of fighting age, and, as part of the "Old Contemptibles", he was involved in the Battle of Mons, the first major confrontation for the British Expeditionary Force.

During the war, Private Roberts took part in some of the most severe fighting on the Western Front, and was wounded three times, as well as being gassed. He was also recommended for the DCM for gallantry in action.

He transferred to the Labour Corps and spent time doing land work in Somerset. It was here that Roland met and married Gladys Pyne, whose family was from Bridgwater, and the couple tied the knot in March 1918.

Sadly, it was during this war service that Private Roberts contracted influenza and pneumonia and he passed away at his in-laws' home on 10th November 1918, the day before the Armistice was signed. He was just 22 years old.

The local newspaper reported on Roland's continued gallantry in its article on his funeral:

> [Roland] held the medal of the Royal Humane Society for saving a woman's life.
>
> He was also the hero of an incident that occurred in Bridgwater a few weeks ago, when he succeeded in checking the career of an infuriated bull through pluckily catching the animal by its horns.
>
> His disposition was always most cheerful, and although suffering from his [war] wounds a good deal, he never complained.
>
> The Cornishman: Wednesday 27th November 1918

Roland Roberts lies at rest in the Wembdon Road Cemetery in his adopted home town of Bridgwater, Somerset.

Name: Roberts, Samuel

Rank: Private

Regiment: Somerset Light Infantry

Date of death: 19th October 1914

Age at time of death: 39

Cause of death: Hodgkin's disease and mania

Grave location: St John's Cemetery, Bridgwater

Samuel Roberts was born in April 1875, one of seven children to William and Harriet Roberts from Bridgwater in Somerset. William worked as a labourer in a timber yard, though sadly he died young, when Samuel was only a child.

In the spring of 1899, Samuel married Rosina (or Rose) James, and the couple went on to have six children. Samuel was supporting his family working as a wicker chair maker, a roaring trade in a part of the county where reed beds were in plentiful supply.

Samuel's war grave suggests that he enlisted in the Somerset Light Infantry; this must have been early in the First World War, given that he passed away in October 1914. His pension records paint a slightly muddier picture, however. They give the cause of Private Roberts' death as Hodgkin's disease and mania, but suggest that:

> As it has not been possible to establish that Private S Roberts
> actually joined for service or was paid as a soldier during the
> war, Mrs Roberts' claim to [a] pension cannot be admitted.

> *WW1 Pension Ledger: Private Samuel Roberts*

Whether Samuel ever enlisted, or whether he only told Rose that he had, or whether, through his mania, he believed that he had, will likely never be uncovered. Either way, what can be established is that he passed away on 19th October 1914, at the age of 39 years old.

He lies at rest in St John's Cemetery in his home town of Bridgwater.

Name: Rochfort-Davies, Wallis

Rank: Second Lieutenant

Regiment: Somerset Light Infantry

Date of death: 8th March 1916

Age at time of death: 20

Cause of death: Overdose of morphia

Grave location: Milton Cemetery, Weston-super-Mare

Wallis Rowland Henry Rochfort-Davies was born August 1895, the youngest of two children to Reverend Charles Rochfort-Davies and his wife, Ethel. Charles was, for some time, the vicar at St Leonard's Church in Shipham, Somerset, and both Wallis and his older sister Agnes, were both at school until at least their late teens.

Details of Wallis' military service are scant. He enlisted in the Somerset Light Infantry and was assigned to the 3rd (Reserve) Battalion, which was based initially in Taunton and then Devonport, near Plymouth.

Sadly, the next information available for Wallis relates to his death. A contemporary local newspaper initially:

> It is reported that Sec.-Lieut. Wallis Rowland Henry Rochfort-Davies, 3rd (Reserve) Batt. Somerset LI, died on March 8th. He was the only son of Rev. CH Rochfort-Davies, of Shipham Rectory, Weston-super-Mare. Aged 20, he obtained his commission in Somerset LI in August 1914.
>
> Western Morning News: Thursday 16 March 1916

No details of the cause of Wallis' death were announced, but a post mortem and inquest were held, and the findings came out later that month:

> At the Coroner's Court yesterday afternoon, Mr AE Baker resumed the inquiry into the circumstances surrounding the death of Wallis Roland [sic] Henry Rochfort-Davies, aged 20, a Second Lieutenant in the Somerset Light Infantry. The inquest was opened on the 9th when evidence was given to the effect

that deceased was found dead at the Royal Hotel on March 8. The adjournment was rendered necessary in order that the contents of the stomach might be analysed.

Mr Russell, the City Analyst, gave evidence as to the examination of the contents of the stomach. This showed the presence of morphia.

Dr PW White said he was called to the Royal Hotel about 3:30 in the afternoon of March 8. He found the deceased lying in bed, life being extinct. Death had taken place probably 8 or 9 hours previously. There were no external marks of violence. The post mortem examination showed some congestion of the internal organs, but nothing to account for death. He had no hesitation in saying that the cause of death was morphia poisoning, probably hypodermically administered.

Charles Greenslade, a plain clothes officer, said he was called to the Royal Hotel on Wednesday 8 March about 4:30pm. Witness made an examination of the room. He found on the dressing table a case containing two small bottles: one was filled with morphia tablets and the other empty. There was also a blue bottle found, which contained a lotion. Needles and a hypodermic syringe were also found...

Reginald Francis Cheese, a friend of the deceased, said he had shown him some drugs on two occasions. He identified a case of drugs produced as having been shown him by the deceased.

The jury returned a verdict of "Death from an overdose of morphia, self-administered". The expressed sympathy with the father of the deceased and desired to severely censure the witness Cheese.

The Coroner spoke of the increased habit of drug taking among officers, and of the amount of drugs which the case that had been produced contained. Deceased, he said, could not have purchased from any chemist such a quantity of drugs, and it must have got into his hands through the medium of a friend. It was a grossly wicked act that such a large quantity of drugs was ever allowed to get into the hands of this unfortunate young man.

Western Daily Press: Friday 31st March 1916

Wallis Rowland Henry Rochfort-Davies was just 20 years old when he died. He was laid to rest in the Milton Cemetery in Weston-super-Mare, in his home county of Somerset.

Name: Rodgers, Percy

Rank: Sapper

Regiment: Canadian Engineers

Date of death: 5th November 1918

Age at time of death: 30

Cause of death: Pneumonia

Grave location: St John the Baptist Churchyard, Pilton

Percy Wright Rodgers was born in June 1888 in Pilton, Somerset. He was the fifth of eleven children to Levi and Elizabeth Rodgers.

In the 1901 census Levi was listed as a butcher and publican; ten years later, he listed himself as a butcher, slaughter man and shopkeeper.

Percy followed in his father's footsteps – by the time of the 1911 census, he was boarding with a family in Swanage, Dorset, and worked as a butcher's assistant.

1913 was a busy year for Percy. He married Frances Bower, they had their first child, Percy Augustus, and he emigrated to the United States (Frances and Percy Jr followed a year later).

In the 1915 New York census, Percy and his family are listed in the town of Cortland, around 200 miles north of New York City. Percy describes himself as a meat cutter – following in his father's footsteps – and he and his wife now have a second child, Vera, who was born in the States.

Sapper Rodgers joined the Canadian Engineers in May 1918; he was shipped abroad, back to Europe, but his service appeared short-lived. He contracted pneumonia, and was admitted to the Canadian Hospital in Eastbourne, East Sussex. He passed away on 5th November 1918, at 30 years of age.

Sapper Percy Wright Rodgers lies at rest in the churchyard of St John the Baptist in his home village of Pilton. His grave is topped with a cross dedicated by his widow, Frances.

Name: Roman, Walter

Rank: Private

Regiment: Somerset Light Infantry

Date of death: 28th July 1916

Age at time of death: 30

Cause of death: Died from wounds and sepsis

Grave location: Wembdon Road Cemetery, Bridgwater

Walter James 'Rattler' Roman was born in July 1880, one of six children to George and Betsy Roman. George was a labourer in a brickyard, and the family lived in Bridgwater in Somerset.

Walter's passion was rugby football, and he made the Bridgwater & Albion first team at the age of 15. Two years later he had reached county level and was playing for Somerset.

Walter enlisted in the army in around 1897, joining the Somerset Light Infantry. He spent several years abroad, serving as a Private in India and South Africa and fighting at Cawnpore and in the Second Boer War.

When Walter's service ended, he returned to England, and continued his rugby career. He was a regular for the Bridgwater and Somerset teams, gaining the nickname 'Rattler', before being signed up by Rochdale Hornets in 1910.

Walter married Henriette Washer in Bridgwater in April 1911, and the couple had two children, Edna – born in 1912 – and Leonard – who was born a year later.

Continuing with rugby union, Walter was called to county level, where he joined Lancashire for a number of games. Walter also played for England, receiving a cap in the international match against Wales in February 1914, and he toured Australia and New Zealand the same year.

War broke out, and Private Roman was re-enlisted, one of twenty-five Hornets players to enlist. He served on the Western Front with the 1st Battalion of the Somerset Light Infantry and was caught up in the engagements at Ypres and Armentieres. Fighting in the Battle of the Somme, he went over the top at Beaumont-Hamel at the start of fighting, on 1st July 1916 – his 36th birthday.

In that initial charge, he was shot several times, in both arms, a leg and the torso. Initially treated at a local field hospital, he was evacuated to England and admitted to the Voluntary Aid Hospital in Cheltenham. His condition initially improved, and he wrote letters to Henrietta, who was living back in Rochdale.

Sadly, Walter's contracted sepsis and his health deteriorated; Henrietta was called to the hospital in Cheltenham on 27th July 1916. It is likely that she didn't make it in time, as Walter passed away at 1pm the following day. He was just 36 years old.

Walter James Roman lies at rest in the Wembdon Road Cemetery in his home town of Bridgwater, Somerset, one of many sporting heroes to perish in the First World War.

Name: Rousell, Arthur

Rank: Private

Regiment: Lincolnshire Regiment

Date of death: 22nd February 1919

Age at time of death: 20

Cause of death: Illness

Grave location: St Mary's Churchyard, Huish Episcopi

Arthur Edward Rousell was born in the summer of 1898, one of five children to Henry and Lucy Rousell. Henry was a police constable in Worle, near Weston-super-Mare, and this is where he initially raised his family. By the time of the 1911 census – when Arthur was a schoolboy of 12 years old – the family had moved to the village of Huish Episcopi, on the outskirts of Langport.

Details of Arthur's military career are sketchy. Initially enlisting with the Royal Lancashire Regiment, he was soon transferred over to the 1st Battalion of the Lincolnshire Regiment. He certainly saw action abroad and was caught up on the Western Front.

Private Rousell was injured on 27th May 1918, this the first day of the Battle of Aisne. His battalion was certainly involved in the battle, but whether this was where he was injured, and what his injuries actually were, cannot be confirmed.

Evacuated back to England for treatment, Private Rousell was admitted to the South African Hospital in Richmond. Whether he was there for a long time, is not recorded, but he was certainly there in the nine months after he was wounded.

It seems that his injuries left him susceptible; his pension record confirms that he *"died of sickness"*, and it seems likely that this was one of the lung conditions – pneumonia, influenza – that was prevalent following the cessation of hostilities.

Private Arthur Edward Rousell died on 22nd February 1919, at the age of

20 years old. His body was brought back to Huish Episcopi, and he lies at rest in the family grave in the graveyard of St Mary's Church.

Name: Rowsell, Cyril

Rank: Private

Regiment: Somerset Light Infantry

Date of death: 30th April 1918

Age at time of death: 21

Cause of death: Died from wounds

Grave location: St Lawrence's Churchyard, Westbury-sub-Mendip

Cyril John Rowsell was born in the spring of 1897, one of four children to John and Edith Rowsell. John had been married previously, to a woman called Martha. She had died in 1893, not long after giving birth to the second of their two children – sadly, the child died when little more than a babe in arms. Cyril, therefore, had a half-sibling in his older brother Albert, as well as two full brothers, Richard and George, and a sister, Irene.

Cyril had been born in the Somerset village of Yeovil Marsh, but his father had moved the family to nearby Haselbury Plucknett, where he was the local miller.

John Rowsell was obviously a man of many talents, because, by the 1911 census, he was listed as a dairy manager. By now Cyril was 14 years old, and the family had moved again, this time to the village of Westbury-sub-Mendip, near Wells.

War was on the horizon, and Cyril seemed keen to play his part as early as he could. Full details of his military service are not readily available, but it is evident that he enlisted soon after the conflict began.

Cyril enlisted in the Somerset Light Infantry in 1914 and was assigned to the 1st Battalion as a Private. The Somerset Light Infantry were involved in a number of the fiercest battles on the Western Front, and he seems to have been lucky enough to escape injury until April 1918.

During the Battle of Bethune, Private Rowsell was shot and injured. Initially treated at the scene, he was evacuated to England and admitted to the General Hospital in Birmingham. Sadly, he did not recover from his wounds, and he passed away on 30th April 1918. He was just 21 years of age.

Cyril John Rowsell lies at peace in the graveyard of St Lawrence's Church in Westbury-sub-Mendip, Somerset.

Name: Russ, Stanley

Rank: Lieutenant

Regiment: Royal Army Service Corps

Date of death: 28th October 1920

Age at time of death: 32

Cause of death: Illness

Grave location: Wells Cemetery

Stanley Hugh Russ was born in 1888, the youngest of five children to Alfred and Elizabeth. The family lived in Wells, Somerset, where Alfred worked as Clerk to the Guardians of the local workhouse. They were doing well for themselves, as they had two domestic servants at the time of the 1891 census.

Stanley seems to have been a studious young man, and by 1911 was boarding in London, where he was a dental student.

Details of Stanley's military service are scant, but he obviously did well at his job, and rose to the rank of Lieutenant. The local newspaper gave a good overview of his life when reporting on his funeral:

> The deceased gentleman was a dentist by profession, and served his apprenticeship with Mr Goddard of Wells. He afterwards went to London, where for some years he had been following his profession at Guy's Hospital.
>
> At the outbreak of war he joined the Middlesex Yeomanry as a trooper. He was later given a commission in the same regiment... After much service in France, he was, by reason of a physical disability incurred whilst on service, transferred to the Royal Army Service Corps (Mechanical Transport).
>
> He again went to France and was attached to the North Somerset Yeomanry. He was invalided home, but went out a third time, being attached to a Canadian Siege Battery. He took part in the great push around Arras and Vimy Ridge.
>
> He returned to England in October 1918, suffering from heart

trouble, severe shell shock, and slight gassing. He was discharged from hospital in January 1919 and demobilised in the following March.

His health gave way, and he was subsequently operated on by a Harley Street specialist. He derived little benefit, and was afterwards removed to a nursing home, where he died.

The deceased gentleman, who was unmarried, was of a very bright and happy disposition, and enjoyed a wide circle of friends.

Wells Journal: Friday 5th November 1920

Stanley Hugh Russ died on 28th October 1920. He was 32 years old. He lies at rest in the cemetery of his home city of Wells.

Name: Russell, John

Rank: Private

Regiment: West Somerset Yeomanry

Date of death: 20th October 1915

Age at time of death: 19

Cause of death: Car accident

Grave location: Churchyard of the Blessed Virgin Mary and All Saints, Meare

Born in September 1896, John Russell was one of thirteen children to Henry and Ellen Russell. Henry worked as a turf cutter on the Somerset levels, and the family lived in the village of Meare, near Glastonbury.

By the time of the 1911 census, John, aged 15, had left school and joined his father's business.

When war broke out, John joined up; sadly, his military records are absent, but what we do know for certain is that he enlisted in the West Somerset Yeomanry and was based at the Stanway Camp near Colchester in Essex.

Sadly, much is written of Private Russell's death. He was acting as a sentry at the camp on the morning of Tuesday 19th October 1915 when he was hit by a car; taken to the Military Hospital in Colchester, he passed away the following morning.

An inquest was held into the incident, and the following was ascertained:

Vera Coysh, aged 19, was driving near the camp with two friends and her gardener; as she was approaching the entrance, a horse-drawn military wagon ahead of her turned and she swerved to avoid it. In doing so, she hit Private Russell *"and carried him some way along the ground"*.

John's injuries were significant. When admitted to hospital, he *"was suffering from bruises on the back of the head and haemorrhage from the right ear and nose. His left hand and the lower part of his left arm were swollen from bruising. He was semi-conscious and restless..."*

The inquest identified some discrepancies in what happened.

Witnesses in the military wagon and a second one following it all saw a turning signal being given, although not necessarily in time for Vera to slow down or stop. All of the army witnesses stated that she was driving at a quick speed, possibly as much as 35mph.

Vera and her passengers all stated that they saw no signal, saying that the wagon pulled across without indication. They also stated that they were not travelling at speed.

The inquest was a lengthy one, but the final verdict was one of accidental death, with a recommendation that signs were put up on the road to warn of the entrance to the camp.

John Russell was just 19 years old when he died. He was laid to rest in the graveyard of the Church of the Blessed Virgin Mary and All Saints in his home village of Meare, Somerset.

It's worth also having a look into the life of the driver of that fated motor car.

Vera Murdoch Coysh was born in September 1896, the eldest child of Commander William Henry Coysh and his wife Beatrice Murdoch. The family lived in Yorkshire and, by the time of the incident, William and Beatrice had had four other children – Humphrey Cecil (who became a Commander), Geoffrey Ernest (who went on to be Sub Lieutenant), John William and Barbara Daphne.

Three months after the accident, Vera married Second Lieutenant Trevor Davidson, of the Essex Regiment, and the couple soon emigrated to Mozambique.

All was not well, however, as, by 1924, Vera has moved back to England, the couple had divorced, and she had remarried, to a Douglas Stuart-Jervis. The couple went on to have two children.

Meanwhile, Vera was also making a bit of a name for herself in the literary world, writing a number of novels under the name of Jane England. While rarely seen nowadays, she wrote books with such 'pulp fiction' titles as *Red Earth*, *Romantic Stranger*, *Flowering Harvest*, *Stormy Passage* and *Winter Jasmine*.

It's bittersweet to see that Vera made a life for herself, in the way that John Russell was sadly unable to.

Name: Sams, Edward

Rank: Private

Regiment: Somerset Light Infantry

Date of death: 5th April 1916

Age at time of death: Unknown

Cause of death: Unknown

Grave location: Milton Cemetery, Weston-super-Mare

In a corner of the Milton Cemetery in Weston-super-Mare, Somerset, stands the gravestone of Edward Sams. It gives little information away, other than the fact that he passed away on 5th April 1916, and that he served as a Private in the Somerset Light Infantry.

There is no documentation – military or otherwise – that can be concretely connected to Private Sams. None of the available documents for Edward Sams include the service number on his gravestone, and there is nothing to provide a definite date of birth or familial connections.

Sams was not an uncommon Somerset name at the start of the twentieth century, and there are a number of men by that name called Edward in the area at the time. Again, however, the information is lacking that allows us to directly connect any of these names with the gravestone in the Weston-super-Mare cemetery.

There is nothing in any contemporary newspapers to suggest that Private Sams' passing was anything out of the ordinary.

Sadly, therefore, he remains a name lost to history. Edward Sams, whoever he was, and however he died, lies at rest in a Somerset cemetery.

Name: Scott, George

Rank: Corporal Wheeler

Regiment: Royal Field Artillery

Date of death: 24th October 1919

Age at time of death: 44

Cause of death: Unknown

Grave location: St Mary's Cemetery, Taunton

George William Scott is destined to be one of those names who is sadly lost to time. While there *is* information relating to him, there is not enough detail to flesh out a concrete history around him.

The facts that we *do* know about George are that his parents were John and Mary who, at the time that his grave was commemorated, were living in County Tyrone in Northern Ireland.

George enlisted in the Royal Field Artillery in November 1914. He was assigned to the 5th Battery of the 45th Brigade and given the rank of Wheeler – one of the positions in a team of horses, pulling the artillery.

During his service, George was awarded the 1914 Star, as well as the Victory and British Medals. He seems to have been in a bit of trouble to begin with, however, as he was reverted down to Gunner because of misconduct. This may only have been temporary, as he ended with the rank of Corporal Wheeler.

And that is it, that is all the concrete information available for George Scott. How he died is a mystery, lost to time.

George William Scott lies at rest in St Mary's Cemetery in Taunton, Somerset.

Name: Scribbens, Cecil

Rank: Leading Stoker

Regiment: Royal Navy

Date of death: 24th June 1919

Age at time of death: 34

Cause of death: Pneumonia

Grave location: St James' Cemetery, Taunton

Cecil Walter Thomas Scribbens was born on 27th June 1885 in Taunton, Somerset. He was one of five children to George and Ann Scribbens. Sadly, George passed away when Cecil was a toddler, leaving his widow to raise her young family alone.

Ann initially found work as a laundress, and her eldest daughter, Alice, began working at the local silk mill when she left school. This brought in a little money, but with five children to feed and clothe, it must have been a struggle.

In 1894, Ann found love again, and married George Sully, a scull labourer, on Christmas Day 1894. The couple went on to have a child together, a son they called Arthur, and the new family set up home in Taunton.

When he left school, Cecil found work as a labourer, but he had a sense of adventure and a life on the ocean was calling him. In July 1903 he joined the Royal Navy as a Stoker 2nd Class and, after his initial training in Plymouth he was assigned to HMS Russell.

Stoker Scribbens' term of service was twelve years, and during that time, he served aboard five vessels, and was promoted to Leading Stoker. War had broken out when his initial contract ended, so it was extended until the end of the hostilities.

After five years aboard HMS Cornwall and eighteen months on HMS Cleopatra, Leading Stoker Scribbens was assigned to HMS Concord, which would turn out to be his last vessel, in December 1916. He stayed with this ship for nearly three years until falling ill in June 1919.

Brought back to England, he was admitted to the Military Hospital in Taunton with pneumonia. Leading Stoker Scribbens died from this lung disease on 24th June 1919, at the age of 34 years old.

Cecil Walter Thomas Scribbens was laid to rest in the St James' Cemetery in his home town.

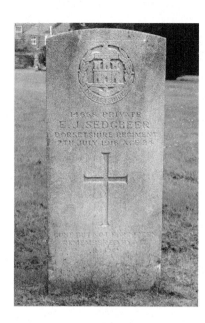

Name: Sedgbeer, Ernest

Rank: Private

Regiment: Dorsetshire Regiment

Date of death: 7th July 1916

Age at time of death: 24

Cause of death: Died of wounds

Grave location: St James' Cemetery, Taunton

Ernest John Sedgbeer was born in Taunton in the summer of 1891, the second of seven children to Henry and Alice Sedgbeer. Henry worked in a foundry, and his son joined him as a labourer.

By the time of the 1911 census, most of the nine members of the family disappear from the records – it is likely that these were lost – but both father and son are to be found living in South Wales – Henry working as a furnace stoker in the Rhondda, Ernest as a labourer below ground in Llanwonno, near Pontypridd.

Ernest seems to have had an opportunity to find other employment and started work for Great Western Railways in February 1914. War was imminent, however, and a little over a year later, he had enlisted.

Ernest first joined the Duke of Cornwall's Light Infantry as a Private but transferred over to the Dorsetshire Regiment. He was certainly involved in fighting on the Western Front, although full details of his military service are not documented.

His records show that he was awarded the Victory and British Medals and the 1915 Star. Private Sedgbeer was wounded in July 1916 and medically evacuated back to England, where he was admitted to King's Hospital in Lambeth. Sadly, he was to die of his injuries on 7th July 1916, aged just 25 years old.

Ernest John Sedgbeer lies at rest in the St James' Cemetery in his home town of Taunton, Somerset.

Name: Selman, Walter

Rank: Private

Regiment: Wiltshire Regiment

Date of death: 7th April 1918

Age at time of death: 18

Cause of death: Unknown

Grave location: Holy Trinity Churchyard, Burrington

Walter Charles Selman was born on 7th June 1899, the youngest of four children to Walter and Annie Selman. Walter Sr was a gardener and, by the time of the 1911 census he had moved the family to the sleepy Somerset village of Burrington.

Sadly, there is little documentation surrounding Walter's young life. His gravestone confirms that he enlisted in the Wiltshire Regiment; although there is no date to confirm when he enrolled, it is likely to have been in the second half of the conflict, given his age.

Private Selman was assigned to the 4th Battalion, but there is no clear confirmation of where he served. The 1/4th Battalion fought in India and Egypt; the 2/4th was also based in India but remained there for the duration. The 3/4th Battalion – the most likely to be Walter's troop – was a reserve troop, based on home soil.

Where little is known about Private Selman's military service, there is similarly little information about his passing. His pension records bluntly put his cause of death as 'disease'; as with many other recruits towards the end of the war, it is likely that this was, in fact, either influenza or pneumonia.

Sadly, the mustering of the Allied armies – and the associated mixing of young men from across the country in crowded barracks – brought a real danger of disease, and lung complaints were commonplace. While there is no definite proof, it appears that Private Selman may have succumbed to one of these conditions; he passed away in a Military Hospital on Salisbury Plain on 7th April 1918, two months short of his 19th birthday.

Walter Charles Selman lies at rest in the graveyard of Holy Trinity Church in his home village of Burrington, Somerset.

Name: Smith, Ernest

Rank: Driver

Regiment: Australian Army Medical Corps

Date of death: 8th October 1919

Age at time of death: 36

Cause of death: Malignant cysts

Grave location: St Mary's Churchyard, Bruton

Ernest John Smith was born in 1883, one of seven children to John Smith and his wife Sarah Jane. John was a coal merchant, and the family lived in the Somerset town of Bruton. When Ernest initially left school, he worked as a farm labourer, but at some point, a sense of adventure caught him, and he emigrated to Australia. Sadly, details of his travels are not available, but he left England at some point before 1915.

When war broke out, however, he was still keen to do his bit. He was living in Queensland when he enlisted on 26th October 1915, and was assigned to the Australian Army Medical Corps.

Driver Smith's battalion left Australia for Europe in March 1916 and served in France for the duration. He was dogged by ill health, catching pleurisy a couple of times, and had a number of fibromas operated on.

In October 1918, he was appointed Lance Corporal, but was shipped back to England later that year with ongoing fibroma issues. He was admitted to Torquay Hospital as dangerously ill in December of that year and spent most of the next nine months in hospital, initially in Torquay, but then when he was able to be moved, he was transferred to the 1st Australian General Hospital near Warminster.

Sadly, the cysts Driver Smith had developed were malignant, and he passed away on 8th October 1919. He was just 36 years old.

Ernest John Smith was brought back to his home town for burial and lies at rest in the graveyard of St Mary's Church in Bruton.

Name: Smith, Francis

Rank: Private

Regiment: Royal Army Service Corps

Date of death: 6th March 1915

Age at time of death: 25

Cause of death: Pneumonia

Grave location: Wells Cemetery

Francis George Smith was born in Glasgow in 1890. Records are scattered, but some of the pieces pull together to give an outline of his life.

The son of William and Mary Smith, Francis was the fourth of six children. His tombstone confirms that William had worked as an optician but passed away when Francis was a young man.

Francis was an electrical engineer and had assisted Mary in her business in Glasgow before signing up.

Private Smith enlisted early on in the war, "*on February 24th of this year [1915], when he left his native city for London, where he joined the motor transport section of the Army Service Corps*" [*Wells Journal, Friday 12th March 1915*].

Billeted in Wells, he had been assigned to the 133 Mechanical Transport Company. Within weeks of moving there, however, it seems that Francis fell ill. Sadly, his was a life cut too short, and he passed away from pneumonia on 6th March 1915, aged just 25 years old.

Francis George Smith lies at rest in the cemetery in Wells.

Name: Southwood, Stanley

Rank: Lance Corporal

Regiment: Somerset Light Infantry

Date of death: 8th September 1919

Age at time of death: 25

Cause of death: Pneumonia

Grave location: Wembdon Road Cemetery, Bridgwater

Stanley James Southwood was born in 1896, the oldest of six children to John and Florence Southwood from Bridgwater, Somerset. John was a labourer and ship's mate, while Stanley, who was the only boy in the family, started work loading barrows in a brickyard.

Military life was pulling Stanley, however. According to another researcher, he enlisted in the Special Reserves of the Somerset Light Infantry in October 1912. Six months later he joined the regular army and was there when the war began.

While I have not been able to corroborate this information, it appears that Southwood was reported missing on 11th September 1915, after being wounded in the chest. He was taken prisoner of war, and, while being held, he developed tuberculosis in both lungs.

After his release (no documents confirm when this was) he was discharged from the army as medically unfit to continue. He was in a Military Hospital at the time – the beginning of November 1918 – suffering from tuberculosis, which had been exacerbated by the chest wound he had received three years earlier. At the time he was discharged, he had the rank of Lance Corporal.

Sadly, it seems that Stanley never fully recovered from his wartime experience. He died on 8th September 1919 from consumption (tuberculosis), aged just 23 years old.

Stanley James Southwood lies at rest in the Wembdon Road Cemetery in his home town of Bridgwater in Somerset.

Name: Spiller, Herbert

Rank: Private

Regiment: Somerset Light Infantry

Date of death: 7th May 1920

Age at time of death: 39

Cause of death: Unknown

Grave location: St James' Cemetery, Taunton

Herbert George Spiller was born in 1881, the second of four children to George and Emily Spiller. George was a timber merchant and ironmonger, born in Taunton, Somerset, who raised his family in his home town.

When Herbert left school, he found work as a clerk in a solicitor's office, and this was the trade he followed, eventually becoming a solicitor in his own right.

In March 1907, he married Winifred Lewis, an outfitter's daughter, and the couple soon emigrated, arriving in Perth, Australia, later that year. They had two children in Australia: a son, who sadly passed as a babe in arms, and a daughter. Within three years, however, the Spillers were back living in England again and went on to have four further children, three of whom survived infancy.

War had arrived, and Herbert enlisted on 11th December 1915, but was initially placed as a reserve. He was finally called to do his duty for King and

Country on 6th September 1917 and joined the 28th Battalion of the London Regiment. After initial training, Private Spiller was sent out to the Front, arriving in France in April 1918.

Herbert was back on home soil after three months, suffering from albuminuria (a disease of the kidneys) and served in territorial depots until he was demobbed in December 1918.

At this point, Herbert disappears from the records. It seems likely that his illness was the cause of his passing, but this cannot be confirmed. Either way, Herbert George Spiller died on 7th May 1920, at the age of 39 years old. He lies at rest in the St James' Cemetery in his home town of Taunton, Somerset.

While Private Spiller was afforded a Commonwealth War Grave, his exact burial location is not identifiable. The image at the top of this post, therefore, is of the other family graves in the cemetery.

Name: Stainton, John

Rank: Private

Regiment: Royal Lancashire Regiment

Date of death: 11th August 1916

Age at time of death: 45

Cause of death: Died of wounds

Grave location: St Andrew's Churchyard, Clevedon

John Stainton was born in the Cumbrian village of Ambleside in January 1871. He was one of seven children to George and Mary Stainton, a labourer and his wife. John followed in his father's footsteps as a labourer, as they took him to where the work was – by the time John was ten, the family were living in Barrow-in-Furness.

The 1911 census found John married to a woman called Mary. The couple wed in 1909 and were boarding with Maybrooke Cole, a fellow labourer, and his family.

The next record for John comes in the form of his enlistment papers. He joined up on 31st August 1914, but the document throws up a couple of anomalies.

To the question "Are you married?" John marked "No". The fact that he didn't confirm he was a widower presents more questions than answers.

The document also confirms that he has previous military experience. He served with 2nd Battalion King's Own (Royal Lancaster Regiment), which fought in the Second Boer War, and was involved in the Battle of Spion Kop in January 1900.

John re-enlisted in the same battalion on 31st August 1914 and remained part of a territorial force for the best part of a year. It was during this time that he married Rhoda Selina Cooper. She was born and brought up in Clevedon, Somerset, and it can only be assumed that John was stationed in the county at this time.

Private Stainton seemed to have a bit of a rebellious streak, and his service records identify three times when he was pulled up for dereliction of duty. In December 1914, he was admonished for overstaying his leave pass; in June 1915 he was reported for being absent from the base; a year later, he was admonished again, this time for losing a pair of handcuffs.

The battalion were sent to France in July 1915, and, in the end, Private Stainton served on the Western Front for just over a year. On 27th July 1916, he was wounded by shrapnel in the right shoulder, face and thigh, and was evacuated back to England for treatment. Admitted to the English General Hospital in Cambridge, sadly his wounds proved too much for him. Private Stainton died on 11th August 1916, at the age of 45 years old.

John Stainton's body was brought back to his widow; he lies at rest in the picturesque churchyard of St Andrew's in Clevedon, Somerset.

The Commonwealth War Grave for John Stainton incorrectly gives his name as T Stainton.

Name: Steadman, Joseph

Rank: Guardsman

Regiment: Coldstream Guards

Date of death: 1st November 1917

Age at time of death: 25

Cause of death: Died of wounds

Grave location: Wembdon Road Cemetery, Bridgwater

Joseph Richard Steadman was born in Ellesmere Port, Cheshire, in 1892. One of seven children to William and Mary Ann Steadman, his father worked as a slab maker for the local council.

Sadly, Joseph's mother died in 1899, at the age of just 40. William had moved the family to Birmingham by this point, and, on leaving school, Joseph found work with a jeweller as a scratch brusher.

Moving to London, Joseph met Ethel May Tambling, who was originally from Somerset, and the couple married at the beginning of 1914. Ethel already had a child – Frederick – and the young couple also had a son, Alfred, who was born in July 1914.

War was on the horizon, and Joseph was quick to enlist. He joined the Coldstream Guards, embarking for France a month after Alfred was born. An elite force, the Guards were involved in some of the heaviest fighting of the war, including the Battles of Mons, Ypres, Loos, Somme, Passchendaele and Cambrai. It is likely that Guardsman Steadman was caught up in many of these engagements.

His luck was to run out, however, and Joseph was injured towards the end of October 1917. Shipped back to England for treatment, he was admitted to the King George Hospital in London. Sadly, Guardsman Steadman did not recover from his wounds; he died on 1st November 1917, aged just 25 years old.

Joseph Richard Steadman lies at rest in the Wembdon Road Cemetery in Bridgwater, Somerset.

Name: Stelling, Ernest

Rank: Serjeant

Regiment: Somerset Light Infantry

Date of death: 18th December 1916

Age at time of death: 38

Cause of death: Influenza and pneumonia

Grave location: St Mary's Cemetery, Taunton

Ernest Leonard Stelling was born in the summer of 1881, the oldest of six children to Charles and Bertha Stelling. Charles was a tailor from London, and while Ernest was born in Suffolk, by the time of the 1891 census, the family had settled in Reading, Berkshire.

Ernest followed in his father's footsteps, becoming a tailor and cutter in his own right. He met a woman from Reading called Lettie Eliza Mazey, and the couple married in 1904. The couple set up home with Lettie's brother and his family in Tilehurst but didn't go on to have any children themselves.

Details of Ernest's military service are a bit scarce. He initially enlisted in the Royal Berkshire Regiment, but quickly moved to the Somerset Light Infantry in the early stages of the First World War.

Sadly, no formal documents of Ernest's time in the army are available, but a local newspaper gave a good insight into his Somerset service:

DEATH OF A MASTER TAILOR

After an illness of only seven days, the death took place at the military hospital on Monday afternoon of Sergeant EL Stelling, who has been master tailor of the Depot for the past two years. The cause of death was pneumonia, and the loss of so popular a member of the Depot staff is deeply regretted by all ranks.

Sergeant Stelling, who was 37 years of age, came to the Somersets from the Royal Berkshire Regiment, and succeeded the late Sergeant-Master-Tailor Chambers. He was a native of

Reading, and one of four brothers serving their King and country. His father, Mr Charles Stelling, for many years carried on business as a master tailor in Reading.

Since he had been at Taunton barracks, Sergeant Stelling had made many friends, and actively identified himself with the social life of the sergeants' mess, taking a prominent part in the arrangement of concerts, etc.

He was of a bright, generous disposition, and before his illness he was making a collection at the Depot on behalf of the Buffaloes' Christmas treat to poor children of the town. He was a valued member of the local Lodge of the Royal Order of Buffaloes, and his death is greatly regretted by all the brethren.

He leaves a widow but no family. Much sympathy is felt for Mrs Stelling, who has for some years been a confirmed invalid.

The funeral took place with full military honours at St Mary's Cemetery on Friday afternoon.

Taunton Courier and Western Advertiser: Wednesday 27th December 1916

This gives a real insight into Ernest's personal life. He was obviously very active socially and committed to the community. Whether Lettie's infirmity contributed to the couple's lack of family will never be known, but, from his support of the poor children of Taunton, it seems evident that he would have been a good family man.

The next document relating to Serjeant Stelling is his pension record; this confirms the news article's report that he contracted pneumonia and influenza, and he succumbed to the conditions on 18th December 1916. He had, in fact, just turned 38 years old.

Ernest Leonard Stelling lies at rest in St Mary's Cemetery in his wartime adopted home town of Taunton, Somerset.

Name: Stephens, Harry

Rank: Serjeant

Regiment: Royal Army Veterinary Corps

Date of death: 5th July 1918

Age at time of death: 45

Cause of death: Heart failure

Grave location: St James' Cemetery, Taunton

Harry Stephens was born in Banwell, near Weston-super-Mare on 4th January 1873. He was one of six children to Frederick Stephens and his wife, Emma. Frederick was a butcher, and this was a trade that both Harry and his older brother, Fred, would go into when they left school.

It appears that being a butcher was not the full-time career that Harry was looking for, and so, in the 1890s, he found other employment as a farmer, and moved to Lynton, on the north coast of Devon.

It was here that he met Norah Watts, another farmer's daughter and, in 1898, the couple married. They set up home at Furzehill Farm, and went on to have four children, Frederick, Alice, Albert and Herbert.

By the time of the 1911 census, Harry had moved his family back to Banwell, where they lived in a four-roomed house on the High Street. Harry was now a cattle dealer, and was presumably supplying meat to his mother who, having been widowed in 1902, was now running the butcher's shop with three of Harry's siblings.

War was coming, though, and on 21st July 1915, Harry enlisted. Given his farming background, he was assigned to the Army Veterinary Corps and, while remaining on the Home Front, over the next few years he gained promotion.

Towards the end of 1917, when Serjeant Stephens was serving in Romsey, Hampshire, he fell ill, complaining of chest pains and breathlessness. He was taken to Hursley Hospital near Winchester for cardiac checks, and it became apparent that he was no longer fit for active duty.

Discharged from military service on 5th July 1918, he returned home. Admitted to the Military Hospital in Taunton, it was only a matter of weeks later that Serjeant Stephens passed away. He was 45 years of age.

Harry Stephens was laid to rest in the St James' Cemetery in Taunton.

Name: Stevens, William

Rank: Corporal

Regiment: Royal Field Artillery

Date of death: 2nd November 1916

Age at time of death: 32

Cause of death: Myalgia

Grave location: Wells Cemetery

William Charles Stevens was born in Wells in 1884. The eldest child of Alfred and Susan, William was one of eleven children. Alfred worked at the local paper mill, while William became a labourer, and found work as a stonemason.

William seemed keen to improve his prospects, however; he enlisted in the army at the start of 1903, serving in the Royal Field Artillery for a period of four years, before being demobbed to the reserves.

On Christmas Day 1907, William married Minnie Bailey; the census four years later gives the young couple as living in their home city. William, by now, was labouring on the railway, and the census shows, they had had a child, who had sadly passed away.

War was looming, and Gunner Stevens was recalled to duty in August 1914. Quickly posted overseas with the 23rd Brigade, he fell ill with myalgia and was shipped home to recover towards the end of the year.

Sent back to the front in 1915, William was promoted to Corporal and transferred to the 51st (Howitzer) Brigade. Sadly, his 'tremble' returned, and he was sent back to England in October 1915. By this point, Minnie had given birth to their second child, a little girl they called Lilian.

Corporal Stevens' condition continued, and he was medically discharged in March 1916. No further records exist, but it seems that he finally succumbed to the condition later that year. He passed away on 2nd November 1916, aged 32 years old.

William Charles Stevens lies at peace in the cemetery of his home city, Wells in Somerset.

Name: Stodgell, Charles

Rank: Private

Regiment: Devonshire Regiment

Date of death: 2nd February 1919

Age at time of death: 40

Cause of death: Influenza

Grave location: St Peter & St Paul's Churchyard, North Curry

Charles William Stodgell was born in Somerset in 1878, the eldest son of Samuel and Mary Stodgell. His father was an agricultural labourer, while his mother was a glover. Charles followed into farm work, becoming a carter by time of the 1901 census.

Charles married Mabel Duke in 1898 and the young couple had two daughters in the following few years.

When war came, Charles was called up. He enlisted in June 1916, joining the Devonshire Regiment before being transferred to the Agricultural Company. His record shows that he stood at 5ft 6ins (1.67m) and weighed 10st 2lbs (64kg) and his build, health and experience is probably why he ended up in service where he did.

Private Stodgell was demobbed at the end of the war and returned home on furlough. Sadly, before he was fully demobbed, he contracted influenza, and died on 2nd February 1919.

Charles William Stodgell lies at rest in his home village of North Curry, in the churchyard of St Peter & St Paul's.

Name: Stone, Frank

Rank: Private

Regiment: Somerset Light Infantry

Date of death: 8th February 1919

Age at time of death: 20

Cause of death: Unknown

Grave location: St Mary's Cemetery, Taunton

Francis Jesse Stone – known as Frank – was born in 1899, one of five children to William and Sarah Stone. William was a general handyman – his census records record him variously as a labourer, carpenter and carman (or carter) – and the family lived in the village of Bishop's Hull, on the outskirts of Taunton, Somerset.

Given when he was born, documentation for Frank's early life is limited to the 1901 and 1911 censuses. We are restricted, therefore, to the information provided by the medal rolls.

Frank was underage when he joined up. He enlisted in the Somerset Light Infantry on 27th December 1914, when he could only have been 15 years old. He was assigned to the Depot Battalion and was shipped to France the following year.

Sadly, there is little other information about Private Stone. He survived the war and returned to England but passed away on 8th February 1919. No cause of death is evident, but it seems likely to have been one of the lung conditions running rampant across the country at the time, probably influenza, tuberculosis or pneumonia. When he died, Frank was just 20 years old.

Frank Jesse Stone lies at rest in St Mary's Cemetery in his home town of Taunton, Somerset.

Name: Stone, George

Rank: Shoeing Smith

Regiment: Royal Army Service Corps

Date of death: 19th November 1918

Age at time of death: 47

Cause of death: Pneumonia

Grave location: St Michael & All Angels' Churchyard, Milverton

George Henry Stone was born in 1872, son of Milverton's blacksmith James Stone and his wife Mary Ann. He followed in his father's footsteps and, by the time he married Mary Florence Paul in 1894, he was also working in the forge in Milverton.

George and Mary had eight children – seven girls and one boy; by the time he signed up in 1915, he listed himself as a blacksmith.

His military records show that he was medically certified as Category B2 (suitable to serve in France, and able to walk 5 miles, see and hear sufficiently for ordinary purposes). He was assigned to the Remount Depot in Swaythling, Southampton, which was built specifically to supply horses and mules for war service. (In the years it was operating, Swaythling processed some 400,000 animals, as well as channelling 25,000 servicemen to the front.)

While serving, George contracted pneumonia. He was treated in Netley Military Hospital, but passed away on 19th November 1918, aged 47.

Shoeing Smith George Henry Stone lies at peace in a quiet corner of St Michael & All Angel's churchyard in his home village of Milverton.

Name: Strong, Percy

Rank: Able Seaman

Regiment: Royal Navy

Date of death: 9th October 1918

Age at time of death: 21

Cause of death: Drowned

Grave location: Shepton Mallet Burial Ground

Percy William Strong was born in April 1897, the youngest of five children to Albert Strong and his wife Elizabeth. The family lived in Shepton Mallet, Somerset, where Albert worked as a mason's labourer.

Percy was keen to make his own way in the world. By the 1911 census, and having left school, he was working as a farm boy on Kingsdown Farm in Shepton, alongside a couple of other paid, and boarding, employees.

He seemed to have been after adventure in his life too; in January 1913, he enlisted in the Royal Navy, getting his training on a number of vessels, even before the start of the Great War. In his six years of service, he was promoted from Boy to Able Seaman, and served on nine ships.

Able Seaman Strong's final assignment was at HMS Idaho, the naval base in Milford Haven, Pembrokeshire, which he joined in May 1918. It was while he was stationed at HMS Idaho that tragedy would strike:

> *A boat belonging to a Government Patrol-boat capsized in Milford Haven, when three members of the crew lost their lives. They were Sub-Lieutenant Lever (20), Birkenhead; Leading Seaman Thomas Palmer (30) Shepton Mallet; and AB Percy Strong (21), Shepton Mallet.*
>
> *The boat, containing six men, had come ashore in a rough sea. It left Milford Haven Naval stage on return to the ship at eleven am. A sharp squall caught the men when well out on their return journey, and this the craft failed to weather, and was capsized. The six occupants were cast into the sea, and despite the efforts*

*of men in boats from other vessels, the three named were
drowned, and the others had a narrow escape.*

Western Mail: Friday 11th October 1918

Able Seaman Strong lost his life on 9th October 1918. He was just 21 years old.

Percy William Strong's body was returned to Shepton Mallet, the town of his birth, and lies at rest in the cemetery there.

Name: Symes, Joseph

Rank: Gunner

Regiment: Royal Field Artillery

Date of death: 4th March 1921

Age at time of death: 44

Cause of death: Unknown

Grave location: Milton Cemetery, Weston-super-Mare

Joseph Symes was born in May 1876 and was the youngest of ten children to Joseph and Caroline Symes. Joseph Sr was a shoemaker who had been born in Shepton Mallet, Somerset, but who had moved to Bristol for work in the late 1860s.

As with some of his older siblings, Joseph Jr followed in his father's shoemaking footsteps. He worked as a boot clicker, punching the eye holes in footwear, and cutter, taking the shaped pieces out of large leather hides.

In June 1905, he married Emily Delling, who was also from Bristol, and the couple went on to have a son, Douglas, a year later. The couple moved into a two-up-two-down terraced house in a cul-de-sac to the north-east of the city centre.

War was coming to the British Isles. Full details of Joseph's military service no longer exist; however, his gravestone confirms that he enlisted in the Royal Field Artillery.

There is no documentation to confirm whether Gunner Symes saw active service abroad; he certainly survived the war, but in February 1919 was discharged on medical grounds, suffering from myalgia. He was granted a pension, and the family soon replaced the busy city life for a quieter one down the coast in Weston-super-Mare.

Joseph's trail goes cold for a couple of years, and he passed away on 4th March 1921, at the age of 44 years old. Sadly, there is nothing to confirm the cause of his death; it seems likely that his ongoing medical condition got the better of him.

Joseph Symes was laid to rest in the Milton Cemetery in Weston-super-Mare.

Name: Symons, George

Rank: Private

Regiment: Somerset Light Infantry

Date of death: 23rd June 1918

Age at time of death: 23

Cause of death: Unknown

Grave Location: St Michael & All Angels' Churchyard, Milverton

George Symons was born in 1895 to Charles and Rosa Symons. He was the third of five sons.

Charles worked as a carter on a farm, and his son became a cowman as soon as he could leave school.

Military records for George Symons are pretty sparse. From his gravestone we know he joined the Somerset Light Infantry; the Army's Register of Soldiers' Effects confirm that he died in a Military Hospital on home soil; £23 7s 11d went to his father.

It can be assumed, therefore, that Private Symons served with his regiment on the Western Front, was injured and brought home for treatment or rehabilitation. He passed on 23rd June 1918, aged 23 years old.

Private George Symons lies at rest in the churchyard of St Michael and All Angels' in Milverton.

Name: Symons, Rudolph

Rank: Lieutenant

Regiment: Army Service Corps

Date of death: 13th September 1915

Age at time of death: 27

Cause of death: Motorcycle accident

Grave location: Wembdon Road Cemetery, Bridgwater

Rudolph Clifford Symons was born in the autumn of 1887, one of ten children to Clifford and Clara Symons. Clifford ran a brick and tile manufacturer's and later became a town councillor in the family's home of Bridgwater in Somerset.

By the time of the 1911 census, Rudolph had become the works manager for his father, but war soon beckoned.

Sadly, Rudolph's full military record has been lost to time, but he enlisted in the Royal Army Service Corps early on in the conflict and was promoted to Lieutenant at the end of September 1914. He was involved in recruiting new soldiers, and it was following one of these meetings that he was involved in an accident.

The local media picked up the story:

> On Friday night, while riding through St Jon Street on his motorcycle, to which a side-car was attached, he collided with a horse and light waggon... Lieutenant Symons appears to have been struck by one of the shafts in the region of the heart, and was rendered unconscious. He was at once conveyed to his home, where he was medically attended and was subsequently removed to the nursing home on Friarn Street. On the following day a specialist was called in, and an operation performed, but the injuries were of so severe a character that death ensured on Monday.
>
> Taunton Courier and Western Advertiser: Wednesday 22nd September 1915

The coroner reported that Rudolph had died from an internal haemorrhage and the inquest recorded a verdict of accidental death and exonerated the waggon driver – a dealer caller Wyatt – from all blame.

Lieutenant Symons was a popular man, a vocalist in the Bridgwater Amateur Operatic Society, and was also heavily involved in the local annual Guy Fawkes celebrations.

He died on 13th September 1915, aged 27 years old, and lies at rest in the Wembdon Road Cemetery in his home town.

Name: Taylor, Arthur

Rank: Private

Regiment: Machine Gun Corps

Date of death: 13th March 1919

Age at time of death: 27

Cause of death: Unknown

Grave location: St Mary's Churchyard, Bruton

Arthur Ernest Taylor was born at the end of 1892, the middle of three children to James and Sarah. James was a baker, and the family lived in Bruton, a small town in the west of Somerset.

Only one of James' three sons followed him into the baking business; this was his youngest, Reginald. The oldest of the three brothers, Oatley, found employment in Wales as a miner. Arthur, on the other hand, stayed in Bruton, but found work as a cycle repairer when he left school.

In December 1913, Arthur married Gertrude James, the daughter of a local carpenter; the young couple went on to have a son, Gerald, the following year.

Sadly, little information about Arthur's military career survives. He enlisted in the Machine Gun Corps, although there is nothing to confirm exactly when he enrolled.

The next time Private Taylor appears in the records is a notice in the Western Gazette on 28th March 1919. The newspaper reports that he passed away in the Military Hospital in Grantham, Lincolnshire. Further documentation shows that he passed away on 13th March 1919, at the age of 27 years old. Sadly, there is no confirmation of the cause of his passing.

Arthur Ernest Taylor was brought back to Somerset, and his body lies at rest in the graveyard of St Mary's Church in his home town of Bruton.

Name: Taylor, Walter

Rank: Private

Regiment: Essex Regiment

Date of death: 14th July 1918

Age at time of death: 35

Cause of death: Kidney sarcoma

Grave location: St John's Cemetery, Bridgwater

Walter Henry Taylor is one of those people whose details are difficult to track down. From his pension card, he is recorded as having been married to a woman called Lilla Rhoda, and that they had a daughter, Joan Valeria, who was born in April 1916.

Walter's war grave confirms that he was a Private in the Essex Regiment; his pension records also support this, showing that he was assigned to the 6th Battalion, then the 10th Battalion. The two troops were positioned in different locations during the conflict – the 6th fought the Turkish, including involvement at Gallipoli, while the 10th was based on the Western Front.

An article in the local newspaper – the Taunton Courier and Western Advertiser – reported his death, confirming that he passed at the War Hospital in Preston, Northampton. He had been in service for more than a year, having previously been employed by Redwood & Sons in Taunton. The newspaper went on to report that Private Taylor had been suffering from ill health and had been hospitalised in both France and England.

The name is a fairly common one, and my usual resources weren't bringing up anything concrete around him. There are no definitive birth or marriage records and the censuses I have been able to locate do not convince me that they relate to the name on the gravestone.

There *is* a Walter Harry Taylor, who was born in Bridgwater in 1883, one of ten children to Henry John Taylor and his wife Emma; Henry was a sailmaker, while Walter went into boot making.

The 1911 census picks up this Walter in St Pancras, London, where he was working as a boot trade shop assistant, while boarding with a dressmaker called Minnie Adelaide Lloyd.

While these seem likely candidates for Walter, there is nothing to definitively connect the documents to the man being researched. What potentially sways it, is that Redwood & Sons (Walter's pre-service employer) were a boot and shoe dealer.

Sadly, the only other definitive documentation of Walter's life is that he passed away on 14th July 1918, from a kidney sarcoma. He was 35 years old.

Walter Henry (Harry) Taylor lies at rest in the St John's Cemetery in his presumed home town of Bridgwater, Somerset.

Name: Thick, John

Rank: Private

Regiment: Hampshire Regiment

Date of death: 8th March 1917

Age at time of death: 34

Cause of death: Bronchitis

Grave location: St Mary's Cemetery, Taunton

John Valentine Thick was born in 1883, the youngest of two children to John Thick and his wife Anna. John Sr was a plumber, and evidently moved around with his work. He was born in Surrey, Anna came from Berkshire; their older child, Grace was born in Hampshire, while John Jr was also born in Berkshire.

By the time of the 1891 census, John Sr had moved the family down to Blandford Forum in Dorset. Little more is known about his son's early life, but by 1907, he was back in Berkshire, and married Henrietta Entwistle, who had grown up in Chelsea.

The young couple went on to have three children – John, Muriel and Margaret – and settled down in Reading, Berkshire. John, by this time, was working as a domestic gardener.

Little documentation exists relating to John's military service. He enlisted in the Hampshire Regiment and was assigned to the 1st Labour Company. Private Thick would have been part of the regiment's territorial force, presumably using his gardening skills to help with the war effort.

While it is difficult to confirm the dates of his service, it seems that John had enlisted towards the end of 1916. It was early the following year that he fell ill and was soon admitted to hospital with bronchitis. Sadly, this condition was to get the better of him, and Private Thick passed away on 8th March 1917. He was just 34 years old.

John Valentine Thick lies at rest in St Mary's Cemetery in Taunton, Somerset.

Name: Thorne, William

Rank: Chief Stoker

Regiment: Royal Navy

Date of death: 29th September 1918

Age at time of death: 37

Cause of death: Unknown

Grave location: St James' Cemetery, Taunton

William Henry Thorne was born on 28th July 1881 in the Somerset village of Milverton. He was the oldest of five children to farm labourer Henry Thorne and his wife Mary.

William was a young man with a keen sense of adventure. In February 1900, he joined the Royal Navy as a Stoker. After his initial training in Devonport, he was assigned to HMS Thunderer and, after six months, joined HMS Hood, where he spent the next two years.

Over the twelve years of his service, Stoker Thorne served on six further vessels, attaining the rank of Stoker Petty Officer.

In 1907, William had married Mabel Cross, a young woman from Taunton. While her husband was away from England – the marriage certificate gives his address as *"on the high seas"* – she set up home near the centre of town. The young couple went on to have two children, twins Phyllis and Doris, who were born in 1911.

Back at sea, and Stoker Petty Officer Thorne's terms of service were extended in 1912, so that he would continue to be a part of the Royal Navy until the cessation of hostilities. He served on a further six vessels and was promoted to Chief Stoker in June 1917.

It was while he was serving on HMS Griffon in the autumn of 1918 that William fell ill. Brought back to shore, he was admitted to the Military Hospital in Taunton. There is nothing to confirm the illness he contracted, but it was one he would succumb to. Chief Stoker Thorne passed away on 29th September. He was 37 years old.

William Henry Thorne lies at peace in the St James' Cemetery in his home town of Taunton.

Name: Tottle, Walter

Rank: Corporal

Regiment: Somerset Light Infantry

Date of death: 5th May 1919

Age at time of death: 26

Cause of death: Influenza

Grave location: St James' Cemetery, Taunton

Walter James Tottle was born in September 1892, one of fourteen children to Charles and Ellen Tottle from Somerset. Charles was a boatman, and their family lived in Salmon Parade along the riverfront in Bridgwater.

When Walter left school, he became an assistant at a market garden; by the 1911 census, he was living with his parents and eight of his siblings, whose jobs included carpentry and laundering. Walter's younger brother Henry was listed as a rink boy, helping with skating at the local ice rink.

Walter's life beyond this is a bit of a mystery. He enjoyed sports and, before the war had been a regular player for Bridgwater Rugby Football Club. He married a woman called Ruth, although I have been unable to track down who she was or when the couple wed.

When war came, Walter enlisted in the Somerset Light Infantry and, according to contemporary newspaper reports, Corporal Tottle had served on both the Eastern and Western Fronts. He was discharged from the army on 13th February 1919, following a severe attack of influenza, but it appeared to get the better of him. He passed away on 5th May 1919, aged just 26 years old.

Walter James Tottle lies at rest in St John's Cemetery in his home town of Bridgwater, Somerset.

Walter's 'rink boy' brother Henry also served in the First World War. He had also enrolled in the Somerset Light Infantry and, as a Corporal in the 1/5th Battalion, he was involved in some of the fierce fighting in the

Middle East. He was injured, either in Gaza or Jerusalem, but sadly Henry died of his wounds on 22nd November 1917; he was buried in the War Cemetery in Jerusalem.

Name: Trayler, John

Rank: Captain

Regiment: Devonshire Regiment

Date of death: 27th November 1915

Age at time of death: 39

Cause of death: Illness

Grave location: St Mary's Churchyard, Clevedon

John Nelson Trayler was born on 2nd December 1876, the oldest of seven siblings. His father, Jonas Trayler, was born in London, but moved to South Wales to become a farmer. He married Elizabeth Green, who was from Haverfordwest, and John was their eldest child, born in Pembrokeshire.

In December 1895, having just turned 19, John joined the 1st Devonshire Volunteer Corps. He seemed eager for a life of action; it's easy to see why given that the 1901 census lists his profession simply as farmer's son. By this time, the family had moved to a farm in Broadclyst, to the north-east of Exeter in Devon.

There was a change of direction for the family, however. By 1908, both father and son were working as tanners; John had moved back to Wales, while Jonas had set up work in Bridgwater, Somerset.

John, by this time, had met Eunice Sully; she was the daughter of a gentleman, and her family lived in Wembdon, near Bridgwater. They married in July 1908 and lived in the village of Lamphey in Pembroke.

John was, by now, the managing director of a tannery and obviously had the business acumen to run a company. He joined the local freemasons – the Lodge of Perpetual Friendship – but, in January 1914, it was reported in the local newspaper that the business was to be voluntarily wound up.

John's father Jonas was also forging ahead with his ambitions and was a councillor for the Bridgwater area.

When the Great War broke out, John's time with the Devonshire Volunteer Corps was such that he had attained the rank of Captain. Assigned to the 11th (Reserve) Battalion, John was based out of Exeter, and it is unlikely that he saw any active service in France.

In August 1915, the Exeter and Plymouth Gazette reported that Captain Trayler had relinquished his commission on account of poor health, and this seems to have been an ongoing issue. In fact, when he was staying with Eunice's parents in Clevedon later that year, he fell seriously ill. While his medical condition is lost to time, sadly it was one he succumbed to. He died at his in-laws' house on 27th November 1915, at the age of 39 years old.

John Nelson Trayler was laid to rest in the picturesque graveyard of St Mary's Church in Clevedon, Somerset.

Name: Treliving, Walter

Rank: Second Lieutenant

Regiment: Royal Army Service Corps

Date of death: 11th October 1918

Age at time of death: 42

Cause of death: Influenza

Grave location: Wembdon Road Cemetery, Bridgwater

Walter Ricks Treliving was born in Bridgwater, Somerset, in 1876, the middle of three children to James and Elizabeth Treliving. James was a commercial traveller in the drapery trade, and this is something his son followed him into.

According to the 1891 census, Walter was a pupil at the Commercial Traveller's School in Pinner, Middlesex, which was, in effect, a boarding school-cum-children's home for the children of commercial travellers and orphans.

Commerce was obviously engrained into Walter by this point and, after leaving school, he followed his father into the trade of trading. He travelled with his work, frequently boarding with others; in 1901, the census recorded him as lodging with his maternal aunt Annie Ricks.

Love beckoned, however, and in 1904, Walter married Mabel Broadrick, the daughter of a Unitarian Minister from Worcestershire. The couple set up home in Weston-super-Mare and had a daughter, Beryl, two years later.

Things were not to go smoothly, however, as an article in the Western Daily Press was to show:

> In the Divorce Court yesterday, a case was heard in which Mr
> Walter Treliving, a commercial traveller of Weston-super-Mare,
> petitioned for a divorce from Mabel Annie Treliving, on the
> ground of her misconduct with Mr Charles E Rust, an engineer.
> The case was undefended.
>
> Mr Treliving said he was married on the 13th August 1904 at

Bridgwater, and afterwards lived at Weston-super-Mare. There was one child of the marriage. The married life was happy until May 1913, when his wife told him that she cared for someone else.

In July 1913, his wife went away to Manchester on a visit, and when she came back, she told him she had stayed with Mr Rust at the Grand Hotel... He forgave her for that, and took her away for a holiday to Lynton. He then discovered that she was still corresponding with the co-respondent, and afterwards that she was meeting him again.

On the 13th September his wife left him, and he heard that she had gone to Khartoum with the co-respondent. He received a letter from her, in which she said:

"Dear Walter. The divorce papers have come. Of course, I cannot defend the case, nor he. Oh you have it all in your power. I hope you will be happy now you are free. If ever I came back to England, may I see Betty [sic]? I cannot marry Mr R. She will not divorce him. I do not know what I shall do now. I hope you will be happy if you marry again, as I hear you will. Oh! if you had only held out one hand to save me, how different it might have been. I am a broken woman. Yesterday, when the petition came, I realised it. You are fully paid back for all your sufferings. Enjoy your victory. Your wife."

Petitioner said it was not his intention to marry again, as his wife suggested. He had done everything in his power to induce her to remain with him.

Western Daily Press: Thursday 1st April 1915

A decree nisi was granted to Walter and he was awarded costs.

Sadly, it has not been possible to track Walter's military history. That he enlisted is evident; he joined the Royal Army Service Corps and rose through the ranks to become Second Lieutenant Treliving. The divorce proceedings did not identify him as serving in the army, so it seems likely that he joined up at some point after April 1915 – his age and his status as a single father seem further proof of this assumption.

Walter returned to Bridgwater in October 1918 to attend his mother's funeral. Elizabeth had contracted influenza and, sadly, after returning home Walter also caught and succumbed to it. He died on 11th October 1918, at the age of 42.

His probate confirms two beneficiaries: his sister Hilda Treliving, and another woman, Kate Symons, presumably as guardians and trustees for Beryl.

Walter Ricks Treliving lies at rest in the Wembdon Road Cemetery in his home town of Bridgwater, Somerset. He was buried on the same day as Elizabeth, the mother whose funeral he had returned to attend.

Name: Tucker, Clifford

Rank: Gunner

Regiment: Royal Field Artillery

Date of death: 28th February 1915

Age at time of death: 18

Cause of death: Pneumonia

Grave location: Othery Cemetery

Clifford Charles Tucker was born in 1896, one of five children to John and Ellen Tucker. John was a shoemaker in the Somerset village of Othery, while Clifford became a farm labourer when he left school.

There is little documented of Clifford's life, and what I have been able to identify about his military career has come from a newspaper article:

> Much regret is felt in Othery at the news of the death of Clifford Tucker, one of the young fellows who volunteered for the service of their King and Country. Deceased, who was only 18 years of age... enlisted in the Royal Artillery about six weeks ago and was stationed at Brighton.
>
> He was taken ill with pneumonia and died, his father arriving in time to see him before he breathed his last.
>
> Taunton Courier and Western Advertiser: Wednesday 17th March 1915.

Gunner Tucker passed away on 28th February 1915, aged just 18 years old. He lies at rest in the cemetery of his home village of Othery.

Name: Tucker, Leonard

Rank: Deck Hand

Regiment: Royal Navy

Date of death: 28th September 1918

Age at time of death: 20

Cause of death: Unknown

Grave location: St Mary's Cemetery, Taunton

Leonard Francis Tucker was born in 1898, the middle of three children to Arthur and Frances Tucker. Arthur was a tailor from Taunton, Somerset, and this is where he brought his young family up.

Sadly, little documentation remains of Leonard's life. His grave confirms that, when war came, he served in the Royal Navy, and, at the time of his death, he was a Deck Hand on HMS Vivid.

His Commonwealth War Graves Record confirms that his parents were living in Melbourne – his pension ledger confirms Arthur as his next of kin, with an Australian address. There is nothing to confirm their emigration, or whether Leonard emigrated as well.

Leonard's young life is summed up in a short notice in the local newspaper, which has the simple comment *"Tucker – Sept. 28th, at 10 Westgate-street, Taunton, Leonard Francis Tucker, aged 20." [Taunton Courier and Western Advertiser: Wednesday 9th October 1918]*

Slightly more confusing is the next name on that list: *"Tucker – Sept. 29, at 10 Westgate-street, Taunton, Frances Ellen Tucker, aged 44."* It would seem that Leonard's mother was in England, not Australia, at the time of his death, and that she passed away a day after him.

Combined with when Leonard died, it would suggest both he and his mother died from one of the respiratory conditions running rampant through England at the time, possibly influenza or pneumonia. There is nothing to confirm this outright, but it seems the likeliest outcome for the poor mother and son.

Leonard Francis Tucker lies at rest in St Mary's Cemetery in his home town of Taunton.

Name: Turner, Sidney

Rank: Lance Corporal

Regiment: Highland Light Infantry

Date of death: 2nd July 1921

Age at time of death: 32

Cause of death: Pulmonary tuberculosis and exhaustion

Grave location: St John's Cemetery, Bridgwater

Sidney Joseph Turner was born in 1888, the oldest of four children to Sidney and Matilda Turner from Bridgwater in Somerset. Sidney Sr was a carter, while his son became a labourer in a local cement works. Sadly, Sidney Sr died in 1903, when Sidney Jr was 15, leaving Matilda with three other children, one of whom was only 18 months old.

Sidney Jr travelled to get work and had moved to South Wales to work as a miner by 1909. Here he married Rose Shattock, who was born in Bristol, although within a couple of years the young couple had moved back to Somerset.

Sidney and Rose had a son, also called Sidney, although sadly he died when he was only a couple of months old. Tragically for Sidney, the records seem to suggest that Rose may have died in childbirth, or shortly after, as her passing was registered in the same quarter as her son's birth.

By this time, Sidney was living in Bailey Street, Bridgwater, a short distance from some railway sidings. This might have driven some determination in him as, by the following year, he was listed as an engine driver. In December 1913 he married his second wife, Bessie Sharman. She was the daughter of a mariner, who had become a machinist in a shirt factory by the time of their marriage.

When war broke out, Sidney enlisted in the Highland Light Infantry, initially in the 12th (Service) Battalion. They landed in France in July 1915 and were there for the remainder of the war. At some point, Lance Corporal Turner transferred to the 53rd (Young Soldier) Battalion. Very much a training brigade, it seems that Sidney's experience of the front line may have proved useful for the upcoming recruits.

Lance Corporal Turner was demobbed on 21st March 1919; his pension record shows that, during the course of his service, he had fractured his tibia and had contracted bronchitis.

This latter condition was to prove Sidney's downfall, as, within two years, he had succumbed to pulmonary tuberculosis and exhaustion. He died on 2nd July 1921, aged just 32 years old.

Sidney Joseph Turner lies at rest in St John's Cemetery in his home town of Bridgwater, Somerset.

Name: Underhill, Henry

Rank: Private

Regiment: Somerset Light Infantry

Date of death: 14th October 1914

Age at time of death: 44

Cause of death: Heart attack

Grave location: St Mary's Cemetery, Taunton

Henry Thomas Underhill is one of those people whose lives are lost to time. Details of his early life were difficult to track down, but snippets helped with some of the mystery.

In late October 1914, a number of Somerset newspapers gave the following report:

SOLDIER'S SUDDEN DEATH

The West Somerset Coroner held an enquiry at Taunton Barracks on Saturday afternoon relative to the death of Private Henry Thomas Underhill, aged 44, of Street, which took place on Wednesday [14th October 1914].

Deceased was talking to Private TF Davis on a landing in the barracks, when he reeled and, throwing up his arms, fell heavily to the ground, his head striking the floor.

Major Stalkartt, RAMC, was at once summoned, but he found that life was extinct. He afterwards made a post mortem examination, which revealed fatty degeneration of the heart, with a fracture of the base of the skull. The doctor considered that death was due to heart failure, and that the skull was fractured in falling to the ground.

The deceased was accorded a military funeral at St Mary's Cemetery the same afternoon. He was an old member of the Somerset Light Infantry, which he recently re-joined on account of the war.

Private Underhill's pension record confirms that he was married to a woman called Mary Ann and that the couple had had a daughter, Beatrice Kate Lavinia Underhill, who had been born in December 1906. While searching for Henry directly drew too many variables to provide any certainty, his daughter proved the key to unlock his story.

Henry Thomas Underhill was born in the summer of 1860. One of nine children, his parents were William Underhill and his wife Elizabeth, who was also known as Betsy. William worked as a clerk for a button maker, and the family lived in Birmingham, which, at the time, was in Warwickshire.

When he left school, Henry found work as a brass tube drawer, making the metal tubes, using a die. He found love too, and, on 13th March 1881, aged just 20, he married Emma Howner. The couple went on to have a son, Ernest, in 1889 although, from the documentation about him, it seems likely that he passed away when only a toddler. Further tragedy was to strike Henry, when Emma also died in 1890, aged just 30 years old.

It may have been around this time that Henry found a focus in military service; he does not appear in the 1891 census and the next set of documentation for him dates from 1900.

It's at this point that Henry married for a second time. Mary Ann Kelly was seventeen years younger than her new husband and was the daughter of a carpenter from Solihull. Her father, Michael, had died when she was only a teenager, and she lived with her mother, Lavinia, helping to support her.

Henry's previous experience with metalwork – and probably his time in the military – found him employment making gun components. The 1901 census finds him and Mary living in Yardley, to the east of Birmingham, with Lavinia and Mary's younger brother William.

This was obviously a suitable and convenient arrangement; the next census, in 1911, shows the family still living together. By this time, Lavinia was still the head of the household, and shared her home with daughter Mary, Henry and four-year-old Beatrice, son William, his wife Ada and their new-born son, William. Making up the household on Census Day was a visitor, Amy.

War was on the horizon, and this is where we return to the initial news report about Private Underhill. It is likely that Henry had re-enlisted – or at least been called back up – as soon as hostilities broke out. Sadly, his service was not to be a long one, as he suffered the fatal heart attack within a couple of months of the start of the war. Private Underhill was 54 years old at the time of his death.

Henry Thomas Underhill's body was buried in St Mary's Cemetery in Taunton, Somerset.

Name: Vagg, Wilfrid

Rank: Private

Regiment: Somerset Light Infantry

Date of death: 11th February 1918

Age at time of death: 18

Cause of death: Appendicitis

Grave location: St Aldhelm's Churchyard, Doulting

Wilfrid Stanley Vagg was born in 1899 in the Somerset village of Doulting. One of six children, his father Albert was the local blacksmith and innkeeper and he lived with his wife Annie and their family in the Waggon & Horses in the village.

When he left school, Wilfrid was keen to follow in his father's footsteps; the Oakhill Brewery Company was just up the road from the family pub, and it was here that he found employment as a clerk. When war broke out, however, he must have wanted to do his bit, enlisting in the Somerset Light Infantry when he turned 18.

It may well have been while he was training on Salisbury Plain that Private Vagg became ill. He was treated at the Fargo Military Hospital, situated just to the north of Stonehenge, and was operated on for appendicitis. Sadly, he did not recover, and passed away on 11th February 1918. He was just 18 years of age.

Wilfrid Stanley Vagg lies at rest in the graveyard of St Aldhelm's Church in his home village of Doulting in Somerset.

Name: Venn, Henry

Rank: Private

Regiment: Devonshire Regiment

Date of death: 10th November 1918

Age at time of death: 18

Cause of death: Influenza and pneumonia

Grave location: St Leonard's Churchyard, Shipham

Henry John Venn was born in September 1900, the youngest of three children to Charles and Mary Venn. Charles was a gardener, and the family lived in the small Somerset village of Shipham.

Sadly, there is little information available about Henry's life, although when war broke out, he enlisted as a Private in the Devonshire Regiment. There is no documentation to confirm exactly when he enrolled, although, given his age when the conflict began, it is unlikely to have been before 1918.

Indeed, later records show that his parents were refused a war gratuity. This was only usually the case where a soldier had completed less than six months' service. It is likely, therefore, that Private Venn did not join up before he turned 18 years old in September 1918.

Henry joined the 53rd Training Reserve Battalion; they were based at the Rollestone Camp near Stonehenge, Wiltshire. It is here that he likely became unwell, as he was subsequently admitted to the Military Hospital on Salisbury Plain. He was suffering from influenza and pneumonia, and this is what he succumbed to. Private Venn passed away on 10th November 1918 – the day before the Armistice that ended the conflict. He was just 18 years old.

Henry John Venn lies at rest in the graveyard of St Leonard's Church in his home village of Shipham in Somerset.

Name: Vernoum, Arthur

Rank: Private

Regiment: The Queen's (Royal West Surrey Regiment)

Date of death: 14th April 1920

Age at time of death: 47

Cause of death: Carcinoma of the tongue, haemorrhage

Grave location: Wells Cemetery

Arthur Edward Vernoum was born in 1874, the second of seven children to David and Sabina Vernoum. David worked on the railways, while Arthur went into labouring, as a stonemason.

He married Elizabeth Parker in 1896, and the couple settled in Wells, Somerset. They had four children – William, Samuel, Richard and Winifred.

Arthur's military service records are a bit scarce; he enlisted in the Royal West Surrey Regiment (The Queen's). Given his age – he was 40 when war broke out – it is likely that this was towards the end of the conflict.

While his troop served in many of the key battles of the Great War, there is no evidence whether Private Vernoum was involved – again, because of his age, it may well have been that he served as part of a territorial, rather than European force.

Arthur's pension records show that he passed away on 14th April 1920, of a carcinoma of the tongue and a haemorrhage. He was 46 years old.

Arthur Edward Vernoum lies at rest in the cemetery of his home city, Wells in Somerset.

Name: Vickery, William

Rank: Private

Regiment: Royal Welch Fusiliers

Date of death: 28th November 1919

Age at time of death: 26

Cause of death: Tuberculosis

Grave location: Wembdon Road Cemetery, Bridgwater

William George Vickery was born in the summer of 1894, the youngest of three children to George and Mary Vickery. George was a labourer in a brickyard, and this is work that his son followed him into once he left school.

William seems to have progressed with work as, by the time he enlisted for military service, he was recorded as a miner, working in the collieries of South Wales. Initially joining up in February 1916, it seems like his job gave him a level of protection for a couple of years at least; he was not formally mobilised by the Royal Welch Fusiliers until May 1918.

Initially serving on the Home Front, Private Vickery was shipped to France in September 1918, serving two months there, before returning home. William was eventually discharged from the army on medical grounds, having contracted tuberculosis while on active duty.

There is little information about William after his discharge. It seems likely that his health deteriorated, however, as he died just a year later, on 28th November 1919. He was just 26 years of age.

William George Vickery lies at rest in the Wembdon Road Cemetery in his home town of Bridgwater, Somerset.

Name: Virgin, Frederick

Rank: Driver

Regiment: Royal Field Artillery

Date of death: 26th November 1918

Age at time of death: 30

Cause of death: Unknown

Grave location: St Mary's Cemetery, Taunton

Frederick Henry Virgin was born in 1888, the second eldest of ten children. His parents were carter Thomas Virgin and his wife, Ellen, and the family lived in Taunton, Somerset.

Frederick craved adventure and this came in the form of military service. In August 1906, he enlisted in the Royal Field Artillery, and was assigned as a driver. Initially serving at home, he was shipped to India for four years, returning to England in December 1912.

Driver Virgin met and married Alice Shattock in April 1914, but had been shipped off to France within months, when war broke out. He served overseas for eighteen months, before transferring back to England again. By this point he was suffering with sciatica, and this is what saw him assigned lighter duties in the Reserve Brigade on the Home Front.

Alice fell pregnant, and the couple had a little boy in February 1917; sadly, his life was brief, and he passed away at the age of just two days. One can only imagine the impact this had on his parents.

Frederick's health issues continued to be a problem, and he was medically discharged from the army later that year. While the sciatica was not solely attributed to his military service, his discharge report confirmed that his time in the army contributed to the issue. Driver Virgin's time with the Royal Field Artillery came to an end in December 1917.

Sadly, it is at this point that Frederick's trail goes cold. His records confirm that he passed away nearly a year later, on 26th November 1918, but there is no record as to the cause of his death. He was 30 years of age.

Frederick Henry Virgin lies at rest in St Mary's Cemetery in his home town of Taunton, Somerset.

Name: Voisey, Robert

Rank: Private

Regiment: Royal Warwickshire Regiment

Date of death: 23rd October 1918

Age at time of death: 25

Cause of death: Influenza and pneumonia

Grave location: St James' Cemetery, Taunton

Robert Voisey was born towards the end of 1891, one of six children to Richard and Sophia. Richard was a tailor and, while both he and Sophia had been born in Cullompton, Devon, by the time Robert was born, they had moved to the Somerset town of Taunton.

When he left school, Robert followed his father's trade and, by the time of the 1911 census, he was living with his parents and two of his sisters in a terraced house not far from the town's station.

With the outbreak of the Great War, Robert was keen to do his bit. While full details of his military service are not available, it seems that he initially enlisted in the Somerset Light Infantry but was subsequently transferred to the Royal Warwickshire Regiment. Joining the 6th Battalion as a Private, he saw action on the Western Front, and was wounded in April 1918.

Evacuated to England for treatment, Private Voisey was admitted to the 5th Northern General Hospital in Leicester. He seemed to be recovering well from his injuries, but then contracted influenza.

Sadly, this developed into pneumonia and Private Voisey subsequently died on 23rd October 1918, at the tender age of 25 years old.

Robert Voisey's body was brought back to Somerset, and he was laid to rest in the St James' Cemetery in the town.

Robert's funeral was written up in the local newspaper, and the report sheds more of a light on the Edwardian attitude towards some medical and mental health conditions than it does on the actual service:

The very fact of [Robert] ever having been a soldier, considering the great disability he was afflicted with through an incurable impediment in his speech, testifies abundantly to his high and noble interpretation of duty and patriotism.

Had he insisted he could at any time have evaded military service, but so eager was he to serve his country that it was not until he had actually been four times rejected as "physically unfit for military service" was he eventually accepted.

To the writer of this brief notice, who was his friend and fellow shop-mate for a long while, but who was at the time doing duty at Castle Green Recruiting Office, he often time used to express his indignation at not being accepted, and on the last occasion he spoke to the writer, it was to emphatically declare himself "as fit to be a soldier as anyone who had yet left Taunton."

He dreaded the thought of being considered a shirker, and his opinion of many who have, even up till now, successfully evaded service, though far more physically fit than he was, was contemptuous to the bitterest extreme.

He was a true Britisher, a faithful friend and shop-mate, and a courageous soldier of whom no fitter epitaph could be written than "he gave himself in defence of home, country and liberty."

Taunton Courier and Western Advertiser: Wednesday 6th November 1918

Name: Wall, Albert

Rank: Corporal

Regiment: Royal Garrison Artillery

Date of death: 18th November 1919

Age at time of death: 29

Cause of death: Kidney disease

Grave location: St James' Cemetery, Taunton

Albert Wall was born in the spring of 1890, one of eight children to James Wall and his wife Louise. James was a mason's labourer from Taunton, Somerset, and brought his family up in his home town.

Details of Albert's life are tantalisingly absent. It appears that he had a sense of adventure and joined the Royal Garrison Artillery when his age allowed. By 1911, he was stationed at Port Royal in Jamaica, and was listed as a Gunner.

Gunner Wall's involvement with the Royal Garrison Artillery extended into the Great War. He was sent to Egypt in April 1915, and, as part of his service, gained the Victory and British Medals and the 1915 Star. Albert seems to have been lucky in that he saw out the war fairly unscathed and was promoted to the rank of Corporal.

In the winter of 1918, Albert married Beatrice Salter. The war over, he was subsequently discharged from active service in April 1919.

Life on civvy street was not destined to be a long one, however, as, on 18th November 1919, he passed away from kidney disease. He was just 29 years of age.

Albert Wall was laid to rest in the St James' Cemetery in his home town of Taunton.

As a sad footnote to this story, on 5th March 1920, Beatrice gave birth to a little boy, who she called Gordon. Albert was never to see his son.

Name: Walsh, Archibald

Rank: Second Lieutenant

Regiment: Royal Horse Artillery

Date of death: 18th March 1915

Age at time of death: 23

Cause of death: Died of wounds

Grave location: St Mary's Cemetery, Taunton

Archibald Charles Mark Walsh was born on 3rd February 1892, the youngest of three children to Henry Alfred Walsh and his wife Ann. Henry had a distinguished military career, and his sons – Archibald and his older brother Theobald – seemed destined to do the same.

Henry's service took him around the world, and, by the time Archibald was born, the family had settled in Devon. In tracing the family's life, however, an unusual quirk arises around the turn of the century.

In 1901, the majority of the Walsh family disappear from census records. For someone like Henry, this would not be unusual; his career took him overseas, and it is likely that records were lost or destroyed.

However, Archibald and his sister Gwladys *do* appear in the records. They are set up in a seafront villa in the Kent town of Hythe, Gwladys is listed as both a school pupil and the head of the household – at the age of 14 – and the two siblings are living there with a governess, Mary Porter.

By the time of the next census, Cadet Walsh had followed his father into the military. He was a student at the Military Academy in Woolwich, and the following year achieved his commission, becoming a Second Lieutenant in the Royal Horse Artillery.

When war broke out, Archibald's regiment were shipped off to the Western Front. In March 1915, he was caught up in the Battle of Neuve Chapelle, and was badly wounded.

Shipped back to England for treatment, he was admitted to the Hall-Walker Hospital for Officers in Regents Park, London. Sadly, Second

Lieutenant Walsh's injuries were too severe, and he passed away on 18th March 1915. He was just 23 years old.

Brought back to Taunton, near his family home, Archibald Charles Mark Walsh lies at rest in St Mary's Cemetery.

Archibald is buried next to his father, Henry Walsh, whose story can be found in the next entry.

Name: Walsh, Henry

Rank: Colonel

Regiment: Somerset Light Infantry

Date of death: 25th November 1918

Age at time of death: 65

Cause of death: Unknown

Grave location: St Mary's Cemetery, Taunton

Henry Alfred Walsh was born near Taunton, Somerset, in September 1853, the eldest of five children to Theobald and Isabel Walsh. Theobald was a magistrate with some military connections, and it was military service that Henry went into.

While full details aren't readily available, the 1881 census finds him living in Devon, with his employment simply as "military". Presumably, he had enrolled in the Somerset Light Infantry, the regiment he had a lifelong commitment to.

By the early 1880s, Henry had married Ann Sparrow. The couple went on to have three children – Theobald, Gwladys and Archibald.

The 1891 census finds Henry and his family in the Somerset Light Infantry Barracks at Farnborough. Henry was a Sergeant Major by this time and was assigned to the 1st Battalion. Also living in the same accommodation – and presumably helping Ann with the running of the household – were a governess and cook.

The census also highlights the transient nature of army life. Henry, as mentioned before, was born in Taunton, while Ann came from Plymouth in Devon. Theobald was born in Taunton, while Gwladys and her younger brother were both born in Devon. Military service brought a sense of stability, but not necessarily geographically.

Henry eventually took a step back from the army; by the time of the 1911 census, he was living back in Bishop's Hull, the village of his birth in Somerset, and listed as a retired colonel. When war broke out, however, he volunteered his services again, and was appointed the officer commanding the No. 8 District in Exeter.

While Henry came out of retirement to serve his country again, his two sons had also forged their own military careers. Theobald also joined the Somerset Light Infantry, also achieving the rank of Colonel. Archibald joined the Royal Horse Artillery.

When Henry passed away in 1918, local newspapers were unanimous in their praise of the long-serving officer, outlining both his military service and his charitable work:

> Colonel Walsh had had a distinguished military career, dating from 1870, when he joined the old Somerset Militia at Taunton. [He] was created a CB in 1905, and held the medal and clasp for Zululand, and the medal and two clasps and the Khedive's Bronze Star for his services in Egypt.
>
> He was a JP for Somerset and a member of the Army and Navy Club. [He] threw himself wholeheartedly into the work of the Boy Scout organisation.
>
> The greatest work in which Colonel Walsh had been identified during the war, however, was undoubtedly that of feeding the Somerset prisoners of war in Germany, and his name will ever be linked in grateful memory with that of his honoured wife for having raised and maintained a fund capable of bearing the strain of over £3,000 expenditure per month to save the Somerset men in Germany from starvation.
>
> Wells Journal: Friday 29th November 1918

Ironically, for all this exultation, there is no immediate record of the cause of Henry's death; given his age – he was 65 when he passed – it seems likely that he died following an illness.

Colonel Henry Alfred Walsh lies at rest in St Mary's Cemetery in Taunton, Somerset.

Henry is buried next to his son, Archibald, whose story can be found in the previous entry.

Name: Walters, Alfred

Rank: Able Seaman

Regiment: Royal Navy

Date of death: 20th February 1919

Age at time of death: 19

Cause of death: Influenza and pneumonia

Grave location: Wembdon Road Cemetery, Bridgwater

Alfred Charles Walters was born in March 1900, one of six children to Alfred and Sarah Walters from Bridgwater, Somerset. Alfred Sr was a labourer in a brickyard, and the family lived in the centre of the town.

When war broke out, Alfred seemed very eager to be involved. Lying about his age (giving his date of birth as 26th August 1898), he enlisted in the Royal Naval Reserve. Training in Portsmouth – on HMS Victory II, HMS Excellent and HMS President III – he was assigned to the SS Tanfield.

The steamer was heading out of London on route for Bombay and Karachi in April 1918 and was making its way west through the English Channel. On 15th April, it was located and tracked by the German U-Boat UB74, under the command of Ernst Steindorff. The German fired a torpedo, which hit and crippled Able Seaman Walters' ship. Thankfully, there was no loss of life, and the Tanfield managed to limp back to port.

Little else remains of Able Seaman Walters' military life. In February 1919, he was admitted to the Dreadnought Seaman's Hospital in Greenwich, suffering from influenza and bronchial pneumonia. Sadly, he succumbed to the disease, passing away on 20th February 1919. He was just 18 years old (although his military record and gravestone give him as 19).

Alfred Charles Walters lies at peace in the Wembdon Road Cemetery in his home town of Bridgwater, Somerset.

Name: Warren, Sidney

Rank: Private

Regiment: Somerset Light Infantry

Date of death: 27th November 1918

Age at time of death: 28

Cause of death: Pneumonia

Grave location: St John's Cemetery, Bridgwater

Sidney John Warren was born in January 1890, one of eleven children to shipwright George Warren and his wife Elizabeth. The family lived in Salmon Parade, on the riverside in Bridgwater, where George would have plied his trade. By the time of the 1911 census, Sidney had found work as a grocer's assistant, and was living with his parents and the youngest of his brothers, Edward.

While exact details of Private Warren's military career are not available, documents confirm that he enlisted in the Somerset Light Infantry. Assigned to the 4th Battalion, he was based in India and Mesopotamia during the conflict. No details are available of his time there, but at some point, he transferred to the Labour Corps back in Somerset.

And there Sidney's trail goes cold. He survived the war, but passed away on 27th November 1918, suffering from pneumonia. He was just 28 years old.

Sidney John Warren lies at rest in the family grave at St John's Cemetery in his home town of Bridgwater in Somerset.

Name: Waterhouse, William

Rank: Serjeant

Regiment: Royal Army Service Corps

Date of death: 30th June 1915

Age at time of death: 40

Cause of death: Pneumonia

Grave location: Wells Cemetery

William James Waterhouse was born in 1875, the eldest of seven children to Richard and Elizabeth Waterhouse. The family lived in Cumberland, where Richard initially worked as a grocer before becoming a music teacher.

William followed his father into food retail, working initially as a butcher's boy in Barrow-in-Furness, before moving 400 miles to the south coast and settling in Eastbourne. Travel was definitely on William's mind, however, as, by the 1911 census, he was a butcher's manager at a hotel in Leicester.

William's service records are limited; he was 39 when war broke out, and enlisted in the Eastern Mounted Brigade, before transferring to the Army Service Corps. During his time, he was promoted to Serjeant, and according to a newspaper report of his funeral "was most popular among the men." [Wells Journal: Friday 9th July 1915]

It seems that, as part of his service, Serjeant Waterhouse had been assisting with haymaking in the Wells area, and it was after this that he fell ill. He developed pneumonia and passed away on 30th June 1915. He 40 years old.

William James Waterhouse lies at rest in the cemetery of his adopted home city of Wells, in Somerset.

Name: Watts, Samuel

Rank: Gunner

Regiment: Royal Garrison Artillery

Date of death: 26th June 1918

Age at time of death: 21

Cause of death: Meningitis

Grave location: St John's Churchyard, Farrington Gurney

Samuel Reginald Watts was born in 1897, the seventh of eight children of Samuel and Augusta Watts.

He followed his father and brothers into the main industry in the area – coal mining – and was certainly working down the pits by the time of the 1911 census.

Samuel enlisted on 21st April 1918, and joined the Royal Garrison Artillery, which focused on heavy, large-calibre guns and howitzers that were positioned some way behind the front line. He was 5'5" (1.65m) tall and weighed 144lbs (65kg). According to his war records, he had brown hair, hazel eyes and a fresh complexion.

His service started the very next day, when he was transferred to the Citadel in Plymouth for training.

After feeling unwell, complaining of headaches and a sensitivity to light, Gunner Watts was admitted to the Netley Hospital in Southampton on 18th June 1918. He was diagnosed with cerebrospinal fever, more commonly known as meningitis, and was treated over the next week.

Sadly, the treatment did not work, and Gunner Samuel Watts passed away on the evening of 26th June 1918. He had been in the army for a little over two months and had not seen active service.

Samuel Watts lies at peace in the graveyard of St John's Church, Farrington Gurney.

Name: Watts, Sidney

Rank: Private

Regiment: Royal Army Medical Corps

Date of death: 24th September 1916

Age at time of death: 24

Cause of death: Pneumonia

Grave location: St James' Cemetery, Taunton

Sidney Gilbert Watts was born in 1892, one of five children to railway inspector Arthur Watts and his wife Laura. Initially brought up in the village of Congresbury, near Bristol, Arthur soon moved the family to nearby Taunton.

A likeable man, Arthur continued working for Great Western Railways. He also became involved in the Taunton Co-operative and Industrial Society and, for a number of years was the Chairman. Suddenly, and unexpectedly, however, on 20th January 1907, he collapsed and died from a heart attack.

Now widowed, Laura's children rallied around her. Most of them had left school; her eldest, Reginald, was a school master, her older daughters Florrie and Mabel worked for a milliner and draper, and two lodgers moved in to help financially support her and her youngest daughter Evelyn.

By this time Sidney had followed in his father's footsteps and found work as a porter for GWR. He had moved to Hayle in Cornwall, where, according to the 1911 census, he was boarding with 33-year-old widow, Lizzie Richards, and sharing the house with another railway worker, Richard Crago.

Sidney seemed to be looking for something more. In February 1912, he enlisted as a Private in the Royal Army Medical Corps. He trained as a cook and, when war broke out, was sent out to France as part of the British Expeditionary Force.

In July 1915, Private Watts contracted pleurisy and was treated in a hospital in Boulogne. He was discharged for duty and assigned to a hospital ship, where he stayed for six months. While there, he contracted pneumonia and was bedridden for six weeks, his lung having collapsed.

Sidney was evacuated to England to recuperate. His health did not improve, however, and he was medically discharged from the army on 31st July 1916. A few months later, he was admitted to Cranham Lodge Sanatorium near Gloucester, but passed away on 24th September 1916. He was just 24 years old.

The body of Sidney Gilbert Watts was brought back to Taunton, and he was laid to rest in the St James' Cemetery in the town.

Name: Welch, John

Rank: Corporal

Regiment: Somerset Light Infantry

Date of death: 13th September 1916

Age at time of death: 50

Cause of death: Died of wounds

Grave location: St James' Churchyard, Milton Clevedon

John Milton Welch was born in Yeovil on 19th February 1866, one of five children to William and Anne Welch. William was a chemist by trade, but John's calling was elsewhere. He became a clerk, initially for a brewery, but by the time of the 1911 census, he was working for a political agency.

In that census, John can be found living with his parents – who were in their 80s by this point – and his two sisters, both school governesses. He is listed as single; although an earlier census suggests he had married a lady from the Isle of Wight called Sarah, I have found nothing to corroborate this, beyond the fact that she had wed a John M Welch, a brewery clerk from Yeovil.

War beckoned and even though he was 48 when the conflict broke out, John enlisted. Private Welch joined the Somerset Light Infantry; his service record no longer exists, but his medal record shows that he arrived in France in May 1915 and was subsequently awarded the Victory and British Medals and the 1915 Star. His service obviously warranted promotion, and he was elevated to Corporal.

His troop – the 6th (Service) Battalion – was involved in several of the skirmishes of the Battle of the Somme, and it is likely that Corporal Welch was injured during one of these – probably either the Battle of Delville Wood or the Battle of Flers-Courcelette. Wherever it happened, he was shipped back to England, and was treated for his injuries at the Royal Victoria Hospital in Netley, Hampshire.

Sadly, Corporal Welch was not to recover; he passed away on 13th September 1916, at the age of 50.

John Milton Welch lies at rest in the graveyard of St James' Church, in the quiet Somerset village of Milton Clevedon.

Name: West, Albert

Rank: Serjeant

Regiment: South Wales Borderers

Date of death: 9th July 1918

Age at time of death: 48

Cause of death: Unknown

Grave location: Wells Cemetery

Albert Charles West was born in Aldershot, Hampshire, in 1870. The second of nine children, his father Charles was in the army, while his mother Hannah is listed on the 1871 census as a soldier's wife.

By the time of the next census, ten years later, Charles had relocated the family to Wells in Somerset – Charles had been born just up the road in Shepton Mallet, so, in effect, he was bringing his family home. By this point, the Wests were a family of seven; Albert had an older sister, Eliza, and three younger siblings, Mary, Joseph and Earnest.

Albert seemed keen to make his own way in the world; by the 1891 census, he had relocated again, this time to South Wales, where he worked as a miner. He boarded with a grocer in the village of Llantwit Fardre. It would have been a bustling house, because Albert was living there with the grocer, his wife and four children and three other lodgers.

The following year, Albert enlisted in the 2nd Battalion Welsh Regiment. Posted to India, he served there for ten of his twelve years' service.

After completing his enlistment, Albert moved back to Somerset and married Emily Sparrow in Wells. They moved back to South Wales for work, however, this time with Albert working in a mine in Llanwonno, ten miles further up the Taff Valley from Llantwit Fardre.

When war broke out, Albert re-enlisted, this time joining the South Wales Borderers. Sadly, little documentation of his second time in the army remains. He is recorded as having served in the 51st (Graduating) Battalion, which was a training unit based in Suffolk; his experience made him ideal to train others and enabled him to take the rank of Serjeant.

There is nothing to confirm how Serjeant West died. All that is known is that he passed on 9th July 1918. The lack of any media reports around his funeral suggests it is likely to have been illness, rather than injury, that took him. He was 48 years old.

Albert Charles West lies at rest in Wells Cemetery in Somerset.

Charles and Hannah had nine children in total. Two years before Albert passed, their youngest son – Alfred Augustus West – died suddenly and unexpectedly. Records confirm that he was working on the lines at Wells Railway Station, when his foot got caught in the points. Unable to free himself, he was hit by a train and killed.

Name: Westcott, Percy

Rank: Private

Regiment: London Regiment

Date of death: 20th March 1916

Age at time of death: 38

Cause of death: Unknown

Grave location: St James' Cemetery, Taunton

Percy George Westcott was born at the end of 1877, the eldest of six children to George and Elizabeth Wescott. George was a police constable who brought his family up in the Somerset town of Frome.

After leaving school, Percy sought a trade and, by 1901, was living in the East End of London, working as a wheelwright, work he continued with until the start of the war.

In November 1911, Percy married Annie Maria Meineke, a widow with a young son. The couple set up home in Clapton, East London.

War was on the horizon, however, and Percy was keen to enlist. He volunteered for the Army Service Corps at the beginning of June 1915. His application was turned down, however, and the reason for his discharge given was "*not being likely to become an efficient soldier*".

Percy appears to have been undeterred, however, and by September 1915 had enlisted successfully. He joined the London Regiment as a Private, but this is as much as is documented about his military service.

Private Westcott's next appearance in records is on the Army Register of Soldiers' Effects. This confirms that he had served in the 3rd/10th Battalion, which was a territorial force. The document also identifies that he passed away on 20th March 1916, at the age of 38.

While a cause of death is not noted, the location given – the London Asylum, Colney Hatch – is perhaps more significant. As the name suggests, this was a mental health facility, which gives an indication as to Private Westcott's state at the time of his passing.

While Percy's widow was still living in London, his body was taken back to Somerset to be laid to rest. Percy George Westcott is buried in St James' Cemetery in Taunton, where his parents lived.

Name: Western, George

Rank: Private

Regiment: Bedfordshire Regiment

Date of death: 29th May 1918

Age at time of death: 36

Cause of death: Illness

Grave location: St Mary's Cemetery, Taunton

George Western was born on 18th September 1881, one of seven children to Alfred and Jane. Alfred worked as a labourer, and the family lived in Taunton, Somerset.

Alfred died when George was only 12 years old, so his mother found work as a hawker to make ends meet. George married local woman Sarah Pinnell in 1900, and the two of them lived with Jane and her younger children, George working as a labourer to help the extended family.

George and Sarah went on to have seven children, and, by the time of the 1911 census, they had set up home in the centre of Taunton, just off the main high roads.

The Great War was on the horizon, though, and George was there to do his duty for King and Country. His service records no longer exist, so it is difficult to pin down any dates, but it seems that Private Western initially served with the Somerset Light Infantry, then transferred to the Bedfordshire Regiment.

George was assigned to the 3rd Garrison Battalion of the Bedfordshire Regiment. While there is nothing to confirm his activities during the war, this particular battalion was formed in January 1917, and was stationed initially in India and then in Burma. Private Western's medal records suggest, however, that he served his time on home soil.

By May 1918, George was definitely back in Somerset. He had caught an undisclosed illness by this point and had been admitted to the Military Hospital in Bristol. Sadly, whatever the illness was (and it seems likely that it would have been one of the many lung conditions that were sweeping the country at the end of the First World War) it got the better of him. Private Western passed away on 29th May 1918 at the age of 36 years old (his gravestone gives the incorrect age).

George Western lies at peace in St Mary's Cemetery in his home town of Taunton, Somerset.

Name: Wheeler, Alfred

Rank: Private

Regiment: Royal Army Service Corps

Date of death: 23rd April 1920

Age at time of death: 34

Cause of death: Influenza

Grave location: St Andrew's Churchyard, Clevedon

Alfred Wheeler was born in Binstead, on the Isle of Wight, in the summer of 1886. One of three children, his parents were John, a labourer from the Isle of Wight, and his wife Emily.

When he left school, Alfred found work at the London City Mission in Ventnor. By this point, tragically, both of his parents had passed away, and the young siblings were finding their own ways in life.

The 1911 census found Alfred living with his uncle back in Binstead. His trade was given as a Motor Car Driver for the local Carriage & Motor Works; while he was obviously brought up with a spiritual side, he seems to have had a sense of adventure too.

When war broke out, Alfred was keen to do his bit. He enlisted in the Gloucestershire Regiment and was attached to the 1st Battalion. Sent to France within weeks of the war commencing, Private Wheeler was awarded the Victory and British Medals and the 1914 Star.

With his background with cars, Alfred subsequently transferred over to the Royal Army Service Corps in the 615th Motor Transport Company. While full dates are not readily available, the 615th were formed in January 1916, so it was likely after this that Private Wheeler moved across. The company were based in Dublin, and it was in Ireland that he saw out the remainder of the conflict.

On 11th July 1919, Alfred married Rose England. She was the daughter of an organ tuner from Bristol, although there is no obvious connection to Clevedon for him. It seems likely, therefore, that the couple may have met through the church, possibly as Private Wheeler was travelling between Ireland and Hampshire.

Alfred wasn't demobbed as soon as the war ended, remaining part of the Royal Army Service Corps through until 1920. It was while he was in Ireland that he contracted influenza. Admitted to hospital in Dublin, he sadly succumbed to the condition on 23rd April 1920. He was 34 years old.

Alfred Wheeler's body was brought back to England. He lies buried in St Andrew's Churchyard in Clevedon, Somerset.

Name: Wilcox, William

Rank: Serjeant

Regiment: Duke of Cornwall's Light Infantry

Date of death: 10th November 1919

Age at time of death: 25

Cause of death: Unknown

Grave location: St Peter & St Paul's Churchyard, Charlton Adam

Soloman William Wilcox – known by just his middle name – was born in 1894 and was one of seven children. His father, James, was a carter from Keinton Mandeville in Somerset, and he and William's mother, Eliza, brought the family up in neighbouring Charlton Mackrell.

By the time of the 1911 census, William had left school, and was working as a farm labourer, with his older brother Sidney. James, meanwhile, had found further employment working in a local bluestone quarry.

War was on the horizon and, while it is evident that he enlisted in the Duke of Cornwall's Light Infantry, there is little further documentation to track his service. Both of the regiment's main battalions fought on the Western Front, though where and when William was involved is lost to time.

He seems to have been an ambitious young man; he rose through the ranks and, at the point he was discharged, he had risen to the role of Serjeant. He was also in receipt of the Military Medal, though there is no further information about the events that led to this.

William may well have been spurred on by family losses he suffered during the conflict. His mother Eliza died in April 1915, his brother Sidney was killed in action on 10th September 1916, and his father James passed away in August 1918.

Serjeant Wilcox survived the war and was eventually discharged from military service in August 1919. Whether he was simply demobbed, or he was medically discharged is unclear, but, given that he died only a few months later, it seems likely that the latter was the case.

Soloman William Wilcox died in Taunton, Somerset, on 10th November 1919, at the age of 25 years old. His body was brought to St Peter & St Paul's Church in Charlton Adam, Somerset, potentially close to where some of his remaining family lived.

Name: Wilkinson, Joseph

Rank: Sergeant

Regiment: Royal Army Service Corps

Date of death: 17th October 1918

Age at time of death: 31

Cause of death: Unknown

Grave location: St Mary's Churchyard, Wedmore

Joseph Wilkinson was born in the village of Greystoke, Cumbria in the summer of 1888. His parents were John and Margaret Wilkinson, and he had two siblings, also called John and Margaret. Joseph's father worked as a railway signalman, and the industry employed a large number of people in the village.

Joseph's life was to take a different turn, however, and it was likely the railway that took him there. He next appears on the 1911 census, boarding in a house in the village of Wedmore in Somerset. At 23 years old, he is listed as a solicitor's cashier.

As with so many other fallen men and women, Joseph's trail goes cold. There is not enough evidence to detail his military career – he joined the Royal Army Service Corps as a Driver and was promoted to Sergeant.

The UK Army Register of Soldiers' Effects show that he was married to a woman called Ethel, although there are no records of their wedding. The document also confirms that he died at the Union Hospital in Winchester, Hampshire on 17th October 1918, but there is no cause of death given. He was 31 years old.

"He did his duty" says his impressive gravestone, but it is tragic that that duty is lost to time.

Sergeant Joseph Wilkinson lies at rest in the churchyard of St Mary's in Wedmore, the Somerset village that came to be his home.

Name: Willcox, Charles

Rank: Serjeant Major

Regiment: Somerset Light Infantry

Date of death: 4th December 1919

Age at time of death: 26

Cause of death: Cerebral haemorrhage

Grave location: Wembdon Road Cemetery, Bridgwater

The early life of Charles Willcox is a bit of a mystery. From fragments of information, we can determine that he was born in 1893 and had a brother called Edmund and a sister called Beatrice. His mother was a Mrs S Willcox, who, by the early 1920s was living in Johannesburg, South Africa.

Piecing together the tiny pieces of information online, it seems likely, therefore, that his parents were Frank and Sarah Willcox. Frank was a cabinet maker and upholsterer, he and Sarah were from Bridgwater in Somerset, and they had eleven children.

By 1895, Frank had moved the family from Somerset to Cardiff; Charles was the last of the siblings to be born in England. The family did eventually move to South Africa – alongside Sarah, both Beatrice and Edmund lived and died there in their later years.

Back to Charles and, once the Great War started, he was quick to enlist. He joined the Somerset Light Infantry in August 1914 and had a narrow escape in October of that year. The *Bridgwater Mercury* reported that he was in the trenches and had had a near miss when his backpack was hit by a shell.

Corporal Willcox was wounded at Ypres in November, when a piece of shrapnel hit him in the shoulder, went through the lung and had to be cut out of the centre of his back. He was expected to make a full recovery within a year. Charles was also awarded the Distinguished Conduct Medal for his actions in the battle.

In September 1915, Sergeant Willcox received another award, the Russian Cross & Order of St George: the *Bridgwater Mercury* noted that he was the first man from the town to be awarded both this and the DCM. The town's mayor also subsequently presented him with a gold watch and chain on behalf of the town.

Promotion continued for Charles, and, by 1917, he had been elevated to Company Sergeant Major. He was heavily involved in recruitment for the Somerset Light Infantry, and it is likely that, standing at a strapping 6ft 4ins (1.93m) tall and weighing in at 17st (107kg), he would have been the perfect advert for the battalion.

When the war came to a close, things quietened down for him. A keen sportsman – he played rugby for Somerset – he had been a gym instructor in the army and had taken up boxing around 1912. He entered a novices' boxing competition in Southampton in December 1919, and found himself up against Seaman Merrilees, from HMS Hearty.

In the fight, Charles received a body blow and a blow to the jaw, he fell to the floor, landed awkwardly and was knocked out. Attended to by doctors in the sports club, he was sent to Charing Cross Hospital when he did not regain consciousness after a couple of hours.

At the hospital, bruising was reported to Charles' eye and cheek, but no skull fracture was found. They operated on him, two pieces of bone were removed, and a large clot on the left-hand side of his brain discovered. Sadly, the operation did no good, and Charles died that afternoon, the 4th December 1919. He was just 26 years old.

His death was recorded as concussion and a cerebral haemorrhage, attributed to the fall he had had in the ring. An inquest was held, although one report suggests a verdict of *accidental death*, while another states *excusable homicide by misadventure*.

Charles Willcox lies at rest in the Wembdon Road Cemetery in his home town of Bridgwater in Somerset. His gravestone remembers that he lived for sport, died for sport and always played the game.

Name: Winter, Thomas

Rank: Private

Regiment: Devonshire Regiment

Date of death: 14th February 1918

Age at time of death: 30

Cause of death: Enteric fever

Grave location: St Mary's Cemetery, Taunton

Thomas Henry Winter was born in 1887, one of six children to James and Mary. James was a farmer, and the family lived in Milverton, in the Somerset countryside to the west of Taunton.

James died in 1900, and Thomas found his way into farm work as well. He met and married a local woman called Ada Thynne in February 1909, and the couple went on to have five children: Beatrice, James, Charles, Frank and Thomas.

There is little confirmed information about Thomas' military career. When he joined up, he enlisted in the 13th Battalion of the Devonshire Regiment, although, as his service records no longer exist, it is not possible to identify when this was.

Private Winter later transferred to the Labour Corps — again there are no records to confirm the dates — and this is the division in which he remained.

Illness dogged Thomas, however; in early 1918, he contracted enteric fever (known nowadays as typhoid) and was hospitalised. Sadly, he succumbed, and passed away on 14th February 1918. He was 30 years of age.

Thomas Henry Winter lies at rest in St Mary's Cemetery in Taunton, Somerset.

An additional tragic turn to Thomas' story is that Ada was pregnant when he passed away. His youngest son, whom Ada named after him, would never know his father.

Name: Wood, Charles

Rank: Private

Regiment: Royal Defence Corps

Date of death: 12th November 1917

Age at time of death: 48

Cause of death: Unknown

Grave location: Milton Cemetery, Weston-super-Mare

Charles Wood is destined to be one of those servicemen whose lives remain shrouded in mystery.

He was laid to rest in the Milton Cemetery in Weston-super-Mare, and his widow, Ellen, is buried with him. There are two headstones on the site – a family one, and a more recent war grave.

The Commonwealth War Graves Commission website gives his age – 48 years old when he died – and states that he was a Private in the 263rd Company of the Royal Defence Corps and gives his service number. This was a territorial force, so it is probable that he served on home soil.

The only remaining military document relating to him is the Army Register of Soldiers' Effects. This confirms that he died in the Red Cross Hospital in Portishead on 12th November 1917, and that his belongings passed to his widow. It *does* highlight that he received a war gratuity, which was only applicable to soldiers who had completed at least six months' service, so we know that he enlisted before May 1917.

There are a number of censuses available for the Weston-super-Mare area, but there are at least two men called Charles Wood who married women called Ellen, so it is a challenge to identify which is the man buried in this grave.

A usual source of information would be his service record – which, in addition to his military activity, would give an address as well as other family members. However, this document is not available for Private Wood.

There is no mention of his passing in any of the contemporary newspapers, so it seems unlikely that his death was anything out of the ordinary.

Charles Wood is, sadly, lost to time, one of the countless men and women who gave up their lives for King and Country.

Name: Wood, Ernest

Rank: Driver

Regiment: Royal Army Service Corps

Date of death: 2nd March 1919

Age at time of death: 28

Cause of death: Unknown

Grave location: St John's Cemetery, Bridgwater

Ernest James Wood was born in 1891, one of ten children to Alfred and Charlotte Wood. Alfred was a carpenter and machinist for a timber merchant, and, by the time of Ernest's birth the family lived in Bridgwater, Somerset.

When hostilities broke out, Ernest was quick to enlist. He joined the Royal Army Service Corps in September 1914. Driver Wood was assigned to the Horse Transport Depot Company at Park Royal in London, and there is a note of him being injured on 29th July 1916. Sadly, little else of his military service remains.

In January 1916, Ernest married Hilda Williams. She was the same age as her new husband, and was the daughter of Thomas and Elizabeth, who were also from Bridgwater.

The trail of Driver Wood goes a little cold after that. He was demobbed on 6th January 1919 and on his discharge documents he confirmed that he was healthy and would not be claiming to be suffering from a disability as a result of his military service.

Frustratingly, the trail goes totally cold at that point. All we know for certain is that Ernest died on 2nd March 1919, two months after leaving the army. There are no records confirming a cause of death but, as he does not appear in any contemporary newspapers, it is likely that the cause was not unusual; perhaps one of the respiratory conditions going around at the time, such as influenza or pneumonia. Whatever the cause, Ernest was just 28 years old when he died (his headstone is based on an incorrect date of birth).

Ernest James Wood lies at peace in the St John's Cemetery in his home town of Bridgwater, in Somerset.

Name: Woodbury, William

Rank: Private

Regiment: Somerset Light Infantry

Date of death: 30th August 1916

Age at time of death: 17

Cause of death: Died of wounds

Grave location: St John's Cemetery, Bridgwater

William Alfred Woodbury was born in the Somerset village of Nether Stowey in April 1899, the oldest of four children to Alfred and Nellie Woodbury. Alfred was a farm labourer, and, by the time William was a couple of years old, he had moved the family to the town of Bridgwater to work as a carter.

After leaving school, William found work at Barham Brothers' Brickworks in the town. When war broke out, he enlisted in the Somerset Light Infantry almost as soon as he was able to, at the beginning of 1916.

Assigned to the 6th (Service) Battalion, Private Woodbury was sent out to the Western Front in April. He would almost certainly have seen action at the Battle of Delville Wood – part of the Somme offensive – and was wounded in the shoulder and arm on 18th August 1916.

Shipped back to the UK for treatment, William was admitted to the Western General Hospital in Cardiff, but tragically died from his wounds less than a fortnight later on 30th August 1916. He was just 17 years old.

His funeral was reported in both the Shepton Mallet Journal and the Central Somerset Gazette; his father, who had been serving in France as part of the Army Veterinary Corps, managed to return home for his son's funeral.

William Alfred Woodbury lies at rest in the St John's Cemetery in his home town of Bridgwater.

Name: Wride, John

Rank: Private

Regiment: Royal Scots Fusiliers

Date of death: 27th July 1921

Age at time of death: 30

Cause of death: Heart disease

Grave location: Baptist Burial Ground, Cheddar

John Wride was born in 1891, one of eleven children to William and Kate Wride from Cheddar in Somerset. William started as an agricultural labourer, but went on to become a market gardener, a trade at least four of his sons, John included, also went into.

Sadly, little of John's life before the outbreak of war is documented. He enlisted on 12th February 1915 and was assigned to the Royal Scots Fusiliers. There is little information about whether he served abroad, although a number of battalions remained based in the UK.

When he enlisted, Private Wride was noted to have an enlarged thyroid and dental deficiencies. He seems to have suffered with his health during the conflict, and the medical report that accompanied his discharge from the army showed that he suffered from VDH – valvular disease of the heart – although the doctor did not attribute this to his military service.

This decision was appealed, and a subsequent report identified that John's heart and kidney disease *were* in fact aggravated by his time in the army. He was medically discharged due to these conditions in February 1919.

Sadly, John's heart condition proved fatal. He passed away on 27th July 1921, aged 30 years old. He lies at rest in the Baptist Burial Ground in his home town of Cheddar.

Name: Wyatt, Quinton

Rank: Private

Regiment: South Staffordshire Regiment

Date of death: 11th November 1918

Age at time of death: 25

Cause of death: Died of wounds

Grave location: St Mary's Churchyard, Charlton Mackrell

Private Quinton Charles Wyatt was born in the Gloucestershire town of Northleach in 1893 to William and Elizabeth. His mother died when he was a toddler, leaving William to look after Quinton and his older sister Agnes.

By the time war was declared, Quinton was working as a farm labourer and waggoner in the Gloucestershire village of Hampnett.

Quinton enlisted in the 8th Battalion of the South Staffordshire Regiment on 22nd November 1915. Appointed Lance Corporal just two months later, he was posted to France in March 1916.

Neglect of duty in June meant that Lance Corporal Wyatt was demoted to Private four months later. His battalion was caught up in a German gas attack in the autumn of 1917, and he was injured; ultimately, he was medically discharged from the army on Boxing Day 1917.

Quinton Charles Wyatt finally succumbed to his injuries on 11th November 1918 – Armistice Day. He was 25 years old.

He is buried in St Mary's Churchyard in the village of Charlton Mackrell in Somerset.

ACKNOWLEDGEMENTS

I am indebted to the following online tools for guiding my research:
- Ancestry: www.ancestry.co.uk
- The British Newspaper Archive: britishnewspaperarchive.co.uk
- Commonwealth War Graves Commission: cwgc.org
- Find A Grave: findagrave.com
- Fold3: fold3.com
- The Long, Long Trail: longlongtrail.co.uk
- National Army Museum: nam.ac.uk

The support of The Friends of Wembdon Road Cemetery (wembdonroadcemetery.com) was invaluable when researching that Bridgwater location.

I am also eternally grateful to my husband, Andrew, for his patience during hours of scrabbling around overgrown and far-flung churchyards locating seemingly random headstones.

FURTHER READING

My interest in war graves extends beyond the Somerset boundaries; my blog – deathandservice.co.uk – includes these and numerous other stories from across the south of England.

Facebook: @deathandservice
Twitter: @deathandservice
Instagram: @deathandservice
Email: deathandservice@outlook.com

BURIAL LOCATIONS

The servicemen and women highlighted in this book were buried in Somerset. Below is a list of the churchyards and cemeteries referenced in this guide:

Ashcott:	All Saints' Church, Vicarage Lane TA7 9LR
Binegar:	Holy Trinity Church, Station Road BA3 4UG
Blagdon:	St Andrew's Church, Church Street BS40 7SJ
Bridgwater:	St John's Cemetery, Bristol Road TA6 4DE
	Wembdon Road Cemetery, Wembdon Road TA6 7DW
Bruton:	St Mary's Church, Silver Street BA10 0EB
Burrington:	Church of the Holy Trinity, Fry's Lane BS40 7AD
Butleigh:	St Leonard's Church, High Street BA6 8SA
Charlton Adam:	St Peter & St Paul's Church, Church Hill TA11 7BW
Charlton Mackrell:	St Mary's Church, Bonfire Lane TA11 7BN
Cheddar:	Baptist Burial Ground, Lower North Street BS27 3HA
	St Andrew's Church, Church Street BS27 3RF
Clevedon:	St Andrew's Church, Old Church Road BS21 7UF
Compton Dundon:	St Andrew's Church, Peak Lane TA11 6PE
Coxley:	Christ Church, Main Road BA5 1RG
Croscombe:	Church of St Mary the Virgin, Church Street BA5 3QS
Dinder:	St Michael's Church, Church Street BA5 3PE

Ditcheat:	St Mary's Church, Lintern Close BA4 6PJ
Doulting:	St Aldhelm's Church, Church Lane BA4 4QE
Draycott:	St Peter's Church, School Lane BS27 3SD
Evercreech:	Evercreech Cemetery, Bruton Road BA4 6HN
Farrington Gurney:	St John's Church, Church Lane BS39 6UH
Glastonbury:	Glastonbury Cemetery, Wells Road BA6 9BB
Huish Episcopi:	St Mary's Church, The Hill TA10 9QR
Kingsdon:	All Saints' Church, Top Street TA11 7JU
Litton:	St Mary the Virgin, Litton Lane BA3 4PW
Long Sutton:	Friends Burial Ground, Langport Road TA10 9NE
	Holy Trinity Church, Martock Road TA10 9HS
Lydeard St Lawrence:	St Lawrence's Church, Lydeard Down Hill, TA4 3SF
Martock:	All Saints' Church, Church Street TA12 6JL
Meare:	Church of the Blessed Virgin Mary and All Saints, St Mary's Road BA6 9SP
Middlezoy:	Holy Cross Church, Church Road TA7 0NU
Milton Clevedon:	St James' Church, Bruton Road BA4 6NS
Milverton:	Church of St Michael & All Angels, St Michael's Hill TA4 1JS
North Curry:	St Peter & St Paul's Church, Church Road TA3 6LJ
North Wootton:	St Peter's Church, Church View BA4 4AD
Othery:	Othery Cemetery, Holloway Road TA7 0QE
Pilton:	St John the Baptist's Church, Shop Lane BA4 4BE
Queen Camel:	St Barnabas' Church, Church Path BA22 7NX
Shepton Mallet:	Shepton Mallet Burial Ground, Meadow Rise BA4 5NS
Shipham:	St Leonard's Church, Cuck Hill BS25 1RA
Somerton:	Somerton Cemetery, Behind Berry, TA11 7PB
Street:	Holy Trinity Church, Church Road BA16 0AD
	Street Cemetery, Cemetery Lane BA16 9PH
Taunton:	St James' Cemetery, Staplegrove Road TA1 1DP
	St Mary's Cemetery, Wellington Road TA1 5AS

Tintinhull:	St Margaret's Church, Church Street BA22 8PW
Ubley:	Church of St Bartholomew, The Street BS40 6PJ
Walton Clevedon:	St Mary's Church, Castle Road BS21 7BX
Wedmore:	St Mary's Church, Church Street BS28 4AB
Wells:	Wells Cemetery, Portway BA5 1LY
Westbury-sub-Mendip:	St Lawrence Church, Wells Road BA5 1HB
Weston-super-Mare:	Milton Cemetery, Bristol Road Lower BS23 2TL
	Westonzoyland: Westonzoyland Cemetery, Main Road TA7 0LE
Wookey:	St Matthew's Church, St Matthew's Terrace BA5 1JR
Yatton:	St Mary's Church, Church Road BS49 4HH

Printed in Great Britain
by Amazon

69523355R00241